Computer Basics

NOW COVERS
Windows® 11

ABSOLUTE
BEGINNER'S
GUIDE

Michael Miller

Pearson

Tenth Edition

Computer Basics Absolute Beginner's Guide, Tenth Edition

ISBN-13: 978-0-13-788577-0
ISBN-10: 0-13-788577-6

Library of Congress Control Number: 2022937763

1 2022

Trademarks

Warning and Disclaimer

Special Sales

For information about buying this title in bulk quantities, or for special sales opportunities (which may include electronic versions; custom cover designs; and content particular to your business, training goals, marketing focus, or branding interests), please contact our corporate sales department at corpsales@pearsoned.com or (800) 382-3419.

For government sales inquiries, please contact governmentsales@pearsoned.com.

For questions about sales outside the U.S., please contact international@pearsoned.com.

Editor-in-Chief
Brett Bartow

Executive Editor
Laura Norman

Associate Editor
Anshul Sharma

Marketing
Stephane Nakib

Development Editor
Charlotte Kughen

Managing Editor
Sandra Schroeder

Senior Project Editor
Tonya Simpson

Technical Editor
Vince Averello

Copy Editor
The Wordsmithery LLC

Indexer
Cheryl Lenser

Proofreader
Sarah Kearns

Publishing Coordinator
Cindy Teeters

Compositor
Bronkella Publishing LLC

Graphics
tj graham art

Contents at a Glance

Table of Contents

About the Author

Michael Miller is a successful and prolific author with a reputation for practical advice, technical accuracy, and an unerring empathy for the needs of his readers.

Mr. Miller has written more than 200 best-selling books over the past three decades that collectively have sold more than 1.5 million copies. Some of his titles are *My Windows 11 Computer for Seniors*, *My iPad for Seniors*, *My Google Chromebook*, *My Video Chat for Seniors*, and *My TV for Seniors*.

He is known for his casual, easy-to-read writing style and his practical, real-world advice—as well as his ability to explain a variety of complex topics to an everyday audience.

Learn more about Mr. Miller at his website, www.millerwriter.com. Follow him on Twitter @molehillgroup.

Dedication

To Sherry—life together is easier.

Acknowledgments

Thanks to the usual suspects, including but not limited to Laura Norman, Anshul Sharma, Charlotte Kughen, and technical editor Vince Averello.

Pearson's Commitment to Diversity, Equity, and Inclusion

Pearson is dedicated to creating bias-free content that reflects the diversity of all readers. We embrace the many dimensions of diversity, including but not limited to race, ethnicity, gender, socioeconomic status, ability, age, sexual orientation, and religious or political beliefs.

Books are a powerful force for equity and change in our world. They have the potential to deliver opportunities that improve lives and enable economic mobility. As we work with authors to create content for every product and service, we acknowledge our responsibility to demonstrate inclusivity and incorporate diverse scholarship so that everyone can achieve their potential through learning. As the world's leading learning company, we have a duty to help drive change and live up to our purpose to help more people create a better life for themselves and to create a better world.

Our ambition is to purposefully contribute to a world where:

- Everyone has an equitable and lifelong opportunity to succeed through learning.

- Our products and services are inclusive and represent the rich diversity of readers.

- Our content accurately reflects the histories and experiences of the readers we serve.

- Our content prompts deeper discussions with readers and motivates them to expand their own learning (and worldview).

While we work hard to present unbiased content, we want to hear from you about any concerns or needs with this Pearson product so that we can investigate and address them. Please contact us with concerns about any potential bias at https://www.pearson.com/report-bias.html.

We Want to Hear from You!

As the reader of this book, *you* are our most important critic and commentator. We value your opinion and want to know what we're doing right, what we could do better, what areas you'd like to see us publish in, and any other words of wisdom you're willing to pass our way.

We welcome your comments. You can email or write to let us know what you did or didn't like about this book—as well as what we can do to make our books better.

Please note that we cannot help you with technical problems related to the topic of this book.

When you email, please be sure to include this book's title and author as well as your name and email address. We will carefully review your comments and share them with the author and editors who worked on the book.

Email: community@informit.com

Reader Services

Visit our website and register this book at informit.com/register for convenient access to any updates, downloads, or errata that might be available for this book.

Figure Credits

Figures 3.1 through 3.13, 4.1 through 4.5, 4.7, 4.8, 5.1 through 5.8, 6.6, 7.1 through 7.4, 9.2, 9.3, 10.1, 11.1 through 11.5, 13.1 through 13.6, 14.5, 14.6, 15.14, 15.15, 16.1 through 16.4, 16.6, 16.7, 17.1 through 17.5, 17.10, 17.11, 18.1 through 18.6, 20.4, 21.1, 22.1 through 22.4: Microsoft

Figure 8.1: James Looker/Future/Shutterstock

Figures 11.6 through 11.8, 13.7, 13.8, 17.6 through 17.9, 19.11, 20.5: Google

Figures 12.1, 19.1: Amazon.com, Inc.

Figure 12.2: Craigslist

Figure 12.3: eBay Inc.

Figure 12.4: Etsy, Inc.

Figures 12.5, 15.1 through 15.6: Meta Platforms, Inc.

Figure 12.6: Reverb.com LLC

Figures 14.1 through 14.4: Zoom Video Communications, Inc.

Figures 15.7, 15.8: Twitter, Inc.

Figures 15.9 through 15.13: Pinterest

Figure 16.5: Intuit Inc.

Figure 19.1: Apple Inc.

Figure 19.3: Discovery, Inc.

Figure 19.4: The Walt Disney Company

Figure 19.5: WarnerMedia Direct, LLC

Figures 19.6, 19.10: Hulu, LLC

Figure 19.7: Netflix

Figure 19.8: Paramount

Figure 19.9: Peacock TV LLC

Figure 20.1: Pandora Media, Inc.

Figure 20.2: Spotify AB

Figure 20.3: TuneIn, Inc.

INTRODUCTION

Because this book is titled *Computer Basics: Absolute Beginner's Guide*, let's start at the absolute beginning, which is this:

Computers aren't supposed to be scary. Intimidating? Sometimes. Difficult to use? Perhaps. Inherently unreliable? Not really, although they used to be.

But scary? Definitely not.

Computers aren't scary because there's nothing they can do to hurt you (unless you drop one on your foot, that is). And there's not much you can do to hurt them either. It's kind of a wary coexistence between person and machine, but the relationship has the potential to be beneficial—to you, anyway.

Many people think that they're scared of computers because they're unfamiliar with them. But that isn't really true.

You see, even if you've never actually used a computer before, you've been exposed to computers and all they can do since at least the mid 1980s. Whenever you make a deposit at your bank, you work with computers. Whenever you make a purchase at a retail store, you work with computers. Whenever you watch a television show, read a newspaper article, or look at a picture in a magazine, you work with computers.

That's because computers are used in all those applications. Somebody, somewhere, works behind the scenes with a computer to manage your bank account and monitor your credit card purchases.

In fact, it's difficult to imagine, here in the twenty-first century, how we ever got by without all those keyboards, mice, and monitors (or, for that matter, the Internet and social networking).

However, just because computers have been around for a while doesn't mean that everyone knows how to use them. It's not unusual to feel a little trepidation the first time you sit down in front of that intimidating display and keyboard. Which keys should you press? What do people mean by double-clicking the mouse? And what are all those little pictures onscreen?

As foreign as all this might seem at first, computers really aren't that hard to understand—or use. You have to learn a few basic concepts, of course (all the pressing and clicking and whatnot), and it helps to understand exactly what part of the system does what. But when you get the hang of things, computers are easy to use.

Which, of course, is where this book comes in.

Computer Basics: Absolute Beginner's Guide, Windows 11 Edition can help you figure out how to use your new computer system. You learn how computers work, how to connect all the pieces and parts (if your computer has pieces and parts, that is; not all do), and how to start using them. You learn about computer hardware and software, about the Microsoft Windows 11 operating system, and about the Internet. And when you're comfortable with the basic concepts (which won't take too long, trust me), you learn how to actually do stuff.

You learn how to do useful stuff, such as writing letters and editing photos; fun stuff, such as listening to music and watching movies and TV shows; online stuff, such as searching for information, sending and receiving email, keeping up with friends and family via Facebook and other social networks, and video chatting with Zoom and Microsoft Teams; and essential stuff, such as copying files, troubleshooting problems, and protecting against malware and computer attacks.

All you have to do is sit yourself down in front of your computer, try not to be scared (there's nothing to be scared of, really), and work your way through the chapters and activities in this book. And remember that computers aren't difficult to use, they don't break easily, and they let you do all sorts of fun and useful things after you get the hang of them. Really!

How This Book Is Organized

This book is organized into eight main parts, as follows:

- **Part I, "Understanding Computers,"** discusses the different types of computers available today; describes all the pieces and parts of desktop, all-in-one, laptop, and 2-in-1 PCs; and talks about how to connect everything to get your new system up and running.

- **Part II, "Using Windows,"** introduces the backbone of your entire system, the Microsoft Windows operating system, now in its eleventh version. You learn how Windows 11 works, how to navigate your way around the desktop and the Start menu, and how to personalize it. You'll also learn how to use Windows to perform basic tasks, such as copying and deleting files and folders.

- **Part III, "Setting Up the Rest of Your System,"** talks about all those things you connect to your computer—printers, external storage drives, USB drives, and the like. You also learn how to connect your new PC to other computers and devices in a home network and how to use your PC to do text messaging and voice calls with your Android phone.

- **Part IV, "Using the Internet,"** is all about going online. You discover how to connect to the Internet and surf the Web. You also learn how to search for information, shop, and even sell things online. This is one of the most fun parts of the book.

- **Part V, "Communicating Online,"** is all about keeping in touch. You find out how to send and receive email, of course, but also how to do video meetings and get started with social networking, on Facebook, Twitter, and other social networks. The Internet is how everyone keeps in touch these days.

- **Part VI, "Getting Productive,"** tells you everything you need to know about using software programs (what some people call "apps"). You learn how software programs work and where to find new ones. You'll also learn how to do office work with Microsoft Office software, and how to edit and share digital photos.

- **Part VII, "Exploring Online Entertainment,"** is all about streaming audio and video over the Internet. You'll learn how to listen to streaming music online and how to stream your favorite TV shows, movies, and other videos.

- **Part VIII, "Keeping Your System Up and Running,"** contains all the boring (but necessary) information you need to know to keep your new PC in tip-top shape. You learn how to protect against Internet threats (including viruses, spyware, and spam), as well as how to perform routine computer maintenance. You even learn how to troubleshoot problems and, if necessary, restore, refresh, or reset your entire system.

Taken together, the 22 chapters in this book can help you progress from absolute beginner to experienced computer user. Just read what you need, and before long, you'll be using your computer like a pro!

Which Version of Windows?

This edition of the *Absolute Beginner's Guide to Computer Basics* is written for computers of all types running the latest version of Microsoft's operating system, dubbed Windows 11.

What if you're running an older version of Windows? In that case, you'll be better off with one of the previous editions of this book. There are editions out there for Windows 10, Windows 8.1, (Microsoft skipped Windows 9), Windows 8, Windows 7, Windows Vista, and even Windows XP. If you can't find a particular edition at your local bookstore, look for it online.

Conventions Used in This Book

I hope that this book is easy enough to figure out without requiring its own instruction manual. As you read through the pages, however, it helps to know precisely how I've presented specific types of information.

Menu Commands

Most computer programs operate via a series of pull-down menus. You use your mouse to pull down a menu and then select an option from that menu. This sort of operation is indicated throughout the book like this:

>Select File, Save.

or

>Right-click the file and select Properties from the pop-up menu.

All you have to do is follow the instructions in order, using your mouse to click each item in turn. When submenus are tacked onto the main menu, just keep clicking the selections until you come to the last one—which should open the program or activate the command you want!

Shortcut Key Combinations

When you use your computer keyboard, sometimes you have to press two keys at the same time. These two-key combinations are called shortcut keys and are shown as the key names joined with a plus sign (+).

For example, Ctrl+W indicates that you should press the W key while holding down the Ctrl key. It's no more complex than that.

Web Page Addresses

This book contains a lot of web page addresses. (That's because you'll probably be spending a lot of time on the Internet.)

Technically, a web page address is supposed to start with http:// (as in http://www.millerwriter.com). Because web browsers automatically insert this piece of the address, however, you don't have to type it—and I haven't included it in any of the addresses in this book.

Special Elements

This book also includes a few special elements that provide additional information not included in the basic text. These elements are designed to supplement the text to make your learning faster, easier, and more efficient.

 TIP   A *tip* is a piece of advice—a little trick, actually—that helps you use your computer more effectively or maneuver around problems or limitations.

 NOTE   A *note* is designed to provide information that is generally useful but not specifically necessary for what you're doing at the moment. Some are like extended tips—interesting, but not essential.

 CAUTION   A *caution* tells you to beware of a potentially dangerous act or situation. In some cases, ignoring a caution could cause you significant problems—so pay attention to them!

There's More Online

If you want to learn more about me and any new books I have in the works, check out my website at www.millerwriter.com. Who knows, you might find some other books there that you would like to read. You can also follow me on Twitter (@molehillgroup) and leave messages to me on my website. I love hearing from readers!

PART I

UNDERSTANDING COMPUTERS

1

HOW PERSONAL COMPUTERS WORK

Chances are you're reading this book because you just bought a new computer, are thinking about buying a new computer, or maybe even had someone give you their old computer. (Nothing wrong with high-tech hand-me-downs!) At this point, you might not be totally sure what it is you've gotten yourself into. Just what is this thing you're holding in your hands, and what can you—or should you—do with it?

This chapter serves as an introduction to the entire concept of personal computers—what they do, how they work, that sort of thing—and computer hardware in particular. It's a good place to start if you're not that familiar with computers or want a brief refresher course in what all those pieces and parts are and what they do.

Of course, if you want to skip the background and get right to using your computer, that's okay, too. For step-by-step instructions on how to connect and configure a new PC, go directly to Chapter 2, "Setting Up and Using Different Types of Computers." Everything you need to know should be in that chapter.

What Your Computer Can Do

What good is a personal computer, anyway?

Everybody has one, you know (including you, now). In fact, it's possible you bought your new computer just so that you wouldn't feel left out. But now that you have a personal computer, what do you do with it?

Good for Getting Online

Most of what we do on our computers these days is accomplished via the Internet. We find friends and communicate with them online; we find useful information online; we watch TV and movies and listen to music online; we play games online; we even shop, order meals, and do our banking online. Most of these activities are accomplished by browsing something called the World Wide Web (or just the "Web"), which you do from something called a web browser.

 NOTE   Learn more about getting online in Chapter 10, "Connecting to the Internet—at Home or Away."

Good for Social Networking

One of the most popular online activities these days involves something called social networking. A *social network* is a website where you can keep informed about what your friends and family are doing, and they can see what you're up to, too. There are several social networks you can use, but the most popular are Facebook, Twitter, Pinterest, and LinkedIn. You can join one or more of these and start sharing your life online.

 NOTE   Learn more about Facebook and other social networks in Chapter 15, "Social Networking with Facebook, Twitter, and Other Social Media."

Good for Communicating

Your new computer is also great for keeping in touch with friends, family, and co-workers. Want to send a note to a friend? Or keep your family informed of what's new and exciting? It's easy enough to do, thanks to your new computer and the Internet. You can drop a note via email, keep folks up to date via Facebook or some similar social networking site, or participate in a real-time video chat (using your computer's microphone and webcam) via Microsoft Teams or Zoom.

 NOTE   Learn more about communicating with email in Chapter 13, "Sending and Receiving Email." Learn more about video chats in Chapter 14, "Video Chatting with Friends and Family."

Good for Sharing Photos and Home Movies

You can also use your computer to store, edit, and share your favorite photos and home movies. When you upload a picture, your friends can view it online. You can even touch up the photo before you share it. Pretty nifty.

 NOTE   Learn more about digital photos in Chapter 18, "Working with Digital Photos."

Good for Entertainment

For many people, a personal computer is a hub for all sorts of online entertainment. You can use your computer to listen to music over the Internet via streaming music services such as Pandora and Spotify. You also can watch movies and TV shows online with streaming video services such as Amazon Prime Video, Disney+, Hulu, and Netflix.

 NOTE   Learn more about watching TV and movies on your PC in Chapter 19, "Watching Movies and TV Shows Online." Learn more about listening to music with your PC in Chapter 20, "Listening to Music Online."

Good for Keeping Informed

Entertainment is fun, but it's also important to stay informed. Your computer is a great gateway to tons of information, both old and new. You can use Google and other search engines to search for just about anything you want online—or use your computer to browse the latest news headlines, sports scores, and weather reports. All the information you can think of is online somewhere, and you use your computer to find and read it.

NOTE Learn more about staying informed online in Chapter 11, "Browsing and Searching the Web."

Good for Work

A lot of people use their home PCs for work-related purposes. You can bring your work (reports, spreadsheets, you name it) home from the office and finish it on your home PC. Or, if you work at home, you can use your computer to pretty much run your small business—you can use it to do everything from typing memos and reports to generating invoices and setting budgets.

In short, anything you can do with a normal office PC, you can probably do on your home PC, using Microsoft Office, Google Docs, and similar productivity software.

NOTE Learn more about using your computer for office work in Chapter 17, "Doing Office Work."

Good for Play

All work and no play make Jack a dull boy, so there's no reason not to have a little fun with your new PC. There are a lot of cool games online, plus you can purchase all manner of computer games to play, if that's what you're into. There's a lot of fun to be had with your new PC!

NOTE This book is written for users of relatively new personal computers—in particular, PCs running the Microsoft Windows 11 operating system. If you have an older PC running an older version of Windows, most of the advice here is still good, although not all the step-by-step instructions will apply. Instead, you may want to pick up a previous edition of this book to match your older operating system.

Inside a Personal Computer

As I discuss momentarily, there are a lot of different types of personal computers—desktops, all-in-ones, laptops, and the like. What they have in common is a core set of components—the computer *hardware*. Unlike computer *software*, which describes the programs and applications you run on your computer, the hardware is composed of those physical parts of your system you can see and touch.

Well, you could see the parts if you opened the case, which you can't always do. Let's take a virtual tour inside a typical PC, so you can get a sense of how the darned thing works.

The Motherboard: Home to Almost Everything

Inside every PC are all manner of computer chips and circuit boards. Most of these parts connect to a big circuit board called a *motherboard*, so named because it's the "mother" for the computer's microprocessor and memory chips, as well as for all other internal components that enable your system to function.

On a laptop or 2-in-1 PC (a laptop that also functions as a tablet), the motherboard is just under the keyboard. On a traditional desktop PC, the motherboard is located somewhere inside the computer's system unit. (In Figure 1.1, it's on the left side of the cabinet.) On an all-in-one desktop, it's typically built into the monitor unit.

FIGURE 1.1

What a typical desktop PC looks like on the inside—a big motherboard with lots of add-on boards attached.

On a traditional desktop PC, the motherboard contains several slots, into which you can plug additional *boards* (also called *cards*) that perform specific functions.

For example, some gaming PCs feature a separate video card that enables your motherboard to transmit high-quality video signals to your monitor. All-in-one, laptop, and 2-in-1 PCs have these functions built into the motherboard and thus aren't expandable like PCs that have separate system units.

Microprocessors: The Main Engine

I'm not done talking about the motherboard just yet. That's because the specific chip that controls your entire computer system is buried somewhere on that big motherboard. This chip is called a *microprocessor* or a *central processing unit (CPU)*.

The microprocessor is the brain inside your system. It processes all the instructions necessary for your computer to perform its duties. The more powerful the microprocessor chip, the faster and more efficiently your system runs.

Microprocessors carry out the various instructions that enable your computer to compute. Every input and output device connected to a computer—the keyboard, printer, monitor, and so on—either issues or receives instructions that the microprocessor then processes. Your software programs also issue instructions that must be implemented by the microprocessor. This chip truly is the workhorse of your system; it affects just about everything your computer does.

Different computers have different types of microprocessor chips. Desktop and laptop computers running the Windows operating system use chips manufactured by either Intel or AMD. (Apple Macintosh computers also use Intel chips, although they're different from the chips used in Windows PCs.)

In addition to having different chip manufacturers (and different chip families from the same manufacturer), you'll run into microprocessor chips that run at different speeds. CPU speed today is measured in *gigahertz (GHz)*. A CPU with a speed of 1GHz can run at one *billion* clock ticks per second! The bigger the gigahertz number, the faster the chip runs.

It gets better. Most computers today incorporate chips with more than one *core*. Each core is the equivalent of a separate CPU on a single chip. You can find chips with two, four, or six cores—the equivalent of two, four, or six CPUs working together to increase your processing power. The more cores, the better—especially for processor-intensive tasks, such as editing digital video files.

If you're shopping for a new PC, look for one with the combination of a powerful microprocessor and a high clock speed for best performance. And don't forget to count all the cores; a quad-core chip with four 2GHz CPUs is more powerful than a single-core chip with a single 4GHz CPU.

Computer Memory: Temporary Storage

Before a CPU can process instructions you give it, your instructions must be stored somewhere in preparation for access by the microprocessor. These instructions—along with other data processed by your system—are temporarily held in the computer's *random access memory (RAM)*. All computers have some amount of memory, which is created by a number of memory chips. The more memory that's available in a machine, the more instructions and data that can be stored at one time.

Memory is measured in terms of *bytes*. One byte is equal to approximately one character in a word processing document. A unit equaling approximately one thousand bytes (1,024, to be exact) is called a *kilobyte (KB)*, and a unit of approximately one thousand (1,024) kilobytes is called a *megabyte (MB)*. A thousand megabytes is a *gigabyte (GB)*.

Most computers today come with at least 4GB of memory, some with much more. To enable your computer to run as many programs as quickly as possible, you need as much memory installed in your system as it can accept—or that you can afford. You can add extra memory to a computer by installing new memory modules, which is as easy as plugging a "stick" directly into a slot on your system's motherboard.

If your computer doesn't possess enough memory, its CPU must constantly retrieve data from permanent storage on its hard disk. This method of data retrieval is slower than retrieving instructions and data from electronic memory. In fact, if your machine doesn't have enough memory, some programs will run very slowly (or you might experience random system crashes), and other programs won't run at all!

Hard Disk Drives: Long-Term Storage

Another important physical component inside many computers is the *hard disk drive*. The hard disk permanently stores all your important data. Some hard disks today can store multiple *terabytes (TB)* of data, each terabyte equaling 1,000 gigabytes. (Contrast this to your system's RAM, which temporarily stores only a few gigabytes of data.)

A hard disk consists of numerous metallic platters. These platters store data *magnetically*. Special read/write *heads* realign magnetic particles on the platters, much like a recording head records data onto magnetic recording tape.

However, before data can be stored on a disk, including your system's hard disk, that disk must be *formatted*. A disk that has not been formatted cannot accept data. When you format a hard disk, your computer prepares each track and sector of the disk to accept and store data magnetically. Fortunately, hard disks in new PCs are preformatted, so you don't have to worry about this. (And, in most cases, your operating system and key programs are preinstalled.)

 CAUTION If you try to reformat your hard disk, you'll erase all the programs and data that have been installed—so don't do it!

Solid-State Drives: Faster Long-Term Storage

Not all long-term storage is hard disk-based. Many of today's laptop and 2-in-1 PCs and an increasing number of desktop and all-in-one models don't have traditional hard disk storage. Instead, they use solid-state flash memory for long-term storage.

A solid-state drive (SSD) has no moving parts. Instead, data is stored electronically on an integrated circuit. This type of storage is much faster than traditional hard disk storage; data stored on a solid-state drive can be accessed pretty much instantly. Plus, laptops with solid-state drives are considerably lighter than laptops with traditional hard drives.

The downside of solid-state storage is that it's a little more expensive than hard drive storage, although it doesn't cost as much today as it did just a few years ago. What this means is that you typically get a little less storage on an SSD than you would on a similar computer with a traditional hard drive—or you pay a little more for a computer with similarly sized SSD.

So, if it's important for your computer to be fast and lightweight, consider a model with solid-state storage. If you prefer a lower-priced model or need more storage space, stick with a traditional hard disk PC.

 NOTE Some computers come with a mix of hard drive and solid state storage. In this type of system, the SSD contains the Windows operating system and other key files for fast startup and operation, whereas the larger hard drive is used for storing large applications and files.

 NOTE Some PCs still come with a combination CD/DVD drive, although they're becoming increasingly rare. A CD/DVD drive enables you to play audio CDs and movie DVDs, install CD- or DVD-based software programs, and burn music, movies, or data to blank CD or DVD discs. However, the industry has moved away from physical media in recent years as most apps and services are now streamed or downloaded from the Internet.

Keyboards: Fingertip Input

Computers receive data by reading it from disk, accepting it electronically over a modem, or receiving input directly from you, the user. You provide your input by way of what's called, in general, an *input device*; the most common input device you use to talk to your computer is the keyboard.

A computer keyboard, similar to the one in Figure 1.2, looks and functions just like an old-fashioned typewriter keyboard, except that computer keyboards have a few more keys. Some of these keys (such as the arrow, Pg Up, Pg Dn, Home, and End keys) enable you to move around within a program or file. Other keys provide access to special program features. When you press a key on your keyboard, it sends an electronic signal to your system unit that tells your machine what you want it to do.

FIGURE 1.2

A keyboard for a desktop PC.

Many keyboards that come with desktop and all-in-one PCs hook up via a cable to the back of your system unit. Some manufacturers make *wireless* keyboards that connect to your system unit via radio signals, thus eliminating one cable from the back of your system. Keyboards on laptop and 2-in-1 PCs are built into the main unit, of course, and the keys are often just a tad smaller than those on desktop PC keyboards.

On a typical Windows PC keyboard, there are a few extra keys in addition to the normal letters and numbers and symbols and such. Chief among these is the Windows key (sometimes called the *Winkey*), like the one shown in Figure 1.3, which has a little Windows logo on it. In Windows 10, many operating functions are initiated by pressing the Windows key either by itself or along with another key on the keyboard.

FIGURE 1.3

The Windows key on a computer keyboard.

Mice and Touchpads: Point-and-Click Input Devices

It's a funny name but a necessary device. A computer *mouse*, like the one shown in Figure 1.4, is a small handheld device that you scoot across your desktop. Most mice consist of an oblong case with two or three buttons on top. When you move the mouse along a desktop, an onscreen pointer (called a *cursor*) moves in response. When you click (press and release) a mouse button, this motion initiates an action in your program.

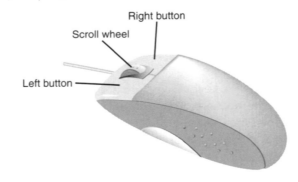

FIGURE 1.4

A typical two-button mouse with scroll wheel.

Mice come in all shapes and sizes. Some have wires, and some are wireless. Some are relatively oval in shape, and others are all curvy to better fit in the palm of your hand. Some even have extra buttons that you can program for specific functions or a scroll wheel you can use to scroll through long documents or web pages.

If you have a laptop or 2-in-1 PC, you don't have a separate mouse. Instead, most laptops feature a *touchpad* pointing device that functions like a mouse (see Figure 1.5). You move your fingers around the touchpad to move the onscreen cursor and then click one of the buttons underneath the touchpad the same way you'd click a mouse button.

FIGURE 1.5

A touchpad on a notebook PC.

 TIP   If you have a laptop PC, you don't have to use the built-in touchpad. Most laptops let you attach an external mouse, which you can use in addition to or instead of the internal device.

If you use a computer with a touchscreen display, you don't need a mouse at all. Instead, you control your computer by tapping and swiping the screen, using specific motions to perform specific operations. With a touchscreen computer, operation is fairly intuitive.

Network Connections: Getting Connected

If you have more than one computer in your home, you might want to connect them to a home network. A network enables you to share files between multiple computers, as well as connect multiple PCs to a single printer or scanner. In addition, you use your home network to share a broadband Internet connection so that all your computers (and other devices, like phones and tablets) connect to the Internet.

You can connect computers via either wired or wireless networks. Most home users prefer a wireless network because there are no cables to run from one room of your house to another. Fortunately, connecting a wireless network is as easy as buying a wireless router, which functions as the hub of the network, and then connecting wireless adapters to each computer on the network. (And if you have a laptop PC, the wireless adapter is already built in.)

 NOTE Learn more about wireless networks in Chapter 9, "Setting Up Whole-House Internet and a Home Network."

Sound Cards and Speakers: Making Noise

Every PC comes with some sort of speaker system. Most traditional desktop systems let you set up separate right and left speakers, sometimes accompanied by a subwoofer for better bass. (Figure 1.6 shows a typical right-left-subwoofer speaker system.) All-in-one, laptop, and 2-in-1 PCs typically come with right and left speakers built in but offer the option of connecting external speakers if you want. You can even get so-called 5.1 surround sound speaker systems, with five satellite speakers (front and rear) and the ".1" subwoofer—great for listening to movie soundtracks or playing explosive-laden video games.

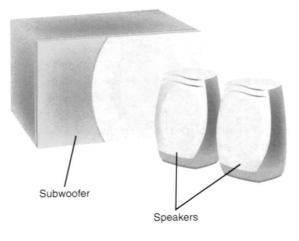

Subwoofer

Speakers

FIGURE 1.6

A typical set of right and left external speakers, complete with subwoofer.

All speaker systems are driven by a sound card or chip that is installed inside your system unit. If you upgrade your speaker system, you also might need to upgrade your sound card accordingly. (You can easily switch sound cards on a traditional desktop PC, but it's really not an option on a laptop or all-in-one.)

Video Cards and Monitors: Getting the Picture

Operating a computer would be difficult if you didn't constantly receive visual feedback showing you what your machine is doing. This vital function is provided by your computer's monitor.

Computer monitors today are built around LCD displays, just like you have on your living room TV. On a laptop PC, this display is built into the unit; on a desktop PC, you connect a separate external monitor. And with an all-in-one unit, the display includes the computer motherboard and connections.

You measure the size of a monitor diagonally from corner to corner. Most free-standing LCD monitors today are in the 24" to 27" diagonal range, although both larger and smaller models are also available.

A flat-screen LCD display doesn't take up a lot of desk space or use a lot of energy, both of which are good things. Most monitors today come with a wide-screen display that has the same 16:9 (or 16:10) aspect ratio used to display wide-screen movies—which makes them ideal for viewing or editing movies on your PC. (You also can find some ultrawide monitors, ideal for doing video editing or accounting work, with a 21:9 aspect ratio—but they're fairly pricey.)

Know, however, that your computer monitor doesn't generate the images it displays. Instead, screen images are electronically crafted by a *video card* or chip installed inside your laptop PC or desktop system unit. To work correctly, both the video card and monitor must be matched to display images of the same resolution.

Resolution refers to the size of the images that can be displayed onscreen and is measured in pixels. A *pixel* is a single dot on your screen; a full picture is composed of thousands of pixels. The higher the resolution, the sharper the resolution—which lets you display more (smaller) elements onscreen.

Resolution is expressed in numbers of pixels, in both the horizontal and vertical directions. Most external monitors today can display 1920×1080 or higher resolution (called full high definition, or FHD). Laptop PC displays are typically smaller (14" to 15.4" diagonal) and sometimes with slightly lower resolution.

Other Parts of Your Computer System

The computer hardware itself is only part of your overall computer system. A typical PC has additional devices—such as printers—connected to it, and it runs various programs and applications to perform specific tasks.

Providing Additional Functionality with Peripherals

There are lots of other devices, called *peripherals*, you can connect to your computer, including the following:

- **Printers:** A printer enables you to make hardcopy printouts of documents and pictures—and some including copying, scanning, and even faxing capability.

- **Webcams:** These are small cameras (typically with built-in microphones) that enable you to send live video of yourself to friends and family. Many laptops and some all-in-ones include built-in webcams.

- **Joysticks and gamepads:** These are alternatives to mice that enable you to play the most challenging computer games.

- **External storage:** These are just like the hard disk or solid state drives inside your computer, but they connect externally to help you back up your precious data.

 NOTE Learn more about installing peripherals in Chapter 6, "Connecting Printers and Other Devices to Your PC." Learn more about using external disks in Chapter 8, "Adding Storage and Backup."

You also can hook up all manner of portable devices to your PC, including smartphones, digital cameras, and camcorders. You can even add the appropriate devices to connect multiple PCs in a network, which is useful if you have more than one computer in your house.

Fortunately, connecting a new device is as easy as plugging in a single cable. Whether you have a desktop or laptop PC, or even a tablet, most printers and other devices connect using a special type of cable called a *USB* cable. Almost all computers have multiple USB connections (sometimes called *ports*), so you can connect multiple peripherals via USB at the same time.

Doing What You Need to Do with Software and Apps

By themselves, the black or white boxes that comprise a typical computer system aren't that useful. You can connect them and set them in place, but they won't do anything until you have some software to make things work.

As discussed earlier, computer hardware refers to those things you can touch—the keyboard, monitor, system unit, and the like. Computer *software*, however, is something you *can't* touch because it's nothing more than a bunch of electronic bits and bytes. These bits and bytes, however, combine into computer programs—sometimes called *applications* or just *apps*—that provide specific functionality to your system.

For example, if you want to crunch some numbers, you need a piece of software called a *spreadsheet* program. If you want to write a letter, you need a *word processing* program. If you want to make changes to some pictures you took with your digital camera, you need *photo-editing* software. And if you want to surf the Internet, you need a *web browser*.

In other words, you need separate software for each task you want to do with your computer. Fortunately, most new computer systems come with a lot of this software already installed. You might have to buy a few specific programs, but it shouldn't set you back a lot of money.

 NOTE   Learn more about computer software and apps in Chapter 16, "Installing and Using Apps."

Making Everything Work—with Windows

Whatever program or app you're using at any time, you interface with your computer via a special piece of software called an *operating system*. As the name implies, this program makes your system operate; it's your gateway to the hardware part of your system.

The operating system is also how your application software interfaces with your computer hardware. When you want to print a document from your word processor, that software works with the operating system to send the document to your printer.

Most computers today ship with an operating system called *Microsoft Windows*. This operating system has been around in one form or another for more than 35 years and is published by Microsoft Corporation.

Windows isn't the only operating system around, however. Computers manufactured by Apple Computing use a different operating system, called *macOS*. Therefore, computers running Windows and computers by Apple aren't totally compatible with each other. Google's *Chrome OS* runs on many low-cost Chromebook computers, which are popular with schools across the country. Then there's *Linux*, which is compatible with most PCs sold today, but it's used primarily by über-techie types; it's not an operating system I would recommend for general users.

But let's get back to Windows and its various versions. The most current version is called *Microsoft Windows 11*. If you've just purchased a brand-new PC, this is the version you're using. If your PC is somewhat older, you might be running *Windows*

10, the immediate predecessor to Windows 11, which was the default OS from July 2015 to October 2021, when Windows 11 was released. If you have an even older computer, it could be running an even older version of Windows.

To some degree, Windows is Windows is Windows; all the different versions do pretty much the same things. Windows 11, however, is much improved over the previous versions, which is why many users have upgraded their older computers to this version.

In any case, you use Windows—whichever version you have installed—to launch specific programs and to perform various system maintenance functions, such as copying files and turning off your computer.

 NOTE   You can learn more about Windows 11 in Part II of this book, "Using Windows."

Different Types of Computers

Although all computers consist of pretty much the same components and work in pretty much the same way, there are several different types to choose from. You can go with a traditional desktop computer, a smaller, more portable laptop model, a touchscreen tablet—or one that combines some or all these features.

Let's look at the different types of computers you can choose from.

Traditional Desktop PCs

A *desktop PC* is one with a separate monitor that's designed to sit on your desktop, along with a separate keyboard and mouse. This was the original PC form factor, and it's still preferred by some old-school users.

A desktop PC is stationary; you can't take it with you. It sits on your desktop, perfect for doing the requisite office work.

A traditional desktop system, like the one shown in Figure 1.7, has a separate system unit that sits either on the floor or beside the monitor. This type of system takes up more space than any other type of system but is the most expandable. Gamers, in particular, like desktop systems that so they can swap graphics and sound boards in and out.

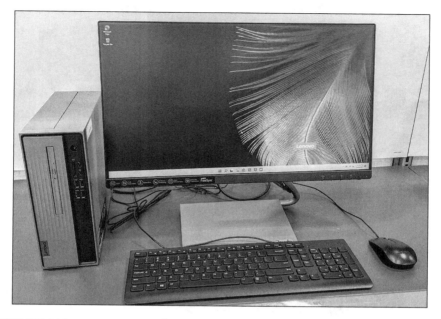

FIGURE 1.7

A traditional desktop PC system unit, complete with monitor, keyboard, mouse, and separate system unit.

All-in-One Desktops

An all-in-one desktop builds the system unit into the monitor for a more compact system, like the one shown in Figure 1.8. Some of these all-in-one PCs feature touchscreen monitors, so you can control them by tapping and swiping the monitor screen.

Many users like the easier setup (no system unit or speakers to connect) and smaller space requirements of all-in-one systems. The drawbacks to these all-in-one desktops are that you can't upgrade internal components, and if one component goes bad, the whole system is out of commission. It's a lot easier to replace a single component in a traditional desktop than the entire system of an all-in-one!

FIGURE 1.8

An all-in-one desktop system, with the system unit and speakers built into the monitor.

Laptop PCs

A *laptop PC*, sometimes called a *notebook PC*, combines a monitor, keyboard, and system unit in a single, compact case. This type of portable PC, like the one shown in Figure 1.9, can operate via normal electrical power or via a built-in battery, so you can take the laptop with you and use it just about anywhere you go.

Just as there are several types of desktop PCs, there are several types of laptops, including the following:

- **Traditional laptops:** These units have screens that run in the 14" to 16" range (15.6" is common) and include decent-sized hard drives (500GB and up). These are typically the least expensive laptops because there's a lot of competition; this category is the most popular.

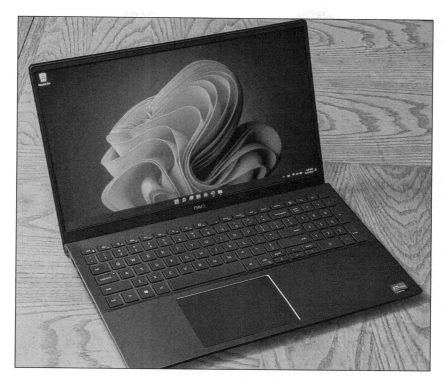

FIGURE 1.9

A traditional laptop PC with 15.6-inch screen.

- **Desktop-replacement laptops:** These are larger laptops, with screens in the 17" range. They're not only bigger; they're also heavier, and the batteries don't last as long. As such, these laptops really aren't designed for true portable use; instead, they're replacements for traditional desktop PCs. Plus, these desktop-replacement models typically cost a bit more than traditional laptops.

- **Ultrabooks:** An ultrabook is a smaller, thinner, and lighter laptop PC. Most ultrabooks have screens in the 10" to 14" range and use solid-state flash storage instead of hard disk storage. All this makes an ultrabook very fast and very easy to carry around without necessarily sacrificing computing power and functionality. However, all this new technology means ultrabooks cost a bit more than more traditional laptops.

With all these choices available, which type of laptop should you buy? It all depends.

Most users choose traditional laptops because they do everything you need them to do at a reasonable price. If you need more computing power but don't plan on taking your PC out of the house, then a desktop-replacement model might make sense. If you're a die-hard road warrior who likes to travel light, consider a more expensive but lighter-weight ultrabook.

Tablet PCs

A tablet PC is a self-contained computer you can hold in one hand. Think of a tablet as the real-world equivalent of one of those communication pads you see on *Star Trek*; it doesn't have a separate keyboard, so you operate it by tapping and swiping the screen with your fingers.

No question about it, the most popular tablet today is the Apple iPad; no other model comes close in terms of number of users. The iPad runs Apple's iPadOS operating system, which is similar to the iOS engine behind the company's iPhones. Also popular are tablets that run Google's Android operating system.

The iPadOS/iOS and Android operating systems, however, are both incompatible with the billion or so computers that run the Windows operating system. If you want a Windows-compatible tablet, the most popular (and often only) choice is the Microsoft Surface, shown in Figure 1.10.

FIGURE 1.10

Microsoft's Surface Pro tablet computer, complete with optional external keyboard.

Tablets are great for consuming media and information, and they're pretty good for web-based tasks, but they're not that great if you have to get serious work done; the lack of a true keyboard is a killer when you need to type long pieces of text and enter a lot of numbers. Still, a Windows tablet can easily supplement a more traditional PC for many types of tasks and is a strong competitor to Apple's iPad.

2-in-1 PCs

A 2-in-1 PC is the newest type of personal computer, a blend of the ultrabook and tablet form factors—literally. Think of a 2-in-1 PC as an ultrabook with a touch-screen, or a tablet with a keyboard.

Most 2-in-1 PCs, like the one in Figure 1.11, come with a swivel or fully removable keyboard, so you can type if you need to or get rid of the keyboard and use the touchscreen display as you would a tablet. Windows 11 is optimized for this new type of PC; depending on how you're using the device, you'll either see the traditional Windows desktop or the newer touch interface.

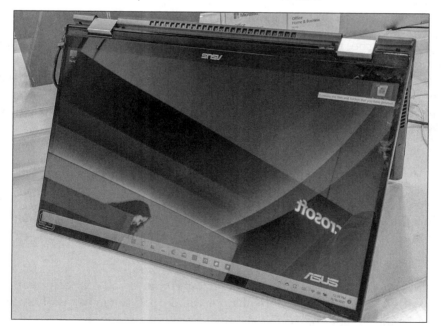

FIGURE 1.11

A 2-in-1 PC that folds from one form factor to another.

With a 2-in-1 PC, you use it like a touchscreen tablet when you watch movies or browse the Web and like a laptop PC when you have office work to do. For many users, it's the best of both worlds.

Which Type of PC Should You Choose?

Which type of PC is best for you? It depends on how you think you'll use your new computer:

- If all you plan to do is check your Facebook feed, watch streaming videos, and maybe send the occasional email, then you don't really need a full keyboard and can make do with a tablet or 2-in-1 PC.

- If you need to do more serious work, then a desktop, all-in-one, or laptop PC, complete with keyboard and mouse, is a must.

- If you plan to do all your computing in one spot, such as your home office, then a traditional desktop or all-in-one PC can do the job.

- If you want more flexibility—and the ability to take your computer with you— then a laptop or 2-in-1 model is a necessity.

As you can see, there are a lot of choices, and even within these general types, more specific considerations to make. The price depends a lot on the amount of hard disk storage you get, the size of the display, the amount of internal memory, the speed of the microprocessor, and other technical details. And don't forget the design; make sure you choose a model with the style and functionality you can live with.

Don't Worry, You Can't Screw It Up—Much

I don't know why, but a lot of people are afraid of their computers. They think if they press the wrong key or click the wrong button, they'll break something or will have to call an expensive repairperson to put things right.

This isn't true.

The important thing to know is that it's difficult to break your computer system. Yes, it's possible to break something if you drop it, but in terms of breaking your system through normal use, it just doesn't happen that often.

It is possible to make mistakes, of course. You can click the wrong button and accidentally delete a file you didn't want to delete or turn off your system and lose a document you forgot to save. You can even take inadequate security precautions and find your system infected by a computer virus. But in terms of doing serious harm just by clicking your mouse, it's unlikely.

So, don't be afraid of the thing. Your computer is a tool, just like a hammer or a blender or a camera. After you learn how to use it, it can be a very useful tool. But it's your tool, which means you tell it what to do—not vice versa. Remember that you're in control and that you're not going to break anything, and you'll have a lot of fun—and maybe even get some real work done!

THE ABSOLUTE MINIMUM

Here are the key points to remember from this chapter:

- There are five main types of computer systems available today: traditional desktops, all-in-one desktops, laptops, tablets, and 2-in-1 models.

- Regardless of type, all personal computers are composed of various hardware components; in a traditional desktop or all-in-one PC, they're separate devices, whereas laptop, 2-in-1, and tablet PCs combine them all into a single portable unit.

- You interface with your computer hardware via a piece of software called an operating system. The operating system on your new computer is probably Microsoft Windows 11.

- You use specific software programs or apps to perform specific tasks, such as writing letters and editing digital photos.

- The brains and engine of your system is the system unit, which contains the microprocessor, memory, disk drives, and all the connections for your other system components.

- To make your system run faster, get a faster microprocessor or more memory.

- Data is temporarily stored in your system's memory; you store data permanently on some type of disk drive—either a hard disk or solid-state drive.

2

SETTING UP AND USING DIFFERENT TYPES OF COMPUTERS

Chapter 1, "How Personal Computers Work," provided the essential background information you need to understand how your computer system works. With that information in hand, it's now time to connect all the various pieces and parts of your computer system—and get your PC up and running!

Before You Get Started

Whatever type of computer you have, it's important to prepare the space where you'll put it. Obviously, the space has to be big enough to hold all the components—though you don't have to keep all the components together. You can, for example, spread out your left and right speakers, place your subwoofer on the floor, and separate the printer from the main unit. Just don't put anything so far away that the cables don't reach. (And make sure you have a spare power outlet—or even better, a multiple-outlet power strip—nearby.)

When preparing your space, you should consider the ergonomics of your setup. For a desktop system, you want your keyboard at or slightly below normal desktop height, and you want your monitor at or slightly below eye level. Make sure your chair is adjusted for a straight and firm sitting position with your feet flat on the floor, and then place all the pieces of your system in relation to that.

This is easier, of course, if you have a laptop PC. All you need is a small amount of desktop space—or you can just hold the thing on your lap. They're that small!

Wherever you put your computer, you should make sure that it's in a well-ventilated location free of excess dust and smoke. (The moving parts in your computer don't like dust and dirt or any other such contaminants that can muck up the way they work.) Because your computer generates heat when it operates, you must leave enough room around the system unit for the heat to dissipate. *Never* place your computer (especially a desktop PC's system unit) in a confined, poorly ventilated space; your PC can overheat and shut down if it isn't sufficiently ventilated.

For extra protection to your computer, connect the PC's power cable to a surge suppressor rather than directly into an electrical outlet. A *surge suppressor*—which looks like a power strip but has an On/Off switch and a circuit breaker button—protects your PC from power-line surges that could damage its delicate internal parts. When a power surge temporarily spikes your line voltage (causing the voltage to momentarily increase above normal levels), a surge suppressor helps to keep the level of the electric current as steady as possible. Most surge suppressors also include circuit breakers to shut down power to your system if a severe power spike occurs.

Setting Up a Laptop or 2-in1 PC

The most popular type of computer today is the laptop (sometimes called notebook) PC. A laptop PC or its 2-in-1 PC cousin does everything a larger desktop PC does but in a more compact package.

Understanding the Elements of a Laptop PC

A typical laptop PC combines the various elements found in a desktop PC system into a single case and then adds a battery so that you can use it on the go. Many users find that portability convenient, even if it's just for using the computer in different rooms of the house.

A laptop PC looks like a smallish keyboard with a flip-up LCD screen attached (see Figure 2.1). That's what you see, anyway; beneath the keyboard is a full-featured computer, complete with motherboard, CPU, memory chips, video and audio processing circuits, hard drive or SSD, and battery.

FIGURE 2.1

The important parts of a laptop PC.

When the screen is folded down on a laptop PC, the keyboard is hidden, and the device is easy to carry from place to place; when the screen is flipped up, the keyboard is exposed. On the keyboard is some sort of built-in pointing device, like a touchpad, which is used in place of a standalone mouse.

On 2-in-1 PCs, the screen may flip or fold in a way to hide the keyboard and make the unit look like and function as a tablet. (On some models, it may be the keyboard that flips.) All 2-in-1 PCs have touchscreen displays, which you can operate with your fingers in either laptop or tablet mode.

Whether you have a traditional or 2-in-1 laptop, you'll likely see two built-in speakers, typically just above the top edge of the keyboard. Most laptops also have an earphone jack, which you can use to connect a set of headphones or earphones. (When you connect a set of headphones or earphones, the built-in speakers are automatically muted.)

 NOTE   Some older laptops have built-in CD/DVD drives. Most newer ones do not, which makes for thinner and lighter devices.

The sides of a laptop PC are where you find all the connecting ports, like what's shown in Figure 2.2. Most laptops have two or more USB connectors, an Ethernet connector (for connecting to a wired network), and an HDMI video connector (for connecting to an external display monitor).

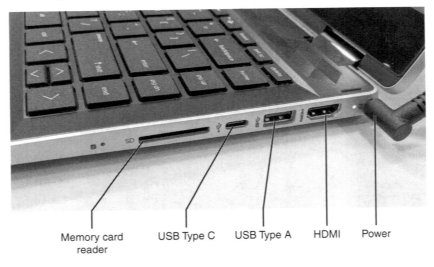

Memory card reader   USB Type C   USB Type A   HDMI   Power

FIGURE 2.2

Connecting ports on a laptop PC.

Inside the laptop case are the guts of the computer—everything you have in a desktop PC's system unit but more compact. In fact, most laptops have *more* inside than a typical desktop does; in particular, most laptop PCs have a built-in Wi-Fi adapter so that the laptop can connect to a wireless home network or public Wi-Fi hotspot.

In addition, virtually all laptop PCs come with some sort of built-in battery. That's because a portable PC is truly portable; in addition to running on normal AC power, a laptop PC can operate unplugged while using battery power. Depending on the PC (and the battery), you might be able to operate a laptop for three or four hours or more before switching batteries or plugging the unit into a wall outlet. That makes a laptop PC great for use on airplanes, in coffee shops, or anywhere plugging in a power cord is inconvenient.

 TIP   When you unpack your new computer, be sure you keep all the manuals, discs, cables, and so forth. Put the ones you don't use in a safe place in case you need to reinstall any software or equipment at a later date.

Getting Connected

One nice thing about laptop and 2-in-1 PCs is that you don't have too much to connect to get your system up and running. Because the monitor, speakers, keyboard, mouse, and Wi-Fi adapter are built in to the laptop unit, the only thing you really have to connect is the power cable.

If you do have peripherals, such as a printer or external mouse or keyboard, you should connect each of them to a USB port on your laptop. Then connect your laptop's power cable to a power strip or surge suppressor, and you're ready to get going. (You can even skip connecting to a power strip if your laptop runs on internal batteries.)

Setting Up an All-in-One Desktop PC

All-in-one desktops combine the system unit, monitor, and speakers into a single unit. These all-in-one desktops take up less space than a traditional desktop PC and, in some instances, provide touchscreen functionality that enables you to use your fingers (instead of a mouse) to navigate the screen.

Understanding the Parts of an All-in-One System

Figuring out an all-in-one computer is easy because practically everything is in the display unit. That includes the monitor screen, of course, but also the motherboard, speakers, microphone, and webcam (if they're included), and all the necessary connections. As you can see in Figure 2.3, an all-in-one typically has four or more USB ports, maybe an Ethernet port (for wired networks), and maybe an HDMI connection for another monitor.

Aside from that, you have an external keyboard and mouse. These typically connect via USB. It's a pretty simple setup.

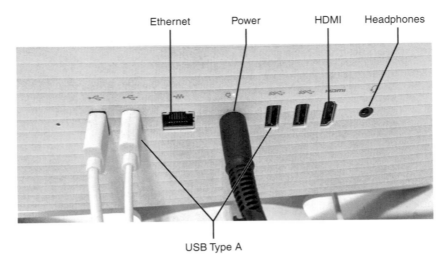

FIGURE 2.3

Ports on the back of an all-in-one desktop PC.

Getting Connected

Connecting an all-in-one desktop is only slightly more difficult than connecting a laptop PC—and a lot easier than connecting a traditional desktop unit. All you need to worry about connecting are the keyboard and mouse, as well as any peripherals you might have. Follow these steps:

1. Connect your mouse to an open USB port on your computer.

2. Connect your keyboard to an open USB port on your computer.

3. If you're connecting your computer to a wired router for network and Internet access, connect an Ethernet cable between the router and the Ethernet connector on the back of your computer. (If you're connecting to a wireless router and network, you can skip this step.)

4. If you have a printer, connect it to an open USB port on your computer.

5. Connect any other external devices to open USB ports on your PC.

6. Plug any powered external components, such as your printer, into a power outlet.

7. Connect the main power cable to the power connector on the back of your PC.

8. Plug your PC's power cable into a power outlet.

Pretty simple—which is one of the advantages of all-in-one units.

Setting Up a Traditional Desktop PC

A traditional desktop computer system is composed of several different pieces and parts. You have to properly connect all these components to make your computer system work.

Understanding the Components of a Desktop System

On a traditional desktop PC, the most important piece of hardware is the *system unit*. This is the big, ugly box that houses your disk drives and many other components. Most system units stand straight up like a kind of tower—and are, in fact, called either *tower* or *mini-tower* PCs, depending on the size.

The system unit is where everything connects; it truly is the central hub for your entire system. For this reason, the back of the system unit typically is covered with all types of connectors. Because each component has its own unique style of connector, you end up with the assortment of jacks (called *ports* in the computer world) that you see in Figure 2.4.

Some PCs put some of these connectors on the front of the case, in addition to the back. This makes it easier to connect portable devices, such as a USB flash drive, without having to muck about behind your PC.

The connections are on the outside, but all the good stuff in your system unit is inside the case. With most system units, you can remove the case to peek and poke around inside.

To remove your system unit's case, make sure the unit is unplugged, and then look for some big screws or thumbscrews on either the side or the back of the case. (Even better—read your PC's instruction manual for instructions specific to your unit.) With the screws loosened or removed, you should then be able to either slide off the entire case or pop open the top or back.

 CAUTION Always turn off and unplug your computer before attempting to remove the system unit's case—and be careful about touching anything inside. If you have any built-up static electricity, you can seriously damage the sensitive chips and electronic components with an innocent touch.

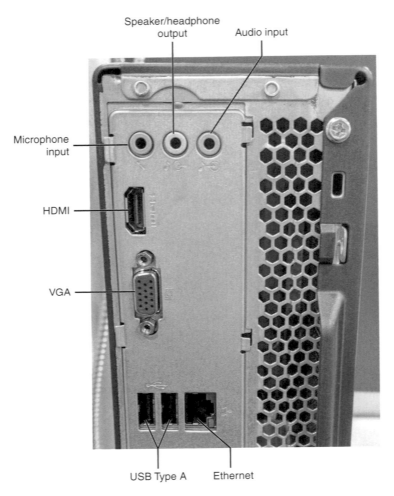

Speaker/headphone output

Audio input

Microphone input

HDMI

VGA

USB Type A

Ethernet

FIGURE 2.4

The back of a typical desktop PC system unit.

Getting Connected

Now it's time to get connected.

Start by positioning your system unit so that you easily can access all the connections on the back. Then you need to carefully run the cables from each of the other components so that they hang loose at the rear of the system unit. Now you're ready to get connected.

CAUTION Before you connect *anything* to your computer, make sure that the peripheral is turned off first.

It's important that you connect the cables in a particular order. To make sure that the most critical devices are connected first, follow these steps:

1. Connect your mouse to an open USB port on your computer.

2. Connect your keyboard to an open USB port on your computer.

3. Connect your video monitor to the video connector on the back of your PC. Most monitors today connect via an HDMI connection, although some older monitors might use a DVI or even a VGA connection. (HDMI is better, if you have it.)

4. If you have external speakers, connect them. Many speaker systems today connect via USB, although some older or lower-priced speakers connect to the "audio out" or "sound out" connector on the back of the system unit. Run the necessary cables between your right and left speakers and your subwoofer, as directed by the manufacturer.

5. If you're connecting your computer to a wired router for network and Internet access, connect an Ethernet cable between the router and the Ethernet connector on the back of your computer. (If you're connecting to a wireless router and network, you can skip this step.)

6. If you have a printer, connect it to an open USB port on your computer.

7. Connect any other external devices to open USB ports on your PC.

8. Plug the power cable of your video monitor into a power outlet.

9. If your system includes powered speakers, plug them into a power outlet.

10. Plug any other powered external components, such as your printer, into a power outlet.

11. Connect the main power cable to the power connector on the back of your PC.

12. Plug your PC's power cable into a power outlet.

 CAUTION Make sure that every cable is *firmly* connected—both to the system unit and to the specific piece of hardware. Loose cables can cause all sorts of weird problems, so be sure they're plugged in really well.

Now that you have everything connected, sit back and rest for a minute. Next up is the big step—turning it all on.

Turning It On—for the First Time

The first time you turn on a new PC is a unique experience. A brand-new, out-of-the-box system has to perform some basic configuration operations, which include asking you to input some key information.

Getting the Right Order

If you have a traditional desktop PC with lots of connected peripherals, it's important that you turn on things in the proper order. (If you have an all-in-one or laptop PC, you just have one thing to power on—the computer itself.)

For a traditional desktop PC, follow these steps:

1. Turn on your video monitor.

2. Turn on your speaker system—but make sure the speaker volume knob is turned down (toward the left).

3. Turn on any other system components that are connected to your system unit—such as your printer, scanner, and so on. (If your PC is connected to an Ethernet network, make sure that the network router is turned on.)

4. Turn on your system unit.

Note that your system unit is the *last* thing you turn on. That's because when it powers on, it has to sense the other components of your system—which it can do only if the other components are plugged in and turned on.

Powering On

This first-time startup operation differs from manufacturer to manufacturer, but it typically includes walking through the configuration process for Windows. You may be asked a series of questions about your location, the current time and date, and other essential information. You'll also be asked to sign in to an existing Microsoft account, if you have one, or create a new one if you don't. You use this account's username (or email address) and password (or PIN) to log in to your computer on subsequent occasions.

 NOTE For full installation, activation, and registration, your PC needs to be connected to the Internet.

Many computer manufacturers supplement these configuration operations with setup procedures of their own. It's impossible to describe all the different options that might be presented by all the different manufacturers, so watch the screen carefully and follow all the onscreen instructions.

After you have everything configured, Windows finally starts, and then you can start using your system.

 NOTE   Some installation procedures require your computer to be restarted. In most cases, this happens automatically; then the installation process resumes where it left off.

THE ABSOLUTE MINIMUM

Here are the key points to remember when connecting and configuring your new computer:

- Most peripherals connect to any USB port on your computer.

- Connecting an all-in-one unit is easier than connecting one with a separate system unit and monitor.

- You don't have to connect anything to your laptop or 2-in-1 PC to get it up and running—save for the power cord, at least until the internal battery is charged up.

- Make sure your cables are firmly connected; loose cables are the cause of many computer problems.

- Connect all the cables to the system unit of a desktop PC before you turn on the power.

- Remember to turn on your printer and monitor before you turn on the system unit.

- For full registration and activation, your computer needs to be connected to the Internet.

PART II

USING WINDOWS

3

GETTING TO KNOW WINDOWS 11

As you learned in Chapter 1, "How Personal Computers Work," Windows 11 is the *operating system* that makes your hardware work. An operating system does what its name implies—*operates* your computer *system*, working in the background every time you turn on your PC.

To use your new computer, you need to learn the ins and outs of operating Windows. Fortunately, it's easy to learn.

Say Hello to Windows 11

The Windows 11 desktop is what you see when you first turn on your computer, after everything turns on and boots up. Windows is your gateway to every program and app you run on your computer and to all the documents and files you view and edit.

Starting and Logging In to Windows

Starting your computer and logging in to Windows is a simple affair that starts when you push the power button on your PC.

 NOTE Technical types call the procedure of starting up a computer *booting* or *booting up* the system. Restarting a system (turning it off and then back on) is called *rebooting*.

After a few seconds (during which your system unit beeps and whirs a little bit), the Windows Lock screen appears. As you can see in Figure 3.1, the Lock screen shows today's date and time against a pretty photographic background while Windows waits for you to log on.

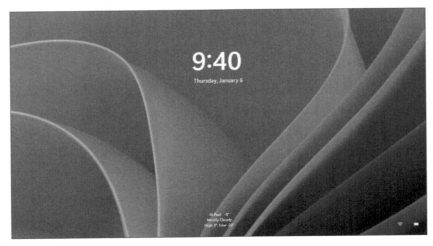

FIGURE 3.1

The first thing you see in Windows 11—the Lock screen.

To log on to your Windows account, all you have to do is press any key on your keyboard or click the mouse. (On a touchscreen display, you swipe your finger up the screen.) This displays the login screen, shown in Figure 3.2.

Enter your PIN or password and then press the Enter key. After you're past the login screen, you're taken directly to the Windows desktop, and your system is ready to use.

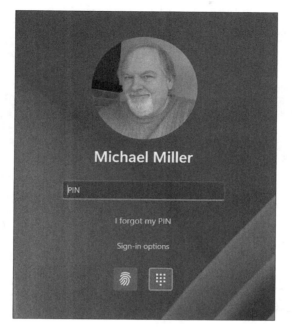

FIGURE 3.2

Enter your PIN or password to proceed.

 NOTE   It's easy to configure Windows 11 for multiple users, each with their own account and settings; I discuss that in Chapter 5, "Personalizing Windows." If you have only a single user on the machine, only one name appears from the Lock screen.

Exploring the Windows Desktop

The desktop is your home base in Windows. It's what you see when you start your computer and Windows launches; it's where all your programs and documents reside.

As you can see in Figure 3.3, the Windows 11 desktop includes a number of key elements. Get to know this desktop; you're going to be seeing a lot of it from now on.

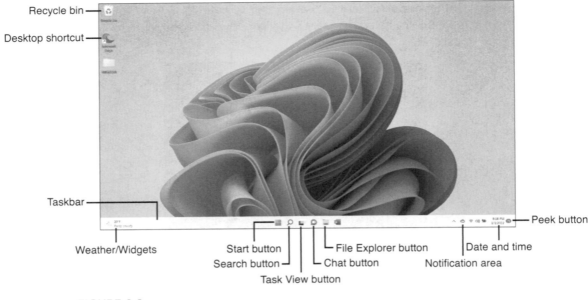

Recycle bin

Desktop shortcut

Taskbar

Weather/Widgets

Start button

Search button

Task View button

Chat button

File Explorer button

Date and time

Notification area

Peek button

FIGURE 3.3

The Windows 11 desktop.

Note the following elements:

- **Taskbar**—Displays icons for your favorite applications and documents, as well as for any open application. Right-click an icon to see a "jump list" of recent open documents and other operations for that application.

- **Weather/Widgets**—Displays current weather conditions and, when clicked or hovered over, displays the Widgets pane.

- **Start button**—Click or tap the Start button to display the Start menu. Right-click the Start button to display an Options menu with links to other important tools and utilities.

- **Search button**—Click or tap the Search button to open the Search pane and search for files and documents on your computer, or topics on the Web.

- **Task View button**—Click or tap the Task View button to view all open applications as thumbnail previews.

- **Chat button**—Click or tap the Chat button to open Microsoft Teams and start or join a text or video chat.

- **File Explorer button**—Click or tap this button to open the File Explorer for managing the files on your PC.

- **Notification area**—This far-right section of the taskbar displays icons for a handful of key system functions, power (on notebook PCs), networking/Internet, and audio (volume). Click or tap this area to display the Quick Setting panel to make quick system adjustments.

- **Date and time**—This displays—you guessed it—the current date and time. Click or tap to display system notifications and messages—and a handy calendar.

- **Peek button**—Hover over this slim little rectangle at the far edge of the taskbar and all open windows go transparent so that you can see what's on the desktop below. Click or tap the Peek button to immediately minimize all open windows.

- **Shortcut icons**—These are links to software programs you can place on your desktop; a "clean" desktop includes just one icon—the one for the Windows Recycle Bin.

- **Recycle Bin**—This is where you dump any files you want to delete.

 NOTE If you've used an older version of Windows, you're probably used to the taskbar being flush left with the Start button in the bottom-left corner. That changed in Windows 11, with the taskbar and all of its elements—including the Start button—centered at the bottom of the screen.

Learning Basic Operations

To use Windows efficiently, you need to master a few simple operations with your mouse or touchpad, such as pointing and clicking, dragging and dropping, and right-clicking. When you use your mouse or touchpad in this fashion, you move the onscreen *cursor*—that pointer thing that looks like a little arrow.

Pointing and Clicking

The most common mouse operation is *pointing and clicking*. Simply move your computer's mouse or, on a notebook PC, drag your finger across the touchpad so that the cursor points to the object you want to select, and then click the *left* mouse or touchpad button once. Pointing and clicking is an effective way to select menu and toolbar items, icons, and the like.

Double-Clicking

In some instances, single-clicking doesn't launch or open an item; it merely selects it. In these instances, you need to *double-click* an item to activate an operation.

This involves pointing at something onscreen with the cursor and then clicking the left mouse or touchpad button twice in rapid succession.

Right-Clicking

Here's one of the secret keys to efficient Windows operation. When you select an item and then click the *right* mouse or touchpad button, you often see a pop-up menu. This menu, when available, contains commands that directly relate to the selected object. So, for example, if you right-click a file icon, you see commands related to that file—copy, move, delete, and so forth.

Refer to your individual programs to see whether and how they use the right mouse button.

Dragging and Dropping

Dragging is a variation of clicking. To drag an object, point at it with the cursor and then press and hold down the left mouse or touchpad button. Move the mouse without releasing the mouse or touchpad button and drag the object to a new location. When you finish moving the object, release the mouse or touchpad button to drop it onto the new location.

You can use dragging and dropping to move files from one location to another.

Mouse Over

When you position the cursor over an item without clicking your mouse or touchpad, you *mouse over* that item. (This is sometimes called *hovering*.) Many operations require you to mouse over an item to display additional options or information.

Moving and Resizing Windows

When you have multiple windows open, your desktop can quickly become cluttered. Fortunately, there are ways to deal with this sort of multiple-window desktop clutter.

One approach is to move a window to a new position. You do this by positioning your cursor over a blank area at the top of the window frame and then clicking and holding down the left button on your mouse or touchpad. As long as this button is depressed, you can use your mouse or touchpad to drag the window around the screen. When you release the mouse or touchpad button, the window stays where you put it.

TIP   The cursor changes shape—to a double-ended arrow—when it's positioned over the edge of a window.

You also can change the size of most windows. You do this by positioning the cursor over the edge of the window—any edge. If you position the cursor on either side of the window, you can resize the width. If you position the cursor on the top or bottom edge, you can resize the height.

After the cursor is positioned over the window's edge, press and hold down the left mouse or touchpad button; then drag the window border to its new size. Release the button to lock in the newly sized window.

Maximizing, Minimizing, and Closing Windows

Another way to manage a window on the Windows desktop is to make it display full screen. You do this by maximizing the window. All you have to do is click or tap the Maximize button in the upper-right corner of the window, as shown in Figure 3.4.

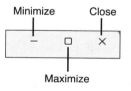

FIGURE 3.4

Use the Minimize, Maximize, and Close buttons to manage your desktop windows.

If the window is already maximized, the Maximize button changes to a Restore Down button. When you click or tap the Restore Down button, the window resumes its previous (premaximized) dimensions.

If you would rather hide the window so that it doesn't clutter your desktop, click or tap the Minimize button. This shoves the window off the desktop, onto the taskbar. The program in the window is still running, however—it's just not on the desktop. To restore a minimized window, all you have to do is click or tap the window's icon on the Windows taskbar (at the bottom of the screen).

If what you really want to do is close the window (and close any program running within the window), just click or tap the window's Close button.

CAUTION   If you try to close a window that contains a document you haven't saved, you're prompted to save the changes to the document. Because you probably don't want to lose any of your work, click Yes to save the document, and then close the program.

Snapping Windows into Position

Any open window can be "snapped" to the left or right side of the desktop so it shares the screen with another app. Windows 11 offers a variety of snapping options, including one that lets you display four different windows onscreen at the same time.

Start by mousing over the Maximize button for the first window. This displays all available snap layouts, as shown in Figure 3.5. Click or tap the position you want this window to be within the given layout.

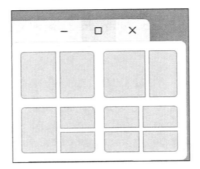

FIGURE 3.5

The different window snap layouts in Windows 11.

The current app is sized and positioned according to the selected layout. Thumbnails of all other open apps also appear on the desktop within the next position in the layout. Click or tap the app you want to appear in this position.

For layouts with three or more apps, the remaining open apps appear in the next open layout position. Click or tap the app you want to appear in this position.

 TIP You can also "snap" a window full screen by using your mouse to drag the window to the top of the desktop. This automatically maximizes the window.

Scrolling Through a Window

Many windows, whether full screen or otherwise, contain more information than can be displayed onscreen. When you have a long document or web page, only the first part of the document or page displays in the window. To view the rest of the document or page, you have to scroll down through the window using the various parts of the scrollbar (shown in Figure 3.6).

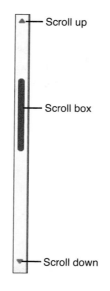

Scroll up

Scroll box

Scroll down

FIGURE 3.6

Use the scrollbar to scroll through long pages.

There are several ways to scroll through a window. To scroll up or down a line at a time, click or tap the up or down arrow on the window's scrollbar. To move to a specific place in a long document, use your mouse or touchpad to grab the scroll box (between the up and down arrows) and drag it to a new position. You can also click or tap the scrollbar between the scroll box and the end arrow so that you scroll one screen at a time.

If your mouse has a scroll wheel, you can use it to scroll through a long document. Just roll the wheel backward or forward to scroll down or up through a window. Likewise, some notebook touchpads let you drag your finger up or down to scroll through a window. And, if your PC has a touchscreen display, you can simply swipe your finger downward in the document to scroll down or swipe upward to scroll up. With a touchscreen display, you also can use your finger to drag or "flick" the screen up or down to scroll.

Peeking at the Desktop

Want to quickly see what's beneath all the open windows on the desktop? Have a gadget you want to look at? Then you'll appreciate the *Peek* feature. With Peek, you can, well, peek at the desktop beneath all that window clutter.

You activate Peek from the little transparent rectangular button at the far right of the Windows taskbar. Click or tap the Peek button, and all open windows are minimized so you see the open desktop.

Using the Start Menu

All the software programs and utilities on your computer are accessed via the Start menu. You display the Start menu by using your mouse or touchpad to click the Start button, located on the left side of the centered taskbar.

Navigating the Start Menu

As you can see in Figure 3.7, the Windows 11 Start menu consists of three parts:

- The top section consists of icons for apps that you've "pinned" to the Start menu. To view an alphabetical list of all the apps installed on your computer, click or tap All Apps.

- The bottom portion consists of icons for recently used files and (sometimes) recommended apps.

- The very bottom slice of the Start menu displays your profile name and picture on the left and a Power button on the right. Click or tap your profile name/ picture to sign out of your account or change users. Click or tap the Power button to shut down or restart your PC or to put it into sleep mode.

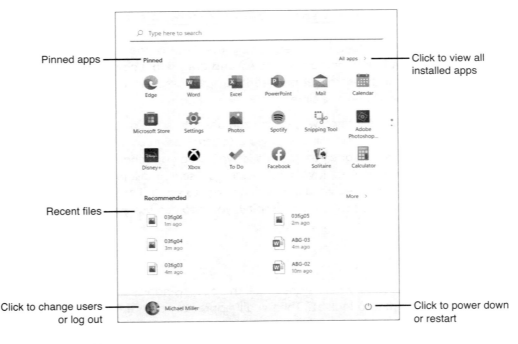

FIGURE 3.7

Access all the programs on your system from the Start menu.

To open a specific program or file, just click the icon for that item.

Launching a Program

Now that you know how to work the Start menu, it's easy to start any particular software program. All you have to do is follow these steps:

1. Click or tap the Start button to display the Start menu.

2. Click or tap the program's name or icon.

Another way to find a program to launch is to use the Search field at the top of the Start menu. Just start entering the program's name into the Search field, and a list of matching programs appears on the Start menu. When the program you want appears, click or tap it to launch it.

Using the Taskbar

That little strip of real estate at the bottom of the Windows desktop is called the *taskbar*. The Windows taskbar lets you open your favorite applications and documents, as well as switch between open windows. For quicker and easier launching, you can even add icons for your favorite programs to the taskbar. Click or tap an icon to launch an app or switch to an open window; taskbar icons exist for both.

Deciphering Taskbar Icons

Because of the multiple functions of the icons on the taskbar, it's difficult to look at an icon on the taskbar and determine whether it represents an open or closed application or document. Difficult, yes, but not impossible. Here's the key.

As you can see in Figure 3.8, an icon for a not-yet-open application or document—essentially a shortcut to that app or doc—appears on the taskbar with no underline. An icon for an open window has a short underline, and the icon for the currently selected open window has a longer underline.

Pinned app ⸻ ⸻ Currently selected open window

Open app

FIGURE 3.8

The Windows taskbar with icons for a (closed) application, open application, and currently selected window.

Opening Applications and Switching Between Windows

Using the taskbar is simplicity itself. Click or tap a shortcut icon to open the associated application or document. Click or tap an open window icon to display that window front and center.

If you click or tap an icon for an app with multiple windows open, something interesting happens: Windows displays thumbnails for each of that application's open windows. (The same thing happens if you mouse over the cursor for any open-window icon, actually.) Move the cursor over a thumbnail, and that window temporarily displays on top of the stack on your desktop, regardless of its actual position. Click a thumbnail to switch to that window, or click the X on the thumbnail to close the window.

Using Jump Lists

The Windows taskbar becomes even more useful with the addition of Jump Lists—kind of context-sensitive pop-up menus for each icon on the taskbar. To display an icon's Jump List, shown in Figure 3.9, right-click the icon.

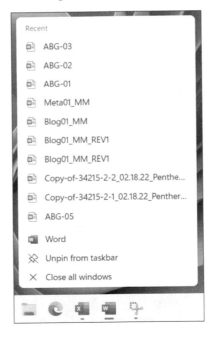

FIGURE 3.9

A Windows taskbar Jump List.

What you see in a Jump List depends to some degree on the application associated with the icon. Most Jump Lists contain the following items:

- The most recent documents opened in this application

- A link to open a new instance of this application

- An option to unpin this item from the taskbar (for shortcut icons)

- An option to close all windows (for open-window icons)

In short, Jump Lists are a lot like traditional right-click pop-up menus in Windows, but with more useful options. They make the new taskbar icons more useful than they would have been otherwise.

Managing Taskbar Buttons

Now that you know what the taskbar does, let's look at how to manage it.

First, know that you have total control over the order of icons on the taskbar. Just drag a taskbar icon from one position to another, and there it stays.

To add an application or document shortcut to the taskbar, just navigate to that item using the Start menu or File Explorer, right-click the item's icon, and select More, Pin to Taskbar. Alternatively, you can drag an icon from any folder to the taskbar. Either approach is quick and easy.

To remove an item from the taskbar, right-click it and select Unpin from Taskbar.

Switching Between Programs

The taskbar is one way to switch between open programs, but it's not the only way. You can also do either of the following:

- Click or tap any visible part of the application's window, which brings that window to the front.

- Hold down the Alt key and then press the Tab key repeatedly until the application window you want is selected. This lets you cycle through thumbnails of all open windows, as shown in Figure 3.10. When you're at the window you want, release the Alt key.

- Click or tap the Task View button on the taskbar. This also displays thumbnails of all open windows. Click a thumbnail to switch to that window.

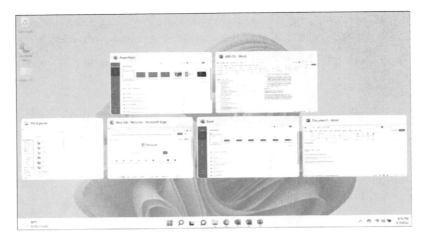

FIGURE 3.10

Press Alt+Tab to cycle through open apps.

Adjusting Quick Settings

Windows 11 has a new Quick Settings panel you use to adjust basic settings—changing volume and brightness levels, connecting to Wi-Fi networks, switching to Airplane mode, and adjusting the screen brightness. To open the Quick Settings panel, click or tap one of the icons the middle of the notifications area on the taskbar. (Figure 3.11 shows the Quick Settings panel.)

FIGURE 3.11

Adjust brightness and volume and connect to Wi-Fi networks from the Quick Settings panel.

Viewing Notifications

If you have any waiting notifications, you see a number next to the date and time area on the taskbar. Click or tap the date and time to display system notifications and notifications from selected apps. There's also a handy calendar if you need it. (Figure 3.12 shows the Notifications panel.)

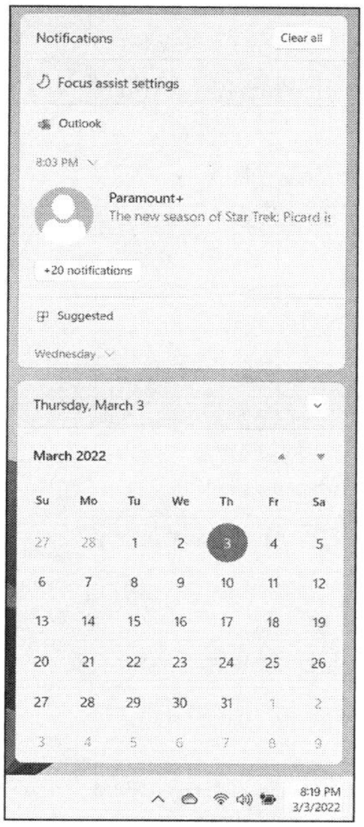

FIGURE 3.12

The Notifications panel.

Learning Important Windows Shortcuts

Now that you know how to use your mouse or touchpad to get around Windows, it's time to learn some shortcuts you can use to speed up important Windows operations. Most of these actions can be initiated with either a mouse, touchpad, or keyboard, as detailed in Table 3.1.

TABLE 3.1 Essential Windows 11 Operations

Operation	Keyboard	Mouse/Touchpad
Close currently running app or window	Alt+F4	Click the X button in top-right corner of window.
Display context-sensitive options menu	Application (menu) key	Right-click.
Display Notifications panel	Windows+N	Click date and time on the taskbar.
Display Quick Settings panel	Windows+A	Click the left side of the notifications area on the taskbar.
Display Start menu	Windows key	Click the Start button.
Lock computer	Windows+L	Click the Start button, click your username, and then click Lock.
Move an item to a new location	N/A	Click and drag, and then release.
Open a program or document	Enter	Click (sometimes double-click).
Open Windows Help	Windows+F1	N/A
Scroll down	Pg Dn or down arrow	Click and drag the scrollbar or click the scroll arrows; use the mouse scroll wheel.
Scroll left	Pg Up or left arrow	Click and drag the scrollbar or click the scroll arrows; use the mouse scroll wheel.
Scroll right	Pg Dn or right arrow	Click and drag the scrollbar or click the scroll arrows; use the mouse scroll wheel.
Scroll up	Pg Up or up arrow	Click and drag the scrollbar or click the scroll arrows; use the mouse scroll wheel.
Search your computer	Windows+S	Click within the Search box on the taskbar.
Shut down Windows	Alt+F4	Click the Start button, click Power, and then click Shut Down.
View or switch to other open apps	Alt+Tab	N/A
View or switch to other virtual desktops	Windows+Tab	Click Task View button on taskbar.

Using Windows with a Touchscreen Display

If you have a computer with a touchscreen display, or if you use a tablet or 2-in-1 PC, you can use your fingers to perform key Windows operations. Table 3.2 details essential touch operations.

TABLE 3.2 Essential Touch Operations

Operation	Does This
Tap	Functions as a mouse click.
Press and hold	Functions as a right-click with a mouse.
Swipe	Performs various functions. For example, swiping in from the right side of the screen opens the Action center. Swiping in from the left side of the screen displays tiles for all open apps.
Pan	Touch and drag a long page to scroll through a series of screens.
Zoom	Pinch two fingers together to zoom out of a page. Spread two fingers apart to zoom into a section.
Rotate	Use two fingers to touch two points on the screen and then turn your fingers to rotate clockwise or counter-clockwise.

Shutting Down Windows—and Your Computer

You've probably already noticed that Windows starts automatically every time you turn on your computer and then displays the Windows desktop.

When you want to turn off your computer, you do it through Windows. In fact, you don't want to turn off your computer any other way—you *always* want to turn off things through the official Windows procedure.

To shut down Windows and turn off your PC, follow these steps:

1. Click or tap the Start button to display the Start menu.

2. Click or tap the Power button to display the pop-up menu of options, as shown in Figure 3.13.

3. Click or tap Shut Down to shut down your computer. You also have the option of putting your computer into Sleep mode (this mode pauses all operations but still consumes some power) or restarting your PC. (This option shuts down the PC and then powers it back up.)

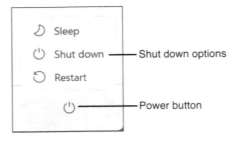

FIGURE 3.13

Shutting down Windows from the Start menu.

That's it. If you have a desktop PC, you then need to manually turn off your monitor, printer, and other peripherals.

THE ABSOLUTE MINIMUM

This chapter gave you a lot of background about Windows 11—your new PC's operating system. Here are the key points to remember:

- You use Windows to manage your computer system and run apps and programs.

- When you start your computer, you see the Windows Lock screen; click or tap this screen to log in to your account and enter Windows.

- Click or tap the Start button to display the Start menu, where all your installed programs are listed.

- The taskbar hosts icons for all open programs, as well as any programs you've "pinned" there for future use.

- To exit Windows and turn off your computer, click or tap the Start button, click the Power button, and select Shut Down.

4

WORKING WITH FILES, FOLDERS, AND ONLINE STORAGE

Managing the data stored on your computer is vital. After you save a file, you might need to copy it to another computer, move it to a new location on your hard drive, rename it, or even delete it. You have to know how to perform all these operations—which means learning how to work with files, folders, and disks in Windows.

Understanding Files and Folders

All the information on your computer is stored in *files*. A file is nothing more than a collection of digital data. The contents of a file can be a document (such as a Word memo or an Excel spreadsheet), a digital photo or music track, or the executable code for a software program.

Every file has a name. A defined structure exists for naming files, and you must follow the naming conventions for Windows to understand exactly what file you want when you try to access one. Each filename must consist of two parts, separated by a period—the *name* (to the left of the period) and the *extension* (to the right of the period). A filename can consist of letters, numbers, spaces, and characters and looks something like this: filename.ext.

Windows stores files in *folders*. A folder is like a parent file; each folder can contain both files and additional folders. The exact location of a file is called its *path* and contains all the folders leading to the file. For example, a file named *filename*.doc that exists in the system folder, which is itself contained in the windows folder on your C: drive, has a path that looks like this: C:\users\ *yourname*\documents\filename.doc.

Learning how to use files and folders is a necessary skill for all computer users. You might need to copy files from one folder to another or from your hard disk to a USB drive. You certainly need to delete files every now and then.

 TIP By default, Windows hides the extensions when it displays filenames. To display extensions in Windows 11, select View, Show, File Name Extensions.

Using File Explorer

In Windows 11, all the items stored on your computer—including programs, documents, and configuration settings—are accessible from *File Explorer*. This is a desktop application that displays all the disk drives, folders, subfolders, and files on your computer system. You use File Explorer to find, copy, delete, and launch programs and documents.

Launching File Explorer

You can launch File Explorer in one of four ways:

- From the taskbar, click or tap the File Explorer icon.
- Click or tap the Start button to display the Start menu; then click or tap the File Explorer icon.

- Right-click the Start menu to display the Options menu; then click or tap File Explorer.

- Press Windows+E on your computer keyboard.

Exploring the File Explorer Window

When you open File Explorer, you see a toolbar on the top, a Path bar beneath that, a Navigation pane on the left, and a contents pane on the right. The Navigation pane is divided into several sections.

The top section, Quick Access, lists your most recently used folders, as well as several folders that are "pinned" to this section: Desktop, Downloads, Documents, Pictures, and Videos. (These are the defaults, but the specific folders listed here can vary.) Next is a OneDrive section, which lists your folders stored on Microsoft's OneDrive Internet-based storage service. Below that is a This PC section, which provides access to all the disk drives and devices connected to your computer. Next is the Network section, which lets you access all your networked computers.

Click any icon in the Navigation pane to view the contents of that item. For example, when you click This PC, you see six pinned folders, as shown in Figure 4.1: Desktop, Documents, Downloads, Music, Pictures, and Videos. There should also be an icon for your computer's C: drive. You may also see icons for any other devices connected to your computer. Double-click or double-tap an icon to view its contents.

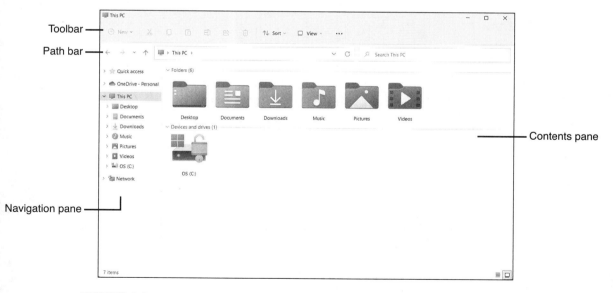

FIGURE 4.1

Navigating through your folders and subfolders with File Explorer.

Displaying File Contents and Details

You can also display a third pane within the File Explorer window. This panel can display the details or a preview of the contents of the currently selected file, depending on what options you select.

To display the Details or the Preview pane, select View, Show and then select either Details Pane or Preview Pane. (Figure 4.2 shows the Details pane in action.)

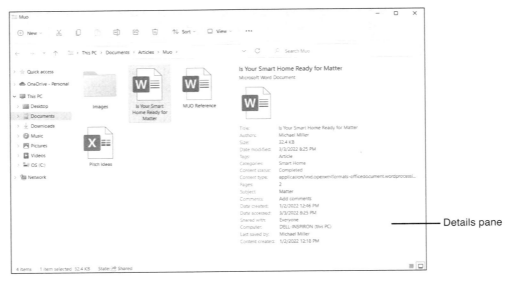
— Details pane

FIGURE 4.2

Displaying file details in the Details pane.

Navigating the Folders on Your PC

After you launch File Explorer, you can navigate through all your folders and sub-folders in several ways:

 NOTE A *subfolder* is a folder that is contained within another folder. Multiple subfolders can be nested in this fashion.

- To view the contents of a disk or folder, double-click or double-tap the selected item.
- To move back to the disk or folder previously selected, click the Back button (left arrow) in the Path bar beneath the toolbar.

- To choose from the history of disks and folders previously viewed, click the down arrow in the Address box in the Path bar and select a disk or folder.

- If you've moved back through multiple disks or folders, you can move forward to the next folder by clicking the Forward button (right arrow) in the Path bar.

- Go directly to any disk or folder by entering the path in the Address box (in the format c:\folder\subfolder) and pressing Enter.

- Move backward through the "bread crumb" path in the Address box. Click any previous folder location (separated by arrows) to display that particular folder.

 TIP   Click any arrow between locations in the Address bar to view additional paths from that location.

Viewing Files and Folders

There's no set way to view the files and folders stored on your computer. In fact, File Explorer has several options to change the way your files and folders display.

Changing the Way Files Display

You can choose to view the contents of a folder in a variety of ways. To change the file view, click or tap View in the toolbar. From here, you can select from eight available views, as shown in Figure 4.3:

- Extra large icons

- Large icons

- Medium icons

- Small icons

- List

- Details

- Tiles

- Content

There's also a Compact view that applies only to the Navigation pane. It squishes together the contents of that pane to take up less room on screen.

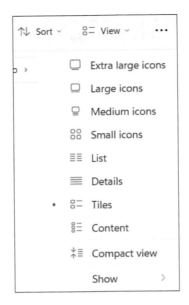

FIGURE 4.3

Use the View menu to change how files display.

 TIP Any of the Icon views are good for working with graphics files or for getting a quick thumbnail glance at a file's contents. The Details view is better if you're looking for files by date or size.

Sorting Files and Folders

When viewing files in File Explorer, you can sort your files and folders in a number of ways. To do this, click or tap Sort in the toolbar and then select Group By. You can then choose to sort by a variety of criteria, including Name, Date Modified, Type, Size, Date Created, Folder Path, Authors, Categories, Tags, or Title.

If you want to view your files in alphabetical order, click or tap Sort in the toolbar and choose to sort by Name. If you want to sort your files by date, select Sort, Date. If you want to see all similar files sorted together, select Sort, Type. Other sort options are available by selecting Sort, More.

To change the sort order of your files, click or tap View on the toolbar and then select either Ascending or Descending.

Grouping Files and Folders

You can also configure File Explorer to group the files in your folder, which can make it easier to identify particular files. For example, if you sort your files by time and date modified, they're grouped by date (Today, Yesterday, Last Week, and so on). If you sort your files by type, they're grouped by file extension, and so on.

To turn on grouping, select View, Group By, and then select the desired parameter. File Explorer now automatically groups your files and folders by the selected criteria.

Searching for Files

As organized as you might be, you might not always find the specific files you want. Fortunately, Windows 11 offers an easy way to locate difficult-to-find files, via the Instant Search function. Instant Search indexes all the files stored on your hard disk (including email messages) by type, title, and contents. So you can search for a file by extension, filename, or keywords within the document.

To use the Instant Search feature, enter one or more keywords into the Search box in the Path bar. Matching files display as you type; you can select one of these or finish entering the keyword(s) and then press Enter. File Explorer displays a list of items that match your search criteria. Double-click or double-tap any icon to open that file.

TIP   You can also search for files from anywhere in Windows 11. Just click or tap the Search icon on the taskbar to display the Search panel and start searching from there.

Performing Basic File and Folder Operations

You can perform most common file and folder operations using the functions available on the File Explorer toolbar, shown in Figure 4.4. These functions include Cut, Copy, Paste, Rename, Share, and Delete; you also can create folders.

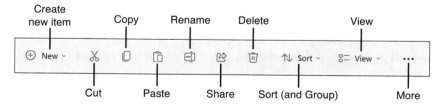

FIGURE 4.4

Use the toolbar in File Explorer to perform basic file and folder operations.

Creating New Folders

The more files you create, the harder it is to organize and find things on your hard disk. When the number of files you have becomes unmanageable, you need to create more folders—and subfolders—to better categorize your files.

To create a new folder, follow these steps:

1. Navigate to the drive or folder where you want to place the new folder.

2. On the toolbar, select New, Folder.

3. A new, empty folder appears within the File Explorer window, with the file-name New Folder highlighted.

4. Type a name for your folder (which overwrites the New Folder name), and press Enter.

 CAUTION   Folder and filenames can include up to 255 characters—including many special characters. Some special characters, however, are "illegal," meaning that you *can't* use them in folder or filenames. Illegal characters include the following: \ / : * ? " < > |.

 CAUTION   The one part of the filename you should never change is the extension—the part that comes after the "dot." That's because Windows and other software programs recognize different types of program files and documents by their extension. This is why, by default, Windows hides these file extensions—so you can't change them by mistake.

Renaming Files and Folders

When you create a new file or folder, it helps to give it a name that somehow describes its contents. Sometimes, however, you might need to change a file's name. Fortunately, Windows makes it relatively easy to rename an item.

To rename a file (or folder), follow these steps:

1. Click or tap the file or folder you want to rename.

2. Click or tap the Rename button on the toolbar.

3. Type a new name for your file or folder (which overwrites the current name), and press Enter.

Copying Files

Copying a file lets you re-create that file in a different location, either on your computer's hard drive or on some sort of external media. Here's how to do it:

1. Select the item you want to copy.

2. Click or tap the Copy button on the toolbar.

3. Navigate to the folder where you want to copy the item.

4. Click or tap the Paste button on the toolbar.

Moving (Cutting and Pasting) Files

Moving a file (or folder) is different from copying it. Moving *cuts* the item from one location and *pastes* it into a new location. Copying leaves the item in its original location *and* creates a copy of the item elsewhere.

In other words, when you copy something, you end up with two of it. When you move something, you have only the one instance.

To move a file, follow these steps:

1. Select the item you want to move.

2. Click or tap the Cut button on the toolbar.

3. Navigate to the new location where you want to move the item.

4. Click or tap the Paste button.

Deleting Files

Too many files eat up too much hard disk space—which is a bad thing because you have only so much disk space. (Music and video files, in particular, can chew up big chunks of your hard drive.) Because you don't want to waste disk space, you should periodically delete the files (and folders) you no longer need.

Deleting a file is as easy as following these simple steps:

1. Select the file or files you want to delete. (To select multiple files, hold down the Ctrl key while clicking or tapping.)

2. Click or tap the Delete button on the toolbar.

This simple operation sends the file to the Windows Recycle Bin, which is kind of a trash can for deleted files. (It's also a trash can that periodically needs to be dumped—as I discuss momentarily.)

TIP You can also delete a file by selecting it and then pressing the Delete key on your computer keyboard.

Working with the Recycle Bin

As just discussed, all recently deleted files are stored in what Windows calls the Recycle Bin. This is a special folder on your hard disk that temporarily stores all deleted items—which is a good thing.

Restoring Deleted Files

Have you ever accidentally deleted the wrong file? If so, you're in luck, thanks to the Recycle Bin. As you now know, Windows stores all the files you delete in the Recycle Bin, at least temporarily. If you've recently deleted a file, it should still be in the Recycle Bin folder.

To "undelete" a file from the Recycle Bin, follow these steps:

1. Double-click or double-tap the Recycle Bin icon on the desktop (shown in Figure 4.5) to open the Recycle Bin folder.

FIGURE 4.5

The Recycle Bin, where all your deleted files end up.

2. Click or tap the file(s) you want to restore.
3. From the toolbar, select More, Restore the Selected Items.

The deleted file is copied back to its original location, ready for continued use.

Emptying the Recycle Bin

Deleted files do not stay in the Recycle Bin indefinitely. When you delete enough files to exceed the space allocated for these files, the oldest files in the Recycle Bin are automatically and permanently deleted from your hard disk.

If you'd rather dump the Recycle Bin manually (and thus free up some hard disk space), follow these steps:

1. Double-click or double-tap the Recycle Bin icon on your desktop to open the Recycle Bin folder.

2. Click or tap the Empty the Recycle Bin button on the toolbar.

3. When the confirmation dialog box appears, click or tap Yes to completely erase the files; click or tap No to continue storing the files in the Recycle Bin.

Working with Compressed Folders

Really big files can be difficult to move or copy. They're especially difficult to transfer to other users, whether by email or USB drive.

Fortunately, Windows includes a way to make big files smaller. *Compressed folders* (sometimes called *zip files*) take big files and compress their size, which makes them easier to copy or move. After you transfer the file, you can uncompress the file to its original state.

Compressing a File

Compressing one or more files is a relatively easy task from within any folder in File Explorer. Just follow these steps:

1. Select the file(s) you want to compress. (Hold down the Ctrl button as you select multiple files.)

2. On the toolbar, select More (three dots), Compress to ZIP file.

Windows creates a new folder that contains compressed versions of the file(s) you selected. (This folder is distinguished by a little zipper on the folder icon.) You can copy, move, or email this folder, which is a lot smaller than the original file(s).

 NOTE The compressed folder is actually a file with a .ZIP extension, so you can use it with other compression/decompression programs, such as WinZip.

Extracting Files from a Compressed Folder

The process of decompressing a file is actually an *extraction* process. That's because you extract the original file(s) from the compressed folder. Follow these steps:

1. Select the compressed folder.

2. From the toolbar, select Extract All. This displays the Select a Destination and Extract Files dialog box.

3. Accept the current location or click the Browse button and choose a different location.

4. Click or tap the Extract button.

Copying Files to Another Computer

Of course, you're not limited to copying and moving files from one location to another on a single PC. You can also copy files to other PCs via either a network connection or some sort of portable disk drive.

Copying Files over a Network

I talk more about network operations in Chapter 9, "Setting Up Whole-House Internet and a Home Network." For now, it's important to know that if your PC is connected to a network and has file sharing activated, you can copy and move files from one network computer to another just as you can within folders on a single computer.

Copying Files with a Portable Drive

If you're not on a network, you can use a portable drive to transport files from one computer to another. The most popular type of portable drive today is the USB drive (sometimes called a flash drive or thumb drive), such as the one shown in Figure 4.6, which stores computer data in flash memory. You can find USB drives with capacities up to 1TB—more than big enough to hold even your biggest files.

FIGURE 4.6

Use a USB drive to transport files from one computer to another.

To use a USB drive, simply insert the device into an open USB port on your computer. After you insert it, the drive appears as a new drive in the This PC section of the File Explorer navigation pane. Double-click or double-tap the USB drive icon to view the contents of the drive; you can then copy and paste files from your hard drive to the USB drive and vice versa. When you finish copying files, just remove the USB device. It's that simple.

Copying Files via Email

Another popular way to send files from one computer to another is via email. You can send any file as an email *attachment*; a file is literally attached to an email message. When the message is sent, the recipient can open or save the attached file when reading the message.

To learn how to send files as email attachments, turn to Chapter 13, "Sending and Receiving Email."

Working with Cloud-Based Storage

In addition to the local storage on your personal computer, Microsoft offers online storage for all your documents and data, via its OneDrive service. When you store your files on OneDrive, you can access them via any computer or mobile device connected to the Internet.

This type of online file storage is called *cloud storage* because the files are stored on the "cloud" of computers on the Internet. The advantage of cloud storage is that you can access files from any computer (work, home, or other) at any location. You're not limited to using a given file on one particular computer.

Cloud storage is also great if you want to share your files with others. You can configure your files so that your friends and family can view them, or so that your work colleagues can edit and collaborate on them. It's all up to you, and all available to any person with a web browser and an Internet connection.

Accessing OneDrive from File Explorer

You can use File Explorer to view and manage the files stored online with OneDrive. Follow these steps:

1. From within File Explorer, click or tap OneDrive in the navigation pane. This displays all your OneDrive files and folders, as shown in Figure 4.7.

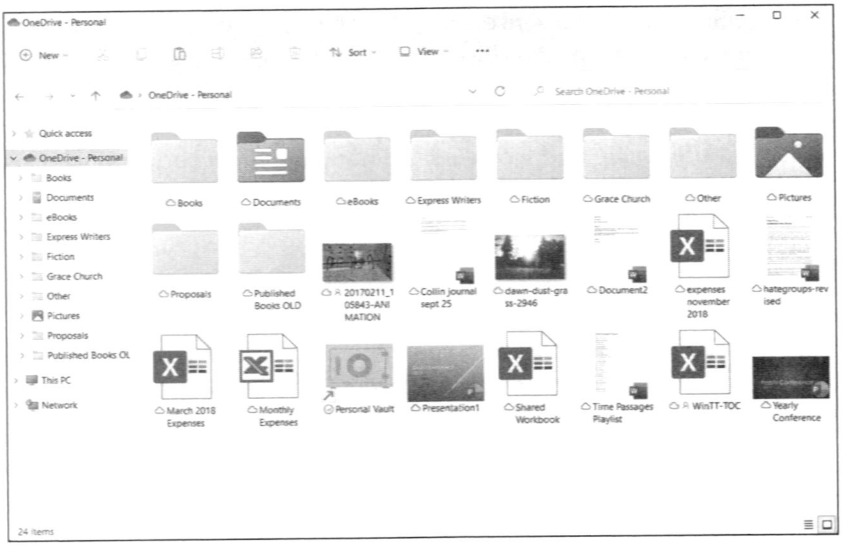

FIGURE 4.7

Viewing OneDrive contents in File Explorer.

2. Double-click or double-tap to open a folder.

3. Double-click or double-tap to open a file.

4. To manage your files, click any file, and then click or tap the appropriate option on File Explorer's toolbar.

Using Microsoft OneDrive

You can also view and manage your OneDrive files from the OneDrive website. Follow these steps:

1. From within any web browser, go to onedrive.live.com and either sign into an existing account or sign up for a new one.

2. As you can see in Figure 4.8, the OneDrive website displays the files you uploaded. If you organized your files into folders, you see those folders on the main page. Click a folder to view its contents.

3. Click a file to view it, or in the case of an Office document, open it in its online application.

4. To copy, cut, or rename a file, mouse over the file to display the selection circle, and then click or tap the circle to select the file. You can then select the action you want from the toolbar.

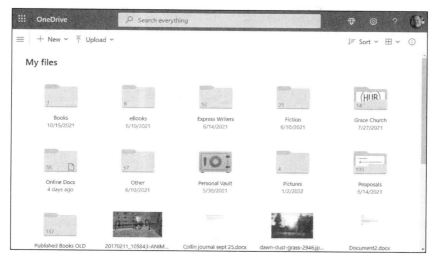

FIGURE 4.8

Viewing online folders and files on the OneDrive website.

5. To download a file from OneDrive to your local hard disk, select the file and then click or tap Download from the toolbar.

6. To upload a file from your computer to OneDrive, click or tap Upload and then select Files; when the Open dialog box appears, select the file to upload and then click or tap Open.

 NOTE   Microsoft gives you 5GB of storage in your free OneDrive account, which is more than enough to store most users' documents, digital photos, and the like. If you need more storage, you can purchase an additional 100GB for $1.99 USD per month. (You also get additional OneDrive storage if you sign up for a subscription to Microsoft 365.)

Syncing Files on Your PC to OneDrive

You can also use OneDrive to synchronize files stored on your computer with those stored in the cloud. You do this by using the OneDrive folder in File Explorer.

To synchronize a file in this fashion, it must be stored in a special OneDrive folder. Then, whenever you connect to the Internet, any changes you make to that file are automatically made to the version of that file stored on OneDrive.

All you have to do is use File Explorer to copy the file in question to the OneDrive folder. Navigate to the file, and then drag it onto the OneDrive folder in the Navigation pane. From then on out, it's easy; OneDrive does all the syncing for you.

 NOTE Microsoft OneDrive is just one of many cloud storage services you can use to store and share your files online. Other popular services include Apple iCloud (www.icloud.com), Box (www.box.com), Dropbox (www.dropbox.com), and Google Drive (www.google.com/drive/). All these services work in a similar fashion. Check out the various services before you commit—especially for a paid plan.

THE ABSOLUTE MINIMUM

Here are the key points to remember from this chapter:

- You manage your files and folders from File Explorer.
- Most common file and folder operations are found on File Explorer's toolbar.
- If you accidentally delete a file, you might recover it by opening the Recycle Bin window.
- If you need to share a really big file, consider compressing it into a compressed folder (also known as a zip file).
- To copy a file to another PC, you can copy the file over a network, send the file as an email attachment, or copy the file to a portable USB drive.
- You can also store your files online, using Microsoft's OneDrive or other cloud-based file storage services.

5

PERSONALIZING WINDOWS

One of the nice things about Windows is that your version of Windows doesn't have to look or feel exactly like your neighbor's version. You can easily personalize various aspects of the operating system by tweaking a handful of configuration settings. Make Windows reflect your personality!

Personalizing the Windows Desktop

Windows 11 enables you to personalize the desktop in a number of ways. You can change the color scheme and the desktop background. You can "pin" your favorite programs to the taskbar or directly to the desktop. There are even special "light" and "dark" modes that completely change how Windows looks.

Changing the Desktop Background

One of the most popular ways to personalize the desktop is to use a favorite picture or color as the desktop background. Follow these steps:

1. Right-click in any open area of the desktop to display the pop-up menu; then click Personalize to display the Personalization tab of the Settings app. (Alternatively, open the Settings app and select Personalization.)

2. Click or tap Background to display the Background page, as shown in Figure 5.1.

FIGURE 5.1

Choosing a desktop background.

3. Use a picture as your desktop background by clicking or tapping the Personalize Your Background control and selecting Picture. Select one of the images displayed or click Browse Photos to select another picture stored on your computer.

NOTE   If the selected image is a different size than your Windows desktop, click the Choose a Fit for Your Desktop Image list and select a display option—Fill (zooms into the picture to fill the screen), Fit (fits the image to fill the screen horizontally but might leave black bars around the image), Stretch (distorts the picture to fill the screen), Tile (displays multiple instances of a smaller image), Center (displays a smaller image in the center of the screen with black space around it), or Span (spans a single image across multiple monitors, if you have multiple monitors on your system).

4. To have a solid-color desktop background instead of a picture, click or tap the Personalize Your Background list and select Solid Color. Select the color you want or click or tap View Colors in the Custom Colors section to choose from a broader palette.

5. To have your desktop background rotate through a variety of pictures in a slideshow, click the Personalize Your Background list and select Slideshow. By default, the slideshow chooses pictures from your Pictures folder; to select a different folder, click Browse. Change how long each photo is displayed by clicking the Change Picture Every list and making a new selection. Display pictures randomly by clicking "on" the Shuffle switch.

Changing to Light or Dark Mode

Windows 11 offers both Light and Dark modes. Dark mode displays a black background in the taskbar, Start menu, and many windows. Light mode displays a light gray background in these same areas.

Follow these steps:

1. Right-click in any open area of the desktop to display the pop-up menu; then click Personalize to display the Personalization tab of the Settings app. (Alternatively, open the Settings app and select Personalization.)

2. Click or tap Colors to display the Colors page.

3. Click the Choose Your Color list and select either Light or Dark.

4. To set one mode for Windows elements and the other for apps, select Custom. You can then click or tap the Choose Your Default Windows Mode list and select either Light or Dark to set the mode for the Start menu, taskbar, and other Windows elements. Click the Choose Your Default App Mode list and select either Light or Dark to set the mode for your Windows apps.

Changing the Accent Color

You can select any accent color for window borders and title bars. In Dark mode, the accent color is also for the Start menu and taskbar. Follow these steps:

1. Right-click in any open area of the desktop to display the pop-up menu; then click Personalize to display the Personalization tab of the Settings app. (Alternatively, open the Settings app and select Personalization.)

2. Click or tap Colors to display the Colors page shown in Figure 5.2.

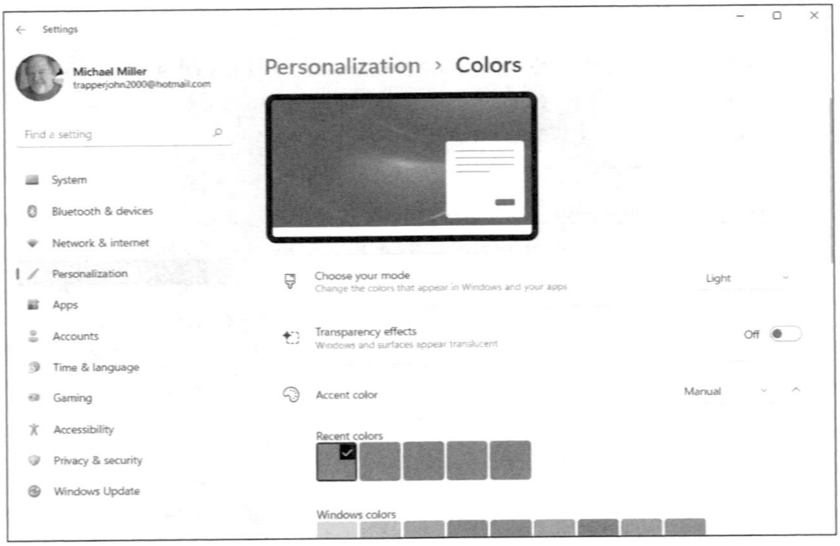

FIGURE 5.2

Choosing an accent color.

3. Make the Windows desktop elements transparent by clicking "on" the Transparency Effects switch.

4. To have Windows automatically choose the accent color based on the color of the desktop image, click the Accent Color control and select Automatic.

5. To manually select an accent color, click the Accent Color control and select Manual; then click to select the color you want.

6. If you're in Windows Dark mode, you can show the accent color on the Start menu and taskbar by scrolling down the window and clicking "on" the Show Accent Color on Start and taskbar switch. Click this switch "off" to show these elements in standard system colors (gray in Light mode, black in Dark mode).

7. Show the accent color on windows' title bars and borders by clicking "on" the Show Accent Color on Title Bars and Window Borders switch. Click this switch "off" to display these elements in standard system colors.

Choosing a Windows Theme

Rather than configuring each desktop element separately, you can choose a pre-designed *theme* that changes all the elements in a visually pleasing configuration. A theme combines background images, color schemes, system sounds, and a screensaver to present a unified look and feel. Some themes even change the color scheme to match the current background picture.

To select a theme, follow these steps:

1. Right-click in any open area of the desktop to display the pop-up menu; then click Personalize to display the Personalization tab of the Settings app window. (Alternatively, open the Settings app and select Personalization.)

2. Click or tap Themes to display the Themes page shown in Figure 5.3.

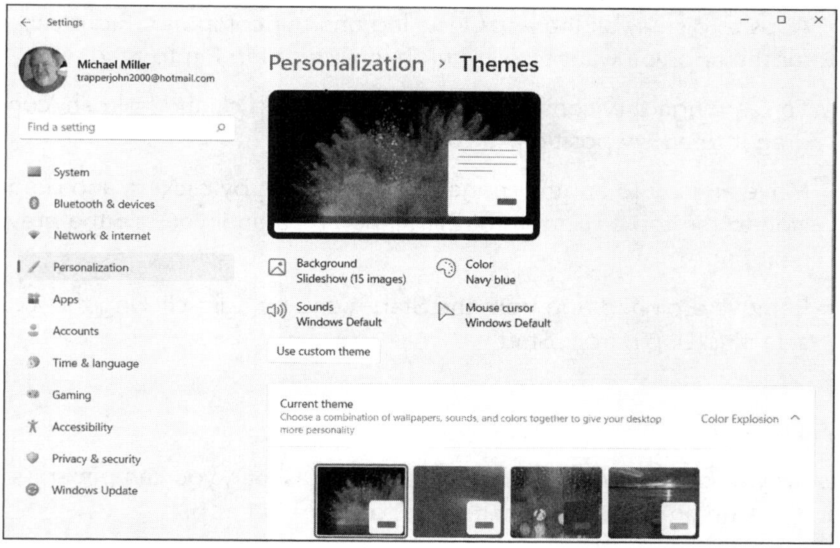

FIGURE 5.3

Choosing a new Windows theme.

3. To save the currently selected background, color, sound, and mouse scheme as a new theme, click Save. When prompted, give this new theme a name.

4. Scroll down to the Current Theme section to view all themes installed on your PC. Click any theme to change to that theme.

5. Additional themes, most free of charge, are available from the Microsoft Store online. Click Browse Themes to view what's available and download new themes.

Customizing the Start Menu

The Windows 11 Start menu is different from the Start menu in Windows 10 in that it displays small icons for your favorite and most-used apps instead of the larger tiles in the older operating system. This makes for a leaner and more efficient Start menu experience that you can still customize by "pinning" icons for your favorite apps.

 NOTE "Pinning" an app creates a shortcut to that app. You can pin programs to either the Start menu or the taskbar. Pins you add can be removed at any time.

1. Click or tap the Start button to open the Start menu.

2. "Pin" a program to the top half of the Start menu by clicking or tapping All Apps to display all the apps installed on your computer. Right-click the icon for the app you want to pin and then click or tap Pin to Start.

3. To rearrange the icons for your pinned apps, click and hold an icon and then drag it to a new position.

4. Move an icon to another page of pinned apps by clicking and dragging the icon to the top or bottom of the Pinned area until you see the previous or next page.

5. Remove a pinned app from the Start menu by right-clicking the icon and selecting Unpin from Start.

Pinning Apps to the Taskbar

Just as you can pin your favorite apps to the taskbar, you can pin apps to the taskbar. Click on an icon for a pinned app to open that app:

1. From the Start menu, navigate to the app you want to pin to the taskbar.

2. Right-click the app icon and select Pin to Taskbar.

3. Rearrange pinned apps on the taskbar by clicking and dragging an icon left or right to a new position.

Customizing the Taskbar

Windows 11 also lets you customize the way the taskbar appears on your computer. You can opt to shift the icons to the left side of the taskbar (instead of centering them) and select which icons appear in the notification area.

 NOTE   In previous versions of Windows, you could move the taskbar to the left, right, or top of the screen. Unfortunately, you can't reposition the taskbar in Windows 11; it's always on the bottom.

1. Right-click any open area of the taskbar; then click or tap Taskbar Settings to display the Taskbar page of the Settings app.

2. Click or tap "on" or "off" to show or not show on the taskbar the four system icons: Search, Task View, Widgets, and Chat.

3. You can also opt to show three additional icons in the corner of the taskbar: Pen Menu, Touch Keyboard, and Virtual Touchpad. Click or tap each item's switch "on" to show it on the taskbar, or click or tap it "off" to hide it.

4. There are several additional icons you can display in the corner of the taskbar by the notification area, including Microsoft OneDrive, Windows Explorer, Windows Security Notification, Microsoft Outlook, and Windows Update Status. Click or tap to expand the Taskbar Corner Overflow section and then click or tap each item "on" or "off."

5. Change the alignment of the taskbar icons by clicking or tapping to expand the Taskbar Behaviors section. Then pull down the Taskbar Alignment list and select either Center (default) or Left.

6. Hide the taskbar when you're not using it (it appears when you mouse over the bottom of the screen) by clicking or tapping to select Automatically Hide the Taskbar.

7. Display a number counter for unread messages (called "badges") on select app icons by clicking or tapping to select Show Badges. This option is on by default; deselect this option to hide those little numbers.

8. To be able to click or tap the far-right corner of the desktop to minimize all open windows and show the desktop, click or tap to select Select the Far Corner of the Desktop to Show the Desktop.

Personalizing Widgets

Windows 11 introduces the concept of *widgets*, which are similar to the Start menu tiles found in Windows 10 (but *not* in Windows 11). A widget is a small panel that displays specific information, such as news, weather, appointments, and the like. Many apps, such as Photos and Weather, have their own related widgets. Other widget content is sourced from around the Web.

Widgets are displayed in a Widgets panel that slides in from the left side of the desktop, as shown in Figure 5.4.

FIGURE 5.4

The Widgets panel in Windows 11.

There are two ways to open the Widgets panel. You can click, tap, or hover over the Weather section on the left side of the taskbar or, on a touchscreen display, swipe in from the left side of the screen.

With the Widgets panel displayed, scroll down to view more widgets. To open the associated app or view more information, click or tap the title of a given widget. To close the Widgets panel, click or tap anywhere else on the screen.

Customizing the Widgets Panel

You can personalize the Widgets panel by resizing, deleting, and rearranging widgets. Here's how it works:

1. Resize a widget by clicking or tapping the More Options (three-dot) button and selecting a different size.

 NOTE Not all widgets can be displayed at all available sizes. Each widget displays in just one of the two columns in the Widgets panel; small widgets are shorter, whereas medium and large ones are taller.

2. Customize the content of a widget by clicking or tapping the More Options button and selecting Customize Widget. (Each widget has its own customization options.)

3. Rearrange widgets by using your mouse or touchpad (or finger on a touch-screen device) to drag a widget to a different location.

4. Remove a widget by clicking or tapping the More Options button and selecting Remove Widget.

Adding a New Widget to the Widgets Panel

Microsoft prepopulates the Widgets panel with a selection of popular widgets. You don't have to limit yourself to these particular widgets, however; it's an easy two-step process to add new widgets to the panel at any time:

1. Scroll down the Widgets panel and click or tap Add Widgets.

2. Select the new widget(s) you want to add.

Customizing Your News Feed

As you scroll down the Widgets panel, you see tiles for news stories. These tiles are part of your News Feed, which is a permanent section of the Widgets panel. Click or tap the tile for any story to read the story in full in the Microsoft Edge web browser.

To customize the news widgets that appear, follow these steps:

1. Scroll down the Widgets panel and click or tap Add Widgets.

2. In the Personalize Your Feed section, click or tap Personalize Your Interests. This opens Microsoft Edge to the My Interests page.

3. Select those topics you're interested in and deselect those that don't interest you.

4. Add a specific interest to your feed by entering that topic into the Discover Interests search box and then selecting the matching interest.

NOTE When you find a story that you don't like, mouse over that story's widget and click the X. You can then select that you're not interested in stories like this or you don't want to see any more stories from this particular source.

Personalizing the Lock Screen

You can also personalize the Lock screen that you see when you first start or begin to log in to Windows. You can change the background picture of the Lock screen, turn the Lock screen into a photo slideshow, and add informational apps to the screen.

Changing the Lock Screen Background

To change the background picture you see on the Lock screen, follow these steps:

1. Right-click in any open area of the desktop to display the pop-up menu; then click Personalize to display the Personalization tab of the Settings app. (Alternatively, open the Settings app and select Personalization.)

2. Click or tap Lock Screen to display the Lock Screen page, shown in Figure 5.5.

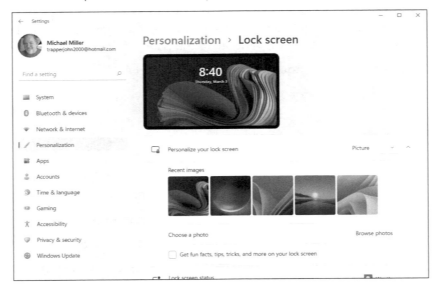

FIGURE 5.5

Personalizing the Lock screen.

3. Choose a specific picture for the Lock screen by clicking the Personalize Your Lock Screen list and selecting Picture.

4. Select the thumbnail for the picture you want to use or click or tap the Browse Photos button to choose a picture stored on your computer.

 TIP   You can let Microsoft select Lock screen photos that display on a rotating basis. Just pull down the Personalize Your Lock Screen list and select Windows Spotlight.

Displaying a Slideshow on the Lock Screen

Windows 11 lets you turn your computer into a kind of digital picture frame by displaying a slideshow of your photos on the Lock screen while your PC isn't used. Follow these steps:

1. Right-click in any open area of the desktop to display the pop-up menu; then click Personalize to display the Personalization tab of the Settings app. (Alternatively, open the Settings app and select Personalization.)

2. Click or tap Lock Screen.

3. Click or tap the Personalize Your Lock Screen list and select Slideshow.

4. By default, Windows displays pictures from your Pictures folder. Click the Browse button to select a different picture folder to use for your slideshow.

5. Click Advanced Slideshow Settings to display additional options.

Changing Your Account Picture

When you first configured Windows, you may have picked a default image to use as your profile picture—or not. You can, at any time, select a new or different profile picture that's more to your liking. Follow these steps:

1. Click the Start button to display the Start menu.

2. Click your name or picture at the bottom of the Start menu to display the options menu.

3. Click Change Account Settings to display the Settings app with the Your Info page selected, as shown in Figure 5.6.

4. Select a picture stored on your computer (or online at OneDrive) by scrolling to the Choose File section and clicking Browse Files. Then navigate to and select the picture you want. *Or...*

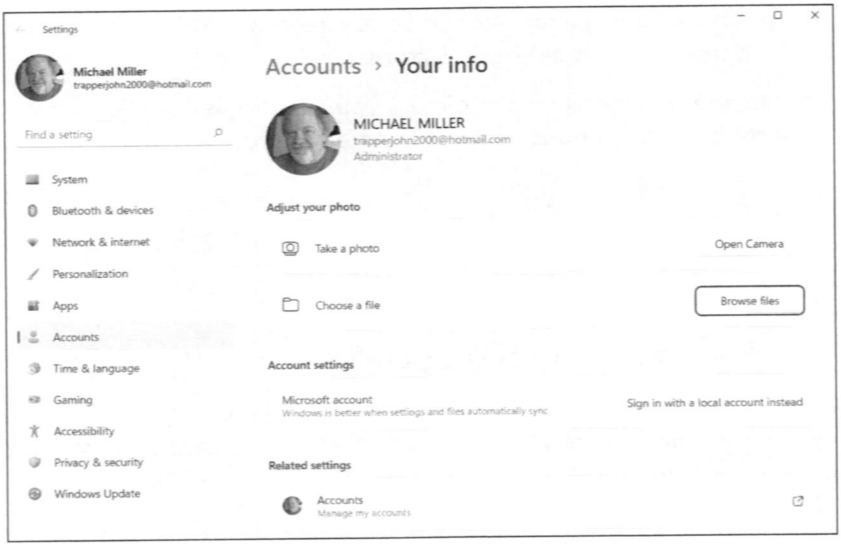

FIGURE 5.6

Changing your account picture.

5. You can take a picture with your computer's webcam to use for your account picture. In the Take a Photo section, click Open Camera and follow the onscreen directions from there.

Setting Up Additional User Accounts

Chances are you're not the only person using your computer; it's likely that you'll be sharing your PC with your spouse or kids, at least to some degree. Fortunately, you can configure Windows so that different people using your computer sign on with their own custom settings—and have access to their own personal files.

The way to do this is to assign each user in your household their own password-protected *user account*. Anyone trying to access another user's account and files without the password is denied access.

NOTE When you set up an account, you can choose from several different ways to log in. You're probably used to signing in with a password, but Microsoft is now encouraging using more secure methods. If your PC is compatible, fingerprint or facial recognition are the most secure ways to log in. Absent those, Microsoft recommends using a five-digit PIN instead of a password because the PIN is more difficult for hackers to guess.

Creating a New User Account

You create one user account when you first launch Windows on your new PC. At any time, you can create additional user accounts for other people using your computer.

By default, Windows uses an existing Microsoft account to create your new Windows user account. So, if you have an Outlook.com, OneDrive, Skype, Xbox Live, or other Microsoft account, you can use that account to sign in to Windows on your computer.

Follow these steps:

1. Open the Start menu and click or tap the Settings icon to open the Settings app.

2. Click or tap Accounts to display the Accounts page.

3. Click or tap Family & Other Users.

4. Scroll to the Other Users section and click or tap Add Account to display the Microsoft Account window.

5. Click or tap I Don't Have This Person's Sign-In Information.

6. Click or tap Get a New Email Address to display the Create Account page.

7. Click to pull down the domain list and make sure Outlook.com is selected.

8. Enter the desired email username into the New Email field and then click Next. (You might have to try several names to get one that isn't already taken.)

9. Enter the desired password into the Create a Password box.

 NOTE   Passwords must be at least eight characters long and contain at least two of the following: uppercase letters, lowercase letters, numbers, and symbols.

10. If you don't want this person to receive Microsoft junk mail, uncheck the I Would Like Information, Tips, and Offers About Microsoft Products and Services box; then click Next.

11. Enter the person's first and last name and then click Next.

12. Select the region where this person lives, enter the person's birthdate, and then click Next. The new account is created, and the new user can now sign in to Windows from the Lock screen.

Switching Users

If other people use your computer, they might want to log in with their own accounts. To switch users on a Windows 11 computer, follow these steps:

1. Click or tap the Start button to display the Start menu.

2. Click or tap your name or picture at the bottom of the Start menu to display a list of other users, as shown in Figure 5.7.

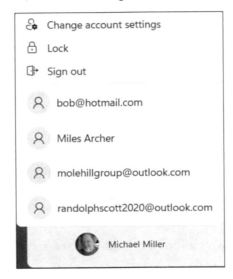

FIGURE 5.7

Switching users from the Start menu.

3. Click or tap the desired user's name.

4. When prompted, enter the new user's sign-in information and then press Enter.

Signing Out

When you switch users, both accounts remain active; the original user account is suspended in the background. If you'd rather log out completely from a given account and return to the Windows Lock screen, follow these steps:

1. Click or tap the Start button to display the Start menu.

2. Click or tap your name or picture.

3. Click or tap Sign Out.

Signing In with Multiple Users

In Chapter 3, "Getting to Know Windows 11," you learned how to sign in to Windows when your computer first starts up. If you have more than one user assigned to Windows 11, however, the sign-in process is slightly different. After you power up your computer, follow these steps:

1. When the Windows Lock screen appears, press any key on your keyboard, click the mouse, touch the touchpad, or swipe the touchscreen display (if you have one) to display the sign-in screen. All users of this computer are displayed here.

2. Click or tap your username to display your personal sign-in screen.

3. Enter your PIN or password (or use another sign-in option); then press the Enter key to display your personal desktop.

Configuring Other Windows Settings

There are many other Windows system settings that you can configure. In most cases, the default settings work fine, and you don't need to change a thing. However, you *can* change these settings, if you want to or need to.

You configure the most common Windows settings from the Settings app, shown in Figure 5.8. This tool offers a series of options that present different types of settings. You open the Settings app by clicking the Settings icon on the Start menu.

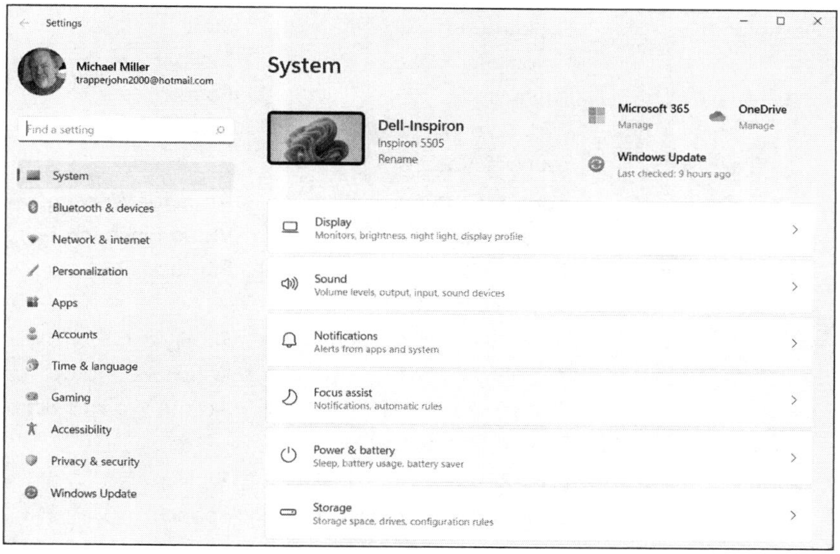

FIGURE 5.8

Configuring Windows from the Settings window.

In Windows 11, there are 11 main configuration options available from the left-side navigation panel of the Settings app. Table 5.1 details these settings.

TABLE 5.1   Windows Settings

Option	Settings	
System	Display	Multitasking
	Sound	Activation
	Notifications	Troubleshoot
	Focus Assist	Recovery
	Power & Battery	Projecting to This PC
	Storage	Remote Desktop
	Nearby Sharing	Clipboard About
Bluetooth & Devices	Bluetooth	Touchpad
	Devices	Touch
	Printers & Scanners	Pen & Windows Ink
	Your Phone	AutoPlay
	Cameras	USB
	Mouse	
Network & Internet	Wi-Fi	Airplane Mode
	Ethernet (if your computer is connected via Ethernet)	Proxy
		Dial-Up
	VPN	Advanced Network Settings
	Mobile Hotspot	
Personalization	Background	Start
	Colors	Taskbar
	Themes	Fonts
	Lock Screen	Device Usage
	Touch Keyboard	
Apps	Apps & Features	Apps for Websites
	Default Apps	Video Playback
	Offline Maps	Startup
	Optional Features	
Accounts	Your Microsoft Account	Family & Other Users
	Your Info	Windows Backup
	Email & Accounts	Access Work or School
	Sign-In Options	
Time & Language	Date & Time	Typing
	Language & Region	Speech

Gaming	Xbox Game Bar	
	Captures	
	Game Mode	
Accessibility	Text Size	Narrator
	Visual Effects	Audio
	Mouse Pointer and Touch	Captions
	Text Cursor	Speech
	Magnifier	Keyboard
	Color Filters	Mouse
	Contrast Themes	Eye Control
Privacy & Security	Windows Security	Calendar
	Find My Device	Phone Calls
	Device Encryption	Call History
	For Developers	Email
	General	Texts
	Speech	Messaging
	Inking and Typing	Radios
	Personalization	Other Devices
	Diagnostics & Feedback	App Diagnostics
	Activity History	Automatic File Downloads
	Search Permissions	Documents
	Searching Windows	Downloads Folder
	Location	Music Library
	Camera	Pictures
	Microphone	Videos
	Voice Activation	File System
	Notifications	Screenshot Borders
	Account Info	Screenshots and Apps
	Contacts	
Windows Update	Check for Updates	Advanced Options
	Pause Updates	Windows Insider Program
	Update History	

THE ABSOLUTE MINIMUM

This chapter showed you pretty much everything you need to know to customize Windows 11. Here are the key points to remember:

- You can personalize the Windows 11 desktop by choosing new background images, color schemes, and even complete system themes.

- Windows 11 lets you choose between Light and Dark modes.

- You can customize the Lock screen with a selected image or display a photo slideshow instead.

- There's a new Widgets panel in Windows 11 you can personalize to display the news and information you want.

- If you have multiple people using your computer, you can create separate user accounts for each person.

- You configure additional Windows settings from the Settings app.

PART III

SETTING UP THE REST OF YOUR SYSTEM

CONNECTING PRINTERS AND OTHER DEVICES TO YOUR PC

If you just purchased a brand-new, right-out-of-the-box personal computer, it probably came equipped with all the components you could ever want—or so you think. At some point in the future, however, you might want to expand your system by adding a printer, a scanner, an external hard drive, better speakers, a different mouse or keyboard, or something equally new and exciting.

Adding new hardware to your system is relatively easy if you know what you're doing. That's where this chapter comes in.

Getting to Know the Most Popular Peripherals

When adding stuff to your PC, what are the most popular peripherals? Here's a list of hardware you can add to or upgrade on your system:

- **Gamepad or other game controller:** Enables you to get better action with your favorite games.

- **Hard disk drive:** Adds more storage capacity to your system or performs periodic backups from your main hard disk. The easiest type of hard drive to add is an external unit, which typically connects via USB and costs less than $100 USD. If you have a traditional desktop PC with a big enough system unit, you might also be able to add a second internal drive inside your system unit, but that's a lot more work.

 NOTE Learn more about adding a hard drive to your system in Chapter 8, "Adding Storage and Backup."

- **Keyboard**—Supplements a notebook's built-in keyboard with a larger, more fully featured model, or upgrades the capabilities of a desktop's included keyboard. Available in either traditional or wireless models.

- **Memory card reader**—Enables you to read data from devices (such as digital cameras) that use various types of flash memory cards.

- **Monitor**—Replaces or supplements the built-in display on a laptop computer or replaces the existing monitor on a desktop system (typically with a larger screen).

- **Mouse**—Provides a more traditional input in place of a laptop PC's touchpad or upgrades the capabilities of a desktop system's mouse. (For example, many users like to upgrade from wired to wireless mice.)

 NOTE Logitech and other companies sell bundles with both a wireless keyboard and wireless mouse in the same package.

- **Printer**—Improves the quality of your printouts, adds color to your printouts, or adds photo-quality printing to your system. (Some multifunction printers also have scanners built in.)

- **Solid-state drive**—On many systems, a replacement for the traditional hard drive. A solid-state drive typically has less storage space than a hard drive but is much faster for accessing that data. Some systems use a solid-state drive to store the Windows operating system (which makes everything run faster) and a separate hard drive to store files and other data. Available in both internal and external models.

- **Sound card**—On traditional desktop PCs, improves the audio capabilities of your systems; this is particularly important if you play state-of-the-art PC games, watch surround-sound DVD movies, or mix and record your own digital audio.

- **Speakers**—Upgrades the quality of your computer's sound system. (Surround-sound speaker systems with subwoofers are particularly popular, especially with PC gamers.)

- **USB memory device**—Provides gigabytes or even terabytes of removable storage; you can transport the USB memory device from one computer to another, connecting to each PC's USB port.

- **Video card**—On traditional desktop PCs, upgrades your system's video playback and graphics, typically for video editing or playing visually demanding PC games.

- **Webcam**—Enables you to send real-time video to friends and family.

- **Wireless network adapter**—Enables you to connect a desktop computer to any wireless network.

- **Wireless router**—Enables you to create a wireless network in your home—and share your broadband Internet connection among multiple computers.

Adding New Hardware to Your System

Everything that's hooked to your PC is connected via some type of *port*. A port is simply an interface between your PC and another device—either internally (inside your PC's system unit) or externally (via a connector on the back of the system unit).

Given the choice, the easiest way to add a new device to your system is to connect it externally. In fact, if you have an all-in-one desktop, laptop, or 2-in-1 computer, it's the *only* way to add new hardware; you can't get inside the case to add anything else. And even if you have a traditional desktop PC with a separate system unit, it's still a whole lot easier to add a new device via an external USB port than it is to open the case and add it that way.

 NOTE   No matter how you connect a new device, make sure to read the installation instructions for the new hardware and follow the manufacturer's instructions and advice.

Understanding USB

The most common external connector today is the Universal Serial Bus, more commonly known as USB, like the one shown in Figure 6.1. USB is a great concept (and truly "universal") in that virtually every type of new peripheral comes in a USB version. Want to add a second hard disk? Don't open the PC case; connect an external drive via USB. Want to add a new printer? Connect a USB printer. Want to connect to a home network? Don't bother with Ethernet cards; get a USB-compatible wireless adapter.

USB port

FIGURE 6.1

USB port on a laptop PC.

 NOTE   There are a few other types of ports that you might occasionally run into or need to use. For example, most computers today include an HDMI port that you can use to connect your PC to your monitor or a big-screen TV, discussed later in this chapter. (HDMI is a special kind of connection for transmitting high-definition audio/video.) But for most purposes, USB is all you need to know about and use.

There are several types of USB connectors in use today. USB Type A, shown in Figure 6.2, is the traditional and most common one, with a large rectangular connector. USB Type B is a six-sided connector used to connect some printers and external drives; you probably won't run into this one. The newer USB Type C, shown in Figure 6.3, is a smaller connector used not just on computers but also on smartphones and other mobile devices.

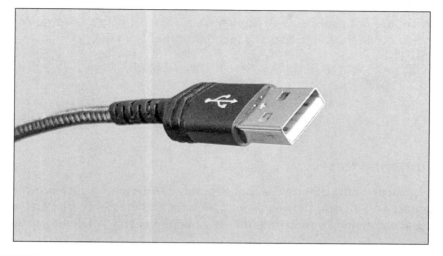

FIGURE 6.2

USB Type A connector.

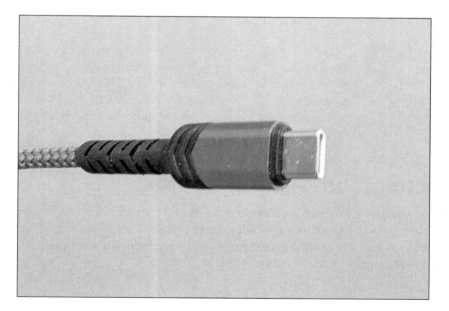

FIGURE 6.3

USB Type C connector.

USB in all of its forms is popular because it's so easy to use. When you connect a USB device, not only do you not have to open your PC's case, but you don't even have to turn off your system when you add the new device. That's because USB devices are *hot swappable*. That means you can just plug the new device into the port, and Windows automatically recognizes it in real time.

 TIP If you connect too many USB devices, you might run out of USB connectors on your PC. If that happens to you, buy an add-on USB hub for $20 USD or so, which enables you to plug multiple USB peripherals into a single USB port.

Connecting via USB

To connect a new USB device, just find a free USB port on your computer and connect a USB cable between your computer and the new peripheral. Windows should automatically recognize the new peripheral and install the proper device driver.

That's it! The only variation on this procedure is if the peripheral's manufacturer recommends using its own installation program, typically provided via download from the company website. If this is the case, follow the manufacturer's instructions to perform the installation and setup.

 NOTE A *device driver* is a small software program that enables your PC to communicate with and control a specific device. Windows includes built-in device drivers for many popular peripherals. If Windows doesn't include a particular driver, you typically can find the driver on the peripheral's installation disk or on the peripheral manufacturer's website.

Connecting and Using a Printer

Your computer monitor displays images in real time, but they're fleeting. To conveniently create permanent visual records of your work, you need to add a printer to your system. Printers create hard copy output from your software programs—or just make prints of your favorite pictures.

Understanding Different Types of Printers

You can choose from various types of printers for your system, depending on your exact printing needs. The two main types of printers today are inkjet and laser, and both are suitable for home use.

The most popular type of printer for home use is the *inkjet* printer, like the one shown in Figure 6.4. An inkjet printer works by shooting jets of ink to the paper's surface to create the printed image.

FIGURE 6.4

A typical all-in-one color inkjet printer.

To work, an inkjet printer needs to be filled with one or more replaceable ink cartridges. The typical inkjet printer has two cartridges—one that contains red, yellow, and blue ink (for color printing) and another with just black ink. You'll likely use up the black ink cartridge first because you'll probably print more single-color text documents than full-color pictures. Your printer should display a message on its front panel when a cartridge is running low; replacement ink cartridges are available at most home office stores.

Inkjet printers are typically lower priced than the other major type of printer, the laser printer. That's because inkjet models are not quite as heavy duty as laser printers, which are more suited for larger print jobs. An inkjet printer is fine for typical home use, but it might not hold up as well in a busy office environment.

Laser printers work a little differently than inkjet models. Instead of shooting liquid ink at the paper, a laser printer works much like a traditional copying machine, applying powdered ink (toner) to paper by using a small laser.

As such, laser printers (like the one in Figure 6.5) typically print a little faster than similar inkjets, and they produce slightly sharper results. This makes laser printers better suited for heavy-duty use, such as what you might get in an office environment.

FIGURE 6.5

An all-in-one black and white laser printer.

Of course, everything comes at a cost, and laser printers tend to be a little bigger and more expensive than comparable inkjet models. In addition, where most inkjets offer full-color printing, not all laser printers do; you can find both black-and-white and color laser printers for home and office use.

 NOTE Most printers sold today are so-called all-in-one or multifunction printers. That is, they combine a traditional desktop printer with a scanner, copier, and (sometimes) a fax machine, all in a single unit.

Connecting a Printer via USB

Most printers connect directly to your computer, typically via USB. Some printers come with their own installation software (or instruct you to download the software from the Internet); this typically includes the latest drivers to install on your system.

In most instances, however, you can skip this process and just connect the printer to your computer via USB. The process goes like this:

1. Connect one end of a USB cable to the USB port on your printer.

2. Connect the other end of the USB cable to a USB port on your computer.

3. Connect the printer to a power outlet.

4. Turn on the printer.

Windows should automatically recognize the new printer and install the proper device driver. Follow the onscreen instructions to finish the installation.

Connecting a Wireless Printer to Your Computer

Many printers also can connect wirelessly, via Wi-Fi, without being connected to a single PC. This lets you place your printer anywhere in your house without having to physically tether it to your PC. (It also makes it easy to share a single printer with multiple computers and other devices.)

Connecting a wireless printer to your PC is a little bit more involved than connecting via a USB cable. It typically goes something like this:

1. Power on your printer and follow the manufacturer's instructions to connect it to your Wi-Fi network.

2. On your computer, click or tap the Start button to open the Start menu; then click or tap Settings to open the Settings app.

3. Click or tap Bluetooth & Devices.

4. Click or tap Printers & Scanners.

5. Click or tap Add Device and let Windows search for your wireless printer.

6. Your wireless printer should appear in the resulting list. Select it and then click or tap Add Device. Follow the onscreen instructions to complete the installation.

Sharing a Network Printer

If you have multiple computers on your home network, you can share a single printer between them over your network.

This printer can be connected to one of your PCs, or directly to your network, typically via Wi-Fi. Once the computer is connected, you then have to install it on your other computers.

Here's how it works:

1. From the second computer, open the Start menu and click or tap Settings to open the Settings app.

2. Click or tap Bluetooth & Devices.

3. Click or tap Printers & Scanners.

4. Click or tap Add Device and let Windows scan your network for the printer.

5. Select the printer you want and then click or tap Add Device.

6. Follow any onscreen instructions to complete the installation.

Printing to Your System's Printer

Printing from a given program is typically as easy as clicking or tapping the Print button in that program. In some instances, the print function might be contained within a pull-down File or Print menu.

In any case, one-click printing is the norm. That is, you click the Print button, and printing ensues. In most programs, however, you can fine-tune your printing options by selecting the File menu and clicking Print. This typically displays a Print Options dialog box or page, like the one shown in Figure 6.6. From here, you can select which printer to print to, which pages to print, how many copies to print, whether to print in portrait (vertical paper) or landscape (horizontal paper) modes, and so forth.

FIGURE 6.6

The Print Options page in Microsoft Word.

Know, however, that print functionality differs from program to program. Make sure you consult a given app's help files if you need assistance in configuring various print options.

Connecting Portable Devices to Your PC

These days, a lot of the devices you connect to your PC actually aren't computer peripherals. Instead, they are gadgets that you use on their own but plug into your PC to share files—smartphones, digital cameras, and USB memory devices.

 NOTE   Learn more about connecting your smartphone to and using it with your computer in Chapter 7, "Using Your PC with Your Mobile Phone."

All these devices connect to a USB port on your PC, which makes for an easy hookup. As mentioned earlier, USB ports are hot swappable, which means that all you have to do is connect the device to the proper port—no major configuration necessary. In some cases, the first time you connect your device to your PC, you need to run some sort of installation utility to install the device's software on your PC's hard drive. Each subsequent time you connect the device, your PC should recognize it automatically and launch the appropriate software program.

After your portable device is connected to your PC, what you do next is up to you. Most of the time, you'll transfer files either from your PC to the portable device, or vice versa. Use the device's software program to perform these operations or use File Explorer to copy files back and forth.

For example, you can use a USB memory device as a removable and portable memory storage system. One of these USB drives is smaller than a pack of chewing gum and can hold several gigabytes' worth of data in electronic flash memory. Plug a USB memory device into your PC's USB port, and your PC recognizes it just as if it were another disk drive. You can then copy files from your PC to the USB drive to take your work (or your digital music or photo files) with you.

For more detailed information, see the instructions that came with your portable device.

Connecting Your PC to Your Living Room TV

As you'll no doubt soon discover, there are a lot of good movies and TV shows on the Internet that you can watch on your PC—often for free. Although you can watch this programming on your computer screen, that might be a little small if you're more familiar with the large screen experience.

NOTE Learn more about finding movies and TV shows on the Internet in Chapter 19, "Watching Movies and TV Shows Online."

Fortunately, there are ways to connect your computer to your TV to watch all your favorite streaming video programming in full big-screen glory. You can connect your computer to your TV via HDMI cable or wirelessly over your home Wi-Fi network.

Connecting via HDMI

HDMI is the easiest way to connect your PC to your TV. HDMI stands for *high-definition multimedia interface*, and it has become the connection standard for high-definition TVs. All newer TV sets have two or more HDMI inputs, which you typically use to connect cable boxes, Blu-ray players, and the like. HDMI transmits both audio and video signals.

Most new computers—both desktops and laptops—have either a full-sized or mini HDMI port, like the one shown in Figure 6.7.

HDMI port

FIGURE 6.7

An HDMI port on a laptop PC.

All you have to do is connect the appropriate HDMI cable between your two devices. Follow these instructions:

1. Connect one end of an HDMI or mini HDMI cable to the HDMI port on your computer.

2. Connect the other end of the HDMI cable to an open HDMI connector on your TV.

3. Switch your TV to the HDMI input you connected to.

4. On your computer, press Windows+P on the keyboard to display options for the external display. Click or tap Duplicate to display content on both your computer screen and the TV screen. *Or...*

5. Click or tap Second Screen Only to display content only on the TV screen while the computer screen is blank.

Wirelessly Mirroring Your Computer Screen

If you have a so-called smart TV or have a streaming media player (such as Amazon Fire TV or Roku) connected to your TV, you can wirelessly mirror the contents of your computer screen to that TV through a technology called Miracast. You just have to have your TV connected to the same Wi-Fi network as your computer.

Follow these steps:

1. Enable the screen mirroring feature on your TV or streaming media player.

2. On your computer, press Windows+K to display screencasting options. Click or tap to select the name of the device you want to cast to. Follow any onscreen instructions to complete the connection.

After you connect your computer to your TV, you can see and hear everything your PC is doing through your TV. Get out the popcorn!

THE ABSOLUTE MINIMUM

Here's what you need to know if you're adding new equipment to your computer system:

- The easiest way to connect a new peripheral is via an external USB connection.

- In most cases, Windows automatically recognizes your new hardware and installs all the necessary drivers.

- There are two types of consumer printers in use today: inkjet and laser.

- A printer can connect directly to a PC via USB or (in some models) wirelessly to your home network.

- To watch streaming video programming on your TV, connect your PC to your TV via HDMI or use screen mirroring to connect wirelessly.

IN THIS CHAPTER

- Linking Your Phone to Your Windows 11 PC
- Texting and Calling from Your PC
- Doing More with Your Phone and Your Windows PC

7

USING YOUR PC WITH YOUR MOBILE PHONE

Did you know that you can use your Windows 11 computer to send and receive text messages? All you need is an Android phone (it doesn't work with Apple iPhones), the Microsoft Phone Link app, and your Windows 11 PC. When everything's synchronized, you can send and receive text messages on your PC, share web pages and other documents between your two devices, and even view all your phone's photos on your big computer screen.

Linking Your Phone to Your Windows 11 PC

For your Android phone and Windows 11 computer to share text messages and other data, you first have to install the Link to Windows app on your phone. You can find the Link to Windows app in your phone's app store; it's free.

 NOTE Windows 11's smartphone features work only with Android phones from Google, Motorola, Samsung, and other manufacturers. These features do not work with Apple iPhones. (Apple and Microsoft don't always play nice with one another.)

Once you've installed the Link to Windows app on your Android phone, you need to link your Windows 11 computer to your phone. You do this by configuring both your computer and your phone. The process is a little involved, but you only have to do it once:

1. On your computer, open the Phone Link app. If you do not yet have your phone linked, click the Get Started button.

2. If you haven't installed the Link to Windows app on your phone, do so now. When the app is installed on your phone, open the app and tap Link Your Phone and PC. (You may be prompted to sign in at this point; if you are so prompted, do it.)

3. Back on your computer, in the Phone Link app, check I Have the Link to Windows App Ready.

4. Click Pair with QR Code.

5. On your phone, when asked if the QR code on your PC is ready, tap Continue.

6. Follow the onscreen instructions to use your phone to scan the QR code displayed on your computer.

7. If the Link to Windows app on your phone prompts you to allow permissions for various activities, click Allow to do so.

Texting and Calling from Your PC

When your phone and your PC are linked, you can use your computer to send and receive text messages—and to make phone calls.

Receiving Text Messages

Once the Phone Link app is linked to your Android phone, you can access all the texts you receive on your phone on your computer, as well. This makes it easier for you to text when you're working with your computer.

To view a text message, open your computer's Phone Link app and select the Messages tab, shown in Figure 7.1. This displays all your text messages. (Unread texts are in bold.) Select a text to read and reply to it.

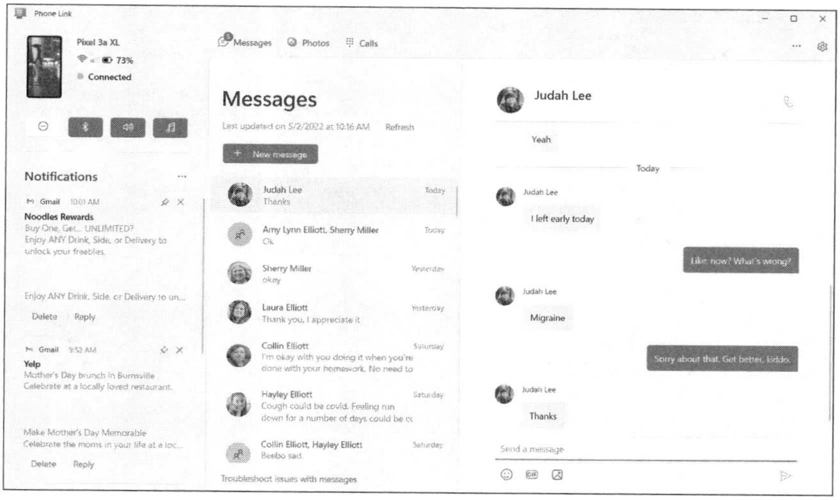

FIGURE 7.1

Sending and receiving text messages in the Phone Link app.

Sending Text Messages

You can initiate new individual texts from within the Phone Link app. Just go to the Messages tab and click or tap the New Message button. Start typing the name or phone number of the person you want to text, and matching names from your contact list are displayed. Click or tap to select the person you want to text and type your message into the Send a Message box. Click or tap the Send icon (or press Enter on your keyboard) to send the text. (You can also send messages to multiple recipients.)

> **TIP**   The Phone Link app lets you add emojis and GIFs to the texts you send. Just click or tap the Emoji or GIF button and choose the one you want. You can also attach photos and other images to texts by clicking or tapping the Attach Image button.

Making a Phone Call

When properly configured, the Phone Link app enables you to make calls on your Android phone from your Windows 11 computer. You do it all from the Calls tab in the app, shown in Figure 7.2.

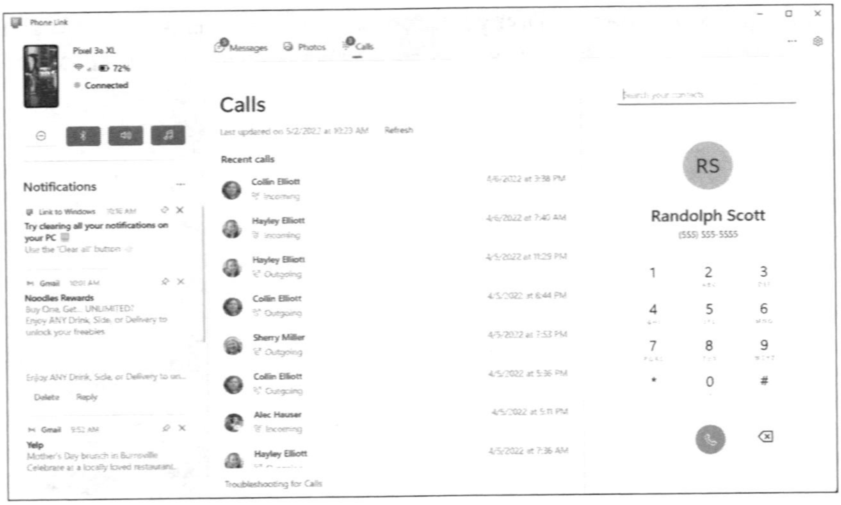

FIGURE 7.2

Making phones calls in the Phone Link app.

You can call anyone from your contacts list by entering that person's name into the Search Your Contacts box. You can also dial up anyone outright by clicking or tapping the numbers on the keypad—or by using your computer keyboard to enter the number manually. Click or tap the green Dial button or press Enter on your keyboard to place the call.

The Phone Link app connects to your phone, initiates the call, and displays a Call panel. Click or tap the Down arrow to expand the panel, which gives you a selection of in-call options, all shown in Figure 7.3:

- Mute mutes the call.

- Keypad displays a keypad in case you need to press any numbers during the call.

- Use Phone transfers the call back to your phone.

- Disconnect ends the call.

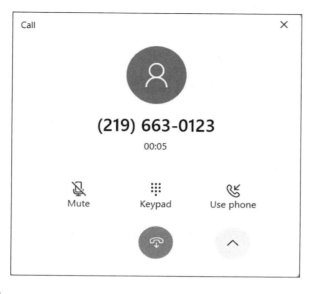

FIGURE 7.3

In-call options while making a phone call.

Doing More with Your Phone and Your Windows PC

When you've paired your Android phone with your Windows 11 PC, you can do more than just text or make phone calls. You can also share web pages between your devices and view your phone's photos on your PC.

Sharing a Web Page from Your Phone to Your PC

Ever find a web page when you're browsing on your phone and want to view it full-size on your computer screen? Windows 11 makes it easy to continue reading interesting web pages when you switch from your Android phone to your PC.

When your phone and computer are synced, all you have to do is tap the Share button in your phone's browser and select Link to Windows. Select the PC you want to link to, and the Microsoft Edge web browser opens on your computer with the web page you were viewing on your phone displayed.

Sharing a Web Page from Your PC to Your Phone

Just as you can share a web page from your phone to your PC, you can also share a page from your PC to your Android phone. Here's how it works:

1. On your computer, use the Microsoft Edge browser to navigate to the web page you want to share; then click or tap the Settings and More (three-dot) button to display the pull-down menu.

2. Select Share to open the Share window.

3. Click or tap Windows Share Options to open the Share Link window.

4. Click or tap Phone Link in the Share with App section.

That's it. You receive an alert on your phone from the Link to Windows app. Tap this alert, and the web page opens in the Link to Windows app.

Viewing Photos from Your Phone on Your PC

If you're like me, you take a lot of pictures with your smartphone. Now, with the Phone Link app, you can easily view all your phone pictures on your computer—and save them to your PC.

All you have to do is select the Photos tab in your computer's Phone Link app (see Figure 7.4).

FIGURE 7.4

Viewing photos on your phone from the Phone Link app.

All the photos on your phone are displayed here. Click or tap a picture to view it larger or perform any of the following actions:

- Click or tap Open to edit the selected photo in the Windows Photos app.

- Click or tap Copy to copy the photo so you can paste it into another application.

- Click or tap Save As to save the photo to a location on your computer.

- Click or tap Share to share the photo with another Windows app.

- Click or tap Delete to delete this photo from your phone.

Running Android Apps on Your PC

There's one more phone-related feature coming to Windows 11. (It's not yet available as I'm writing these words but should be by the time you read them.) This new functionality lets you run Android mobile apps within Windows 11. These are the same apps that run on Android phones and tablets and should give you a lot more options for your Windows 11 PC.

When this feature is activated, you'll need to install the Amazon Appstore app on your computer. This app should be available in the Microsoft Store. Once it's installed, you'll need to sign in to or create a new Amazon account, and then you'll be able to browse the Amazon Appstore for Android apps. Download and install an app to use it on your PC just like you do on an Android phone. Look for this new functionality in the near future!

THE ABSOLUTE MINIMUM

Here's what you need to know to use your Android phone with your Windows 11 PC:

- Use the Phone Link app to connect your Android smartphone to your Windows 11 PC.

- Once connected, you can send and receive text messages from your computer.

- You can also use your computer to make phone calls.

- You can share web pages between your phone's web browser and your Windows 11 PC.

- The Phone Link app also lets you view all of your phone's photos on your computer.

8

ADDING STORAGE AND BACKUP

Most desktop and traditional laptop computers these days come with a fairly large amount of internal storage, anywhere from 500GB (for a basic laptop) up to 10TB (that's 10 *terabytes*—one of which is equivalent to 1,000 gigabytes) or more. That's plenty of storage for most people, even if you download a lot of music and videos or store a ton of digital photos.

Some smaller notebook PCs don't have that much internal storage, however, especially if they use solid state drives. Since SSD storage costs a little more than traditional hard disk drive storage, you typically get a little less storage capacity for the same list price.

What do you do if the storage capacity on your computer isn't quite enough to store your photos, videos, and other valuable files? The solution is to add more capacity with an external drive, either hard disk or SSD. (And you can use that same external drive to back up your data.)

Understanding External Storage

Traditionally, personal computers have used internal hard disk drives to store digital data: software applications, documents, photos, music, and so forth.

Many newer computers, both laptop and desktops, either supplement or replace hard disk storage with solid state storage, which operates much faster. A computer with SSD storage boots up and opens apps a lot faster than one with hard drive storage.

Both hard disk drives and SSDs are also available in external versions that connect to your computer via USB. When it's connected, an external drive appears as another drive in the Computer section of File Explorer. You can access it just like your internal drive, and you can use it to store files or software programs.

You can find external drives in a variety of capacities, starting at 1TB or so and going all the way up to 16TB or more. Most manufacturers offer traditional desktop drives as well as smaller portable drives, like the one in Figure 8.1. As you might suspect, the portable drives are designed to work better with portable laptop PCs.

FIGURE 8.1

A portable hard drive that connects to your PC via USB.

Connecting an External Drive

In most instances, connecting an external drive (hard disk or SSD) is a simple two-step process:

1. Connect the external hard drive to a power source. (Not necessary if you're connecting a portable drive, which typically gets its power from the computer via USB.)

2. Use a USB cable to connect the external hard drive to a USB port on your computer.

Some desktop drives have power switches. If yours does, you need to turn it on, as well.

When the hard drive is powered up and connected to your computer, it should appear in the This PC section of File Explorer as a new drive. It should take the next available letter; for example, if your internal drive is drive C: and your CD/DVD drive is drive D:, then the new external drive should be labeled as drive E:.

Backing Up Your Important Files

Protecting your valuable data—including all your music and personal photos—is something you need to do. After all, what would you do if your computer crashed or your hard disk died? Do you really want to lose all your valuable documents and files?

Of course, you don't—which is why you need to back up your key files on a regular basis.

Backing Up to an External Drive

The easiest way to back up your files is with an external drive. Get a big enough external drive (about the same size as your main internal drive), and you can copy your entire internal drive to the external drive. Then, if your system ever crashes, you can restore your backed-up files from the external drive to your main system.

Most external drives come with some sort of backup software installed, or you can use a third-party backup program. The backup process can be automated to occur only once a day or once a week and to back up only those files that are new or changed since your last backup.

Whichever program you use, you should back up your data at least weekly—if not daily. That way, you won't lose much fresh data if the worst happens.

 TIP   Given the affordability of external drives and how easy most backup programs make the process, there's no excuse *not* to back up your data on a regular basis. It's cheap protection in case something bad happens to your computer.

Backing Up Online

An even more convenient way to back up your data is to do it over the Internet, using an online backup service. This type of service copies your important files from your computer to the service's servers over the Internet. This way, if your local data is lost or damaged, you can restore the files from the online backup service's servers.

The benefit of using an online backup service is that the backup copy of your library is stored offsite, so you're protected in case of any local physical catastrophe, such as fire or flood. Most online backup services also work in the background, so they're constantly backing up new and changed files in real time.

The downside of an online backup service comes if you need to restore your files. It takes a long time to transfer a lot of big files to your computer over an Internet connection. Plus, you have to pay for the backup service on an ongoing basis. Most online backup services run $50 USD or more per year, per computer.

If online backup appeals to you, check out these popular online backup services designed for home users:

- BackBlaze (www.backblaze.com)

- Carbonite (www.carbonite.com)

- IDrive (www.idrive.com)

 NOTE You can also use cloud storage services, such as Microsoft OneDrive or Google Drive, to store backup copies of your files. Unfortunately, these services don't offer the same type of automatic backup functionality as the full-featured backup services, which means you need to manually copy your files to these services, and that's not nearly as convenient. Learn more about these services in Chapter 4, "Working with Files, Folders, and Online Storage."

THE ABSOLUTE MINIMUM

Here are the key points to remember when connecting and configuring your new computer:

- External hard disk and SSD drives let you add extra storage capacity to your system—up to 16TB extra.

- You can find both desktop-type external drives and smaller, portable drives for use with laptop PCs.

- Connecting an external drive is typically as easy as connecting it to one of your PC's USB ports.

- An external drive shows up in File Explorer as just another drive on your system.

- You can use an external drive to back up valuable data from your main internal drive.

- Also available are online backup services, which back up your data over the Internet.

9

SETTING UP A HOME NETWORK

When you need to connect two or more computers or to share an Internet connection in your home, you need to create a computer *network*.

Why would you want to connect two computers? Maybe you want to transfer files or digital photos from one computer to another. Maybe you want to share an expensive piece of hardware (such as a printer) instead of buying one for each PC. Or most likely, you want to connect all your computers to the same Internet connection. Whatever your reasons, it's easy to set up and configure a simple home network. Read on to learn how!

How Networks Work

To physically connect your network, you have two ways to go—wired or wireless. A wireless network is more convenient (no wires!), but a wired network is faster and more secure. Which you choose depends on how you use the computers you network.

Most homes today have wireless networks. A wireless network is easier to set up and maintain than a wired network. However, if you need the fastest possible speeds (for multiplayer online gaming, perhaps) or added security for highly sensitive files, the extra effort of stringing Ethernet cable for a wired connection may be worth the while.

Wired Networks

A *wired network* is the kind that requires you to run a bunch of cables from each PC to a central hub or router. In a wired network, all your PCs connect through a central *network router* via Ethernet cables. (Most new PCs come with built-in Ethernet capability, so you don't have to purchase anything additional to connect to the network—other than the cables and router, that is.) Although this type of network is fast and easy enough to set up, you still have to deal with all those cables—which can be a hassle if your computers are in different areas of your house.

The speed you get from a wired network depends on the type of Ethernet technology used by each piece of equipment. The oldest Ethernet technology (1BASE5) transfers data at just 1 Mbps; so-called Fast Ethernet transfers data at 100 Mbps; and the newest Gigabit Ethernet transfers data at 1 *gigabit* per second. (That's 1,000 Mbps.) Either Fast Ethernet or Gigabit Ethernet is fine for transferring really big files between computers or for playing real-time PC games.

 NOTE   How quickly data is transferred across a network is measured in megabits per second, or Mbps. The bigger the Mbps number, the faster the network—and faster is always better than slower.

Wireless Networks

The popular alternative to a wired network is a *wireless network*. Wireless networks use radio frequency (RF) signals to connect one computer to another. The advantage of wireless, of course, is that you don't have to run cables. This is a big plus if you have a large house with computers on either end or on different floors.

A wireless network is a necessity if you have other non-PC devices in your home that need to connect to the Internet. If you want to surf the Internet from your smartphone or iPad, play online games with your Xbox or PlayStation, or watch streaming video on your Roku streaming media player, you need a wireless network.

Today's wireless network technology is known as Wi-Fi, and there have been several Wi-Fi standards over time, each faster than the previous:

- 802.11b, the original Wi-Fi standard, transferred data at 11Mbps—slower than Fast Ethernet, but fast enough for most practical purposes.

- 802.11a and 802.11g, which transferred data at 54Mbps.

- 802.11n (also known as Wi-Fi 4), with rates up to 600Mbps.

- 802.11ac (also known as Wi-Fi 5), with a theoretical maximum speed of 1.3GBps—that's gigabytes per second.

 NOTE Wi-Fi is short for *wireless fidelity*.

The latest version does away with all the numbers and dots and letters and is simply known as Wi-Fi 6. (The technical designation is 802.11ax.) An updated version of that standard, dubbed Wi-Fi 6E, was released in 2020 and promises speeds up to 9.6GBps.

Setting Up a Wireless Network in Your Home

Connecting multiple computers in a home network is fairly simple. Just make sure that you do the proper planning and buy the appropriate hardware and cables; everything else is a matter of connecting and configuring.

 NOTE For the purposes of this chapter, the assumption is that you're setting up a wireless network because that's what most people today use. Connecting a wired network is equally easy; the big difference is that you have to connect Ethernet cables between your router and each computer instead of making a wireless connection.

How It Works

A wireless network revolves around a device called a *wireless router*. This device functions like the hub of a wheel and serves as the central point in your network; each computer on your network connects through the wireless router.

NOTE   Most wireless routers can make both wireless and wired connections. A typical wireless router includes four or more Ethernet ports on the back in addition to having wireless capabilities.

Every computer in a wireless network connects to the router wirelessly—assuming, that is, that each computer contains wireless functionality. All notebook PCs (as well as tablets and smartphones) have built-in wireless connectivity, but many desktop PCs don't (although some do, of course). You can add wireless functionality to a desktop PC via a wireless adapter, which is a small device that connects to your PC via USB.

When complete, your network should look something like the one in Figure 9.1.

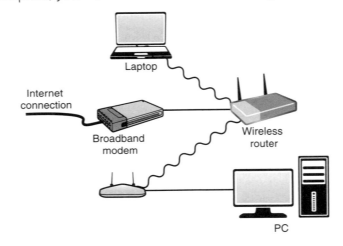

FIGURE 9.1

A typical wireless network.

 NOTE   So-called *mesh networks* expand on the traditional single router approach to include a main router and a group of Wi-Fi nodes, small devices that pick up and extend the router's signal. A mesh network is scalable; add more nodes to extend the reach of your network throughout a larger home.

What You Need

Here's the specific hardware you need to set up your network:

- Wireless router (one for the entire network)
- Broadband modem (typically supplied by your Internet service provider, or ISP)

NOTE   Many ISPs supply devices, called Internet *gateways*, that combine a broadband modem with a wireless router in a single box. If you have one of these devices, you don't need a separate wireless router; it's all built into the gateway.

- Wireless network adapter if you have a desktop or all-in-one PC without built-in Wi-Fi

Making the Connections

Naturally, you should follow the instructions that come with your networking hardware to properly set up your network. In general, however, here are the steps to take:

1. Run an Ethernet cable from your broadband modem to your wireless router and connect it to the port on your router labeled Internet or WAN. (If your router doesn't have a dedicated Internet port, you can connect it to any port.) Naturally, if you have a gateway instead of a modem, you don't need to perform this step.

2. Connect your wireless router or gateway to a power source.

3. Power on your broadband modem and wireless router or your single Internet gateway device.

4. Connect the first PC in your network to the router, as discussed in the "Connecting Your Computer to Your New Network" section, later in this chapter.

5. Follow the instructions provided by the router's manufacturer to create and configure a new wireless network. Make sure you configure your network to use wireless security, which requires a password (sometimes called a *network key*) before a device can connect to the network.

6. Connect all your remaining PCs to your new network.

TIP   When you first connect a new router to your network, you should configure the router using the software or mobile app that came with the device. Follow the manufacturer's directions to configure the network and wireless security.

After you connect all the computers on your network, you can proceed to configure any devices (such as printers) you want to share over the network. For example, if you want to share a single printer over the network, you can connect it to one of the network PCs and then share it through that PC. (You can also install network printers that connect directly to your wireless router, not to any specific PC.)

Connecting Your Computer to Your New Network

After your network hardware is set up, you have to connect all your computers to the network. With Windows 11, this is a relatively painless and practically transparent step.

Connecting via Ethernet

If you connect to your network via Ethernet, you don't have to do a thing. After you connect an Ethernet cable between your PC and your router, Windows 11 recognizes your new network and starts using it automatically.

Connecting Wirelessly

If you connect via a wireless connection, the setup is only slightly more involved. All you have to do is select which wireless network to connect to. Follow these steps:

 NOTE Your computer's Wi-Fi needs to be switched on to connect to the Internet. It's typically switched on by default, but you can switch it on and off manually if you want. Click or tap the middle of the notification area of the taskbar to display the Quick Settings panel and click the left side of the Wi-Fi button. The button is blue when Wi-Fi is on.

1. Click or tap the middle of the notification area of the taskbar to display the Quick Settings panel.

2. Click or tap the right arrow on the Manage Wi-Fi Connections button. You see a list of available wireless networks, as shown in Figure 9.2.

FIGURE 9.2

Select your wireless network from the list.

 NOTE A wireless network that is secured by a password, such as your home network, is displayed with a lock icon next to its name. A network that doesn't require a password, such as a public Wi-Fi hotspot, doesn't display the lock icon.

3. Click or tap to select your wireless network. This expands that network's section.

4. Check the Connect Automatically option to connect automatically to this network in the future.

5. Click or tap the Connect button. This expands this section.

6. When prompted, enter the password (called the *network security key*) for your network. This password is provided with your network router, either printed on the router itself or in the router's instructions, or it may be manually assigned.

7. Click or tap Next. Your computer is now connected to the network.

Accessing Computers on Your Network

After you have your home network set up, you can easily access shared content stored on other computers on your network.

All you have to do is follow these steps:

1. Click the File Explorer icon on the taskbar.

2. Go to the Network section of the Navigation pane, as shown in Figure 9.3.

3. Click the computer you want to access.

4. Windows displays the shared folders on the selected computer; double-click or tap a folder to view that folder's content.

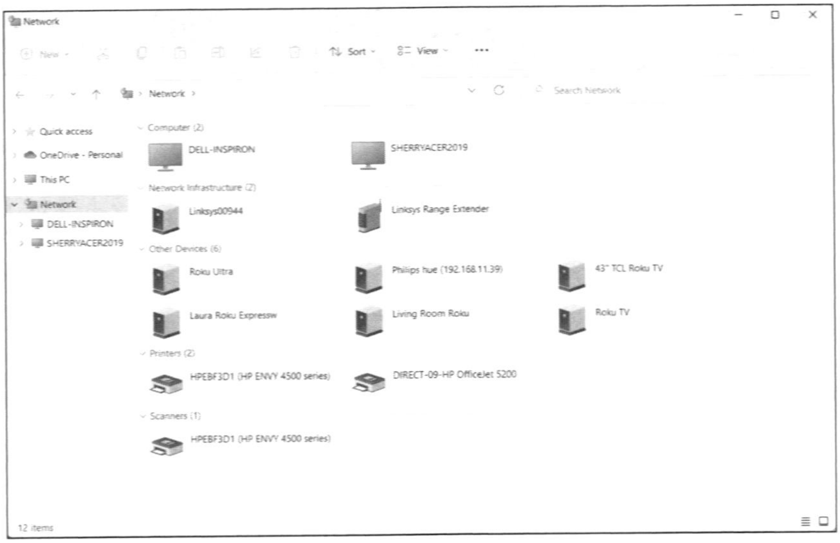

FIGURE 9.3

Viewing computers connected to your home network.

THE ABSOLUTE MINIMUM

Here are the key things to remember about creating a home network:

- To share information or hardware between two or more computers, as well as to share an Internet connection, you have to connect your computers in a network.

- There are two basic types of networks: wired and wireless (Wi-Fi).

- A wireless network uses a wireless router or Internet gateway to serve as the hub for all connected devices.

- After you connect your computers in a network, you access other connected computers via File Explorer.

PART IV

USING THE INTERNET

10

CONNECTING TO THE INTERNET—AT HOME AND AWAY

It used to be that most people bought personal computers to do serious work—word processing, spreadsheets, databases, the sort of programs that still make up the core of Microsoft Office. But today, more people buy PCs to access the Internet—to surf the Web, watch movies and listen to music, send and receive email, and socialize with other users on Facebook and other social networks.

To do this, of course, you first have to connect your computer to the Internet. Fortunately, Windows makes this easy to do.

Different Types of Home Internet

The first step in going online is establishing a connection between your computer and the Internet. When you connect from home, you need to sign up with an Internet service provider (ISP). This is a company that, as the name implies, provides your home with a connection to the Internet.

Although some of us might remember slow-as-molasses dial-up access, ISPs today offer various types of *broadband* access. Broadband is the fastest type of Internet connection available to homes today, and it comes in many flavors: cable, digital subscriber line (DSL), fiber optic, and even satellite. You get the type of service that your chosen ISP offers.

When you sign up with an ISP, you typically have a choice between various plans that offer various broadband speeds. (Not all broadband Internet is created equal, you see.) For example, my ISP in the suburban Twin Cities area is Xfinity by Comcast, which offers Internet packages ranging in speed from 50Mbps to 1,200 Mbps (1.2Gbps). That last service is known as *gigabyte Internet*, and it's super fast. Pricing for these plans, in my area, anyway, ranges from $19.99 USD per month to $79.99 USD per month.

That said, how much speed do you need?

It all depends on what you're doing on the Internet. Browsing the web or scrolling through Facebook posts takes relatively little bandwidth. Watching streaming movies and TV shows takes a lot more.

Table 10.1 details the typical bandwidth required for some common uses of the Internet.

TABLE 10.1 Typical Internet Bandwidth Requirements

Use	Minimum Bandwidth
Web browsing	1Mbps
Zoom video meeting	2.5Mbps
Online gaming	3Mbps
Streaming HD video	5Mbps
Streaming 4K video	25Mbps

All of this starts to add up, especially when you consider all the other devices in your home that connect to the Internet—not just computers but also smartphones, tablets, smart speakers, smart home hubs, and the like.

Consider this example. You watch 4K video on the big TV in your living room while your spouse is watching normal HD video on the bedroom TV. Your daughter is chatting with friends over Zoom in her bedroom, and your son is playing games on his Xbox over the Internet in the basement. At the same time, all four of you are browsing the web or social media on your phones, plus you have an Amazon Echo smart speaker listening for commands. Add this all up and you're going to need 50Mbps of bandwidth, easy.

So, while an ISP's top gigabit plans may be overkill for most users, you'll probably find that the most basic plans aren't fast enough. If you experience freezes, long load times, and pixelated pictures, it may be time to upgrade your Internet plan. If you're watching mostly HD programming and have two or three people in your home watching simultaneously, I recommend at least a 50Mbps plan; 100Mbps if you can afford it. If you have a lot of users in your household and watch a lot of streaming video, you may need to go even higher than that.

 CAUTION   Just because your ISP promises speeds of up to a given number doesn't mean that your actual connection speed will be that fast, at least all the time. Lots of factors, including inefficient equipment and other users online in your neighborhood, can negatively affect Internet connection speed. The speed listed by your ISP is a theoretical maximum; your actual speed will probably be lower. In addition, some ISPs employ "speed caps" for customers who download too much data, effectively throttling their use or charging extra for excessive data usage. It pays to check the fine print for these items before you sign up.

Understanding Internet Hardware

Once you pick your ISP and your monthly plan, you need to pick up the necessary equipment—or have your ISP deliver and install it for you. Broadband Internet comes into your home via a wire or cable and connects to a device called a *modem*. This little black box then connects either directly to your computer or to a wireless router, so you can share the connection with all the computers and wireless devices in your home.

Of course, you'll want to share your Internet connection among all the connected devices used by your family, including other computers, mobile phones, tablets, and gaming consoles. You do this by connecting your broadband modem to your home network.

It doesn't matter whether you have a wired or a wireless network; the connection is similar in both instances. All you have to do is run an Ethernet cable from your broadband modem to your network router, and then Windows does the rest, connecting your modem to the network so that all your computers can access the connection.

 NOTE Some ISPs provide a combination modem and router, sometimes called an Internet *gateway* device. If you get this combo box, you don't need a separate wireless router; the wireless networking functionality is built in.

To work through all the details of this type of connection, turn to Chapter 9, "Setting Up a Home Network." It's really quite easy!

Connecting to a Public Wi-Fi Hotspot

If you have a laptop, 2-in-1, or tablet PC, you can connect to the Internet when you're away from home. Most coffeehouses, restaurants, hotels, and public spaces offer wireless Wi-Fi Internet service, either for free or for an hourly or daily fee. Assuming that your laptop has a built-in Wi-Fi adapter (which almost all do), connecting to a public Wi-Fi hotspot is a snap.

 NOTE A *hotspot* is a public place that offers wireless access to the Internet using Wi-Fi technology. Some hotspots are free for all to access; others require some sort of payment.

When you're near a Wi-Fi hotspot, your PC should automatically pick up the Wi-Fi signal. Make sure that your PC's Wi-Fi adapter is turned on, and then follow these steps:

1. Click or tap the middle of the notification area of the taskbar to display the Quick Settings panel.

2. Click or tap the right arrow on the Manage Wi-Fi Connections button. You see a list of available wireless networks, as shown in Figure 10.1. (Public networks should not have lock icons next to their names.)

3. Click or tap to select the wireless network.

4. If the hotspot has free public access, click the Connect button. You can now open your web browser and surf normally.

5. If the hotspot requires a password, payment, or other logon procedure, Windows displays an Open Browser and Connect link. Click or tap this link to open your web browser to display the hotspot's logon page and enter the appropriate information or click the appropriate button to begin surfing.

FIGURE 10.1

Choosing from available Wi-Fi hotspots.

THE ABSOLUTE MINIMUM

When you configure your new PC system to connect to the Internet, remember these important points:

- You connect to the Internet through an Internet service provider, or ISP; you need to set up an account with an ISP before you can connect.

- When you sign up for Internet service, you need to choose a specific level of speed. Know that you pay more for higher-speed connections.

- If you have more than one computer at home, you can share your Internet connection by connecting your broadband modem to your home network.

- If you have a laptop or 2-in-1 PC, you can connect to the Internet wirelessly at any public Wi-Fi hotspot, such as those offered by Starbucks, Panera Bread, and similar establishments.

11

BROWSING AND SEARCHING THE WEB

Now that you've connected to the Internet, either at home or via a public wireless hotspot, it's time to get busy. The World Wide Web is a particular part of the Internet with all sorts of cool content and useful services, and you surf the Web with a piece of software called a *web browser*.

Windows includes its own web browser, called Microsoft Edge, but you can use other browsers if you like, such as the popular Google Chrome.

Understanding the Web

Before you can surf the Web, you need to understand a little bit about how it works.

Information on the World Wide Web is presented in *pages*. A web page is similar to a page in a book, made up of text and graphics. A web page differs from a book page, however, in that it can include other elements, such as audio and video, and links to other web pages.

It's this linking to other web pages that makes the Web such a dynamic way to present information. A *link* on a web page can point to another web page on the same site or to another site. Most links are included as part of a web page's text and are called *hypertext links*, or just *hyperlinks*. (If a link is part of a graphic, it's called a *graphic link*.) These links are usually in a different color from the rest of the text and often are underlined; when you click a link, you're taken directly to the linked page.

Web pages reside at a *website*. A website is nothing more than a collection of web pages (each in its own computer file) residing on a host computer. The host computer is connected full time to the Internet so that you can access the site— and its web pages—anytime you access the Internet. The main page at a website is called the *home page*, and it often serves as an opening screen that provides a brief overview and menu of everything you can find at that site. The address of a web page is called a *URL*, which stands for *uniform resource locator*. Most URLs start with http://, add a www., continue with the name of the site, and end with a .com, .org, or .net.

 TIP You can normally leave off the http:// when you enter an address into your web browser. In most cases, you can even leave off the www. and just start with the domain part of the address.

Using Microsoft Edge

Microsoft includes its own web browser in Windows 11, called Microsoft Edge. You launch Edge from the taskbar or Start menu.

As shown in Figure 11.1, when you click at the top of the browser, you see an Address box, where you enter the address (URL) of the web page you want to visit. You can display multiple web pages on multiple tabs, and all your controls are located to the right of the Address box.

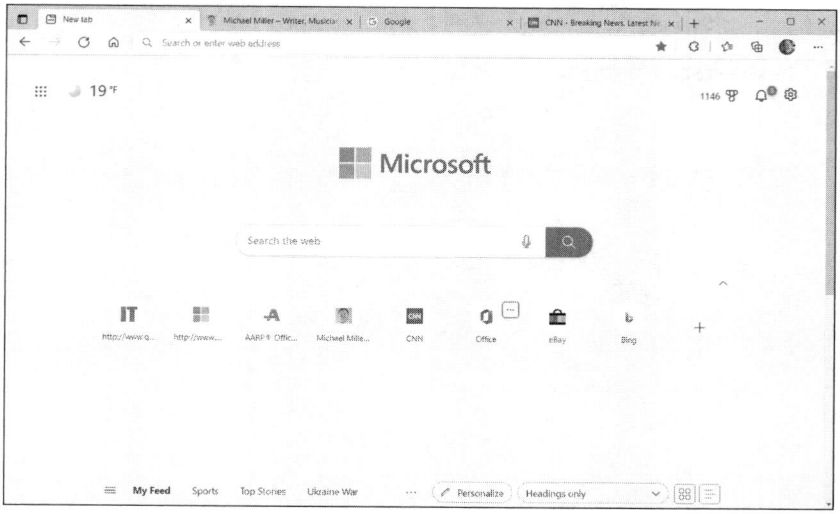

FIGURE 11.1

The Microsoft Edge browser in Windows 11.

Browsing the Web with Edge

Browsing the Web with Edge is easy. Just do the following:

1. To go to a specific web page, click or tap within the Address box; then enter that page's address and press Enter.

2. To return to the previous web page, click or tap the Back (left arrow) button beside the Address box.

3. To reload or refresh the current page, click or tap the Refresh button.

4. To jump to a linked-to page, click or tap the hyperlink on the current page.

> **NOTE**   If you've backed up several pages and want to return to the page you were on last, click the Forward button.

Revisiting History

What do you do if you remember visiting a page earlier in the day, or even in the past few days, but can't get there by clicking the Back button? Now's the time to revisit your browsing history. Follow these steps:

1. Click or tap the Settings and More (three-dot) button on the toolbar; then select History to display the History pane, shown in Figure 11.2.

2. Click or tap a day to display all pages visited that day.

3. Click or tap a page to revisit it.

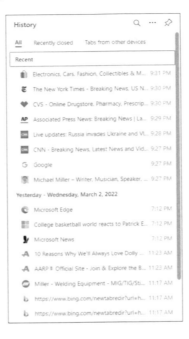

FIGURE 11.2

Revisiting browser history.

TIP   If you want to delete your browsing history—say you've visited a web page you don't want anyone to know you visited—you can do that, too. Open the History pane, click or tap the More Options (three-dot) button, and then click or tap Clear Browsing Data. This displays the Clear Browsing Data pane; check those items you want to delete (typically Browsing Data, Cookies and Other Site Data, and Cached Images and Files); then click or tap the Clear Now button. (You can also delete an individual item from the History list by hovering over it and clicking the X next to the name.)

Opening Multiple Pages in Tabs

Microsoft Edge enables you to display multiple web pages as separate tabs in the browser to easily switch between web pages—which is great when you want to reference different pages or want to run web-based applications in the background.

Here's how to work with tabs in Edge:

1. To switch to another open tab, click or tap that tab.

2. To close an open tab, click or tap the X on that tab.

3. To open a new tab, click or tap the + next to the last open tab.

4. Click a tile on the new tab page or…

5. …enter a new web page address into the Address box.

 TIP By default, Edge displays in whatever the default color scheme you've set for Windows. You can change it to display in either Light or Dark mode, however, by clicking or tapping the More Actions (three-dot) button on the toolbar, clicking Settings, selecting the Appearance tab, and then making a new selection from the Customize Appearance list.

Saving Your Favorite Pages

You can save your favorite pages in what Edge calls the Favorites list. Follow these steps:

1. Navigate to the web page you want to pin, and then click or tap the Add This Page to Favorites (star) button on the right side of the Address box (see Figure 11.3) to display the Favorite Added box.

2. Confirm or enter a name for this page.

3. Pull down the Folder list and select where you want to save it.

4. Click or tap Done.

Add This Page to Favorites

https://www.millerwriter.com

FIGURE 11.3

Adding a new web page to your Favorites list.

Returning to a Favorite Page

To return to a page you've saved as a favorite, follow these steps:

1. Click or tap the Favorites button to display the Favorites pane, as shown in Figure 11.4.

2. Click to open any folder you've created.

3. Click the page you want to revisit.

FIGURE 11.4

Revisiting favorite pages in the Favorites list.

Displaying the Favorites Bar

For even faster access to your favorite pages, display the Favorites bar at the top of the browser window, beneath the Address bar. You can then click or tap any site on the Favorites bar to go directly to that site. Follow these steps:

1. Click or tap the Favorites button to display the Favorites panel.

2. Click or tap the More Options (three-dots) button; then select Show Favorites Bar, Always.

Displaying a Page with Immersive Reader

Edge offers an Immersive Reader view that lets you display certain web pages without ads or other distracting subsidiary content, as shown in Figure 11.5. This is great for reading news stories, articles, and similar content.

Immersive Reader button

FIGURE 11.5

Reading a web article in Immersive Reader view.

To switch to Immersive Reader view, go the web page you want to read and then click or tap the Immersive Reader button on the right side of the Address box or press the F9 button on your keyboard. Click or tap the button again (or press F9 again) to return to normal web view. (Note that reading view is not available for all web pages.)

Browsing in Private

You may want to visit web pages that you'd rather your friends or family not know about. To that end, Edge lets you browse anonymously via the InPrivate Browsing mode. Here's how to activate it:

1. Click or tap the Settings and More (three-dot) button on the toolbar to display the menu of options.

2. Click or tap New InPrivate Window.

This opens a new browser window with InPrivate Browsing turned on. You can now browse anonymously; the pages you visit will not be tracked.

Setting a Different Start Page

By default, Edge displays its own Start page when it launches. You can, however, specify a different page to display on launch. Follow these steps:

1. Click or tap the Settings and More (three-dot) button to display the menu of options.

2. Click or tap Settings to display the Settings panel.

3. Click or tap to select the Start, Home, and New Tabs tab.

4. In the When Edge Starts section, select Open These Pages.

5. Click or tap Add a New Page.

6. Enter the URL for the page you want; then click or tap Add.

Using Google Chrome

Edge is the default browser that's built into Windows 11. You don't have to use it, however. There are several other third-party web browsers available, and some users prefer them for their simplicity and speed.

The most popular of these non-Microsoft web browsers—and the most popular browser period—is Google Chrome. You can download Chrome for free from www.google.com/chrome/. (Yes, you can use Edge to go to another browser's web page.)

Figure 11.6 shows the Google Chrome browser. It looks a lot like Edge, which isn't surprising; both browsers use the same basic code.

Using Chrome is pretty much like using Microsoft Edge. You have tabs for different web pages, Forward and Back buttons, a button for reloading the current web page, and an Address box for entering URLs. You find all the other controls by clicking the Customize and Control (three-bar) button at the far right of the tabs; the resulting menu lets you access all Chrome's various configuration options.

"Favorites" in Chrome are called bookmarks. To bookmark a favorite page, click or tap the star at the right side of that page's Address box. To access bookmarked pages, click or tap the Customize and Control button; then click or tap Bookmarks. (You also can display a Bookmarks bar beneath the Address box; click or tap the Customize button, select Bookmarks, and then click or tap Show Bookmarks Bar.)

FIGURE 11.6

The Google Chrome web browser.

 TIP Chrome also has an anonymous browsing mode, dubbed Incognito mode. To open a page in Incognito mode, click or tap the Customize and Control menu and select New Incognito Window.

Searching the Web with Google

Now that you know how to surf the Web, how do you find the precise information you're looking for? Fortunately, there are numerous sites that help you search the Web for the specific information you want. Not surprisingly, these are among the most popular sites on the Internet.

The sites you use to search the Web are commonly called Internet *search engines*. These sites, such as Google and Bing, employ special software programs (called *spiders* or *crawlers*) to roam the Web automatically, feeding what they find back to a massive bank of computers. These computers then build giant *indexes* of websites; these indexes are what you actually search when you use their sites.

Using Google Search

The most popular search engine is Google (www.google.com). Google is easy to use, extremely fast, and returns highly relevant results. That's because it indexes more pages than any other site—billions and billions of pages, if you're counting.

Most users search Google several times a week, if not several times a day. The Google home page, as shown in Figure 11.7, is a marvel of simplicity and elegant web page design. All you have to do to start a search is enter one or more key-words into the Search box and then press Enter or click or tap the Google Search button. This returns a list of results ranked in order of relevance, such as the one shown in Figure 11.8. Click or tap a results link to view that page.

FIGURE 11.7

Searching the Web with Google.

FIGURE 11.8

The results of a Google search.

TIP Other popular search engines include Microsoft's Bing (www.bing.com) and DuckDuckGo (www.duckduckgo.com).

Constructing a Query

When you search Google (or any search site), the quality of your results depends on the accuracy of your query. It's kind of a "garbage in, garbage out" thing; the better you describe what you're looking for, the more likely that Google will return the results you want.

It's important to focus on keywords because Google looks for these words when it processes your query. Your keywords are compared to the web pages that Google knows about; the more keywords found on a web page, the better the match.

Choose keywords that best describe the information you're looking for—using as many keywords as you need. Don't be afraid of using too many keywords; in fact, using too *few* keywords is a common fault of many novice searchers. The more words you use, the better idea the search engine has of what you're looking for.

 TIP You can use Google to display stock quotes (enter the stock ticker), answers to mathematical calculations (enter the equation), and measurement conversions (enter what you want to convert). Google can also track USPS, UPS, and FedEx packages (enter the tracking number), as well as the progress of airline flights (enter the airline and flight number).

Fine-Tuning Your Search Results

Google offers a variety of options to help you fine-tune your search. Click Tools at the top of the search results page to see these options, which are fine-tuned for specific types of searches. For example, you may have the option to filter your search results by time (Past 24 Hours, Past Week, and so on), reading level, and location (show nearby results only).

If you're looking for pictures or illustrations, Google can help with that, too. Just look for the list of categories at the top of the screen and click the Images link. You then see a page full of images that match your original query.

THE ABSOLUTE MINIMUM

Here are the key points to remember from this chapter:

- You surf the Web with a web browser, such as Microsoft Edge (built into Windows 11) or Google Chrome (downloadable for free).

- To go to a particular web page, enter the page's address in the Address box, and then press Enter. (You also can click or tap a hyperlink on a web page to jump to the linked page.)

- Microsoft Edge and Chrome both offer tabbed browsing, where you can open new web pages in additional tabs; click or tap a tab to switch to that web page.

- When you need to search for specific information on the Internet, you can use one of the Web's many search engine sites, such as Google.

12

BUYING AND SELLING ONLINE

Many users have discovered that the Internet is a great place to buy things—all kinds of things. All manner of online merchants make it easy to buy books, clothing, and other merchandise with the click of a mouse. You can even order meal and grocery delivery online!

The Web isn't just for shopping, however. You also can use sites like Craigslist to sell your stuff online. It's a great way to get rid of all that old stuff cluttering your attic—or a few unwanted Christmas presents!

How to Shop Online

If you've never shopped online before, you're probably wondering just what to expect. Shopping over the Web is easy; all you need is your computer and a credit card—and a fast connection to the Internet!

Online shopping is pretty much the same, no matter which retailer website you visit. You proceed through a multiple-step process that goes like this:

1. **Find an online store** that sells the item you're shopping for.

2. **Find a product**, either by browsing or searching through the retailer's site.

3. **Examine the product** by viewing the photos and information on a product listing page.

4. **Order the product** by clicking a "purchase this" or "buy it now" button on the product listing page that puts the item in your online shopping cart.

5. **Check out** by entering your payment (credit card) and shipping information.

6. **Confirm the order** and wait for the merchant to ship your merchandise.

Let's look at each of these steps separately.

Step 1: Find an Online Store

The first step in online shopping is finding where you want to shop. Most major retailers, such as Target and Walmart, and catalog merchants have websites you can use to shop online. In addition, there are online-only retailers that offer a variety of merchandise, such as Amazon.com. You should find no shortage of places to shop online.

If you're looking for a particular store, just enter its URL into your web browser. This is typically the company's name followed by .com. For example, Target's URL is www.target.com; Walmart's URL is **www.walmart**.com. If you're not sure of a store's URL, just use Google to search for it.

Step 2: Find a Product

After you determine where to shop, you need to browse through different product categories on that site or use the site's search feature to find a specific product.

Browsing product categories online is similar to browsing through the departments of a retail store. You typically click a link to access a major product category and then click further links to view subcategories within the main category. For example, the main category might be Clothing; the subcategories might be

Men's, Women's, and Children's clothing. If you click the Men's link, you might see a list of further subcategories: outerwear, shirts, pants, and the like. Just keep clicking until you reach the type of item that you're looking for.

Searching for products is often a faster way to find what you're looking for if you have something specific in mind. For example, if you're looking for a women's leather jacket, you can enter the words **women's leather jacket** into the site's Search box and get a list of specific items that match those criteria.

The only problem with searching is that you might not know exactly what it is you're looking for; if this describes your situation, you're probably better off browsing. But if you *do* know what you want—and you don't want to deal with lots of irrelevant items—then searching is the faster option.

Step 3: Examine the Product (Virtually)

Whether you browse or search, you'll probably end up looking at a list of different products on a web page. These listings typically feature one-line descriptions of each item—in most cases, not nearly enough information for you to make an informed purchase.

The thing to do now is to click or tap the link for the item you're particularly interested in. This should display a dedicated product page, complete with a picture and full description of the item. This is where you can read more about the item you selected. Some product pages include different views of the item, pictures of the item in different colors, links to additional information, and maybe even a list of optional accessories that go along with the item.

If you like what you see, you can proceed to the ordering stage. If you want to look at other items, just click or tap your browser's Back button to return to the larger product listing.

 TIP   Many online retailers feature customer reviews of their products. Look to see how many stars a product has received (the higher the number, the better) and read some of the individual reviews to see how other consumers liked it.

Step 4: Order the Product

Somewhere on each product description page should be a button labeled Purchase, Buy Now, Add to Cart, or something similar. This is how you make the actual purchase: by clicking or tapping that Buy button. You don't order the product just by looking at the product description; you have to manually click or tap the Buy button to place your order. (Figure 12.1 shows a product page on Amazon.com; click or tap the Add to Cart button to purchase this item.)

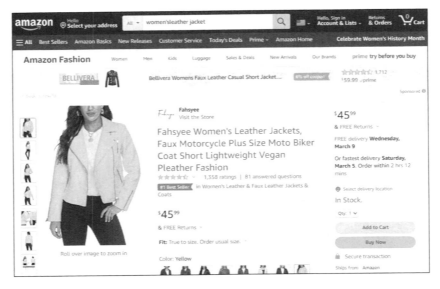

FIGURE 12.1

Getting ready to purchase a jacket on Amazon.com.

When you click or tap the Buy button, that particular item is added to your *shopping cart*. That's right, the online retailer provides you with a virtual shopping cart that functions just like a real-world shopping cart. Each item you choose to purchase is added to your virtual shopping cart.

After you order a product and place it in your shopping cart, you can choose to shop for other products on that site or proceed to the site's checkout. It's important to note that when you place an item in your shopping cart, you haven't actually completed the purchase yet. You can keep shopping (and adding more items to your shopping cart) as long as you want.

You can even decide to abandon your shopping cart and not purchase anything at this time. All you have to do is leave the website, and you won't be charged for anything. It's the equivalent of leaving your shopping cart at a real-world retailer and walking out the front door; you don't actually buy anything until you walk through the checkout line. (Although, with some sites, the items remain in your shopping cart—so they'll be there waiting for you the next time you shop!)

Step 5: Check Out

To finalize your purchase, you have to visit the store's *checkout*. This is like the checkout line at a traditional retail store; you take your virtual shopping cart through the checkout, get your purchases totaled, and then pay for what you're buying.

The checkout at an online retailer typically consists of one or more web pages with forms you have to fill out. If you've visited the retailer before, the site might remember some of your personal information from your previous visit. Otherwise, you have to enter your name, address, and possibly email address and phone number, as well as the address you want to ship the merchandise to (if that's different from your billing address). You also have to pay for the merchandise, typically by entering a credit card number.

The checkout provides one last opportunity for you to change your order. You can delete items you decide not to buy or change quantities on any item. At some merchants, you can opt to have your items gift-wrapped and sent to someone as a present. You should find all these options somewhere in the checkout process.

You might also have the option of selecting different types of shipping for your order. Many merchants offer both regular and expedited shipping—the latter for an additional charge.

 TIP   The better online retailers tell you either on the product description page or during the checkout process whether an item is in stock and when to expect shipment.

Step 6: Confirm the Order

After you enter all the appropriate information, you're asked to place your order. This typically means clicking or tapping a button that says Place Your Order or something similar. You might even see a second screen asking you whether you *really* want to place your order, just in case you have second thoughts.

After you place your order, you see a confirmation screen, typically displaying your order number. Most online merchants also send you a confirmation message, including this same information, via email.

That's all there is to it. You shop, examine the product, place an order, proceed to checkout, and then confirm your purchase. It's that easy!

How to Shop Safely

Shopping online is every bit as safe as shopping at a traditional brick-and-mortar retailer. The big online retailers are just as reputable as traditional retailers, offering safe payment, fast shipping, and responsive service.

How do you know that you're shopping at a reputable online retailer? Simple—look for the following features:

- **Payment by major credit card:** Credit cards offer ample consumer protection in case of fraud. Some merchants might accept credit cards via PayPal or a similar online payment service; this is also acceptable.

- **A *secure server* that encrypts your credit card information—and keeps online thieves from stealing your credit card numbers:** You know that you're using a secure site when the little lock icon appears next to the URL in your web browser.

- **Good contact information—email address, street address, phone number, so on:** You want to be able to contact the retailer if something goes wrong, even if it's just by online chat.

- **A stated returns policy and satisfaction guarantee:** You want to be assured that you'll be taken care of if you don't like whatever you ordered.

- **A stated privacy policy that protects your personal information:** You don't want the online retailer sharing your email address and purchasing information with other merchants—and potential spammers.

- **Information *before you finalize your order* that tells you whether the item is in stock and how long it will take to ship:** More feedback is better.

 TIP   Credit card purchases are protected by Federal law. In essence, you have the right to dispute certain charges, and your liability for unauthorized transactions is limited to $50. In addition, some card issuers offer a supplemental guarantee that says you're not responsible for *any* unauthorized charges made online. (Make sure that you read your card's statement of terms to determine the company's exact liability policy.)

Ordering Meal and Grocery Delivery Online

During that period of the COVID-19 crisis when we were all stuck at home, people starting using their computers not just for online shopping but also for ordering meals, groceries, and other items to be delivered. Many people got really used to convenience of ordering their food and other sundries online and having them delivered direct to their doors. You never have to leave home again.

Most grocery stores, pharmacies, and restaurants either offer their own delivery services or partner with local or national delivery services. You typically order from the grocery or restaurant website and choose the delivery option.

Ordering Meals Online

Thanks to COVID, many restaurants today offer delivery. This delivery is seldom free; you have to pay a delivery fee and perhaps even specify a tip to the driver. All of these fees—as well as the cost of the meal—are paid online when you place your order. You can pay by entering your credit or debit card number.

Some restaurants hire their own drivers and do their own deliveries. Others employ the services of third-party services such as DoorDash (www.doordash.com), Grubhub (www.grubhub.com), and UberEats (www.ubereats.com).

You can order direct from the restaurant or, in some cases, from the delivery site. After you place your order and pay online, the site tells you approximately when your order will be delivered. You may also receive an email or see a link to an online page that displays the status of your order and sometimes even a map with the position of the delivery driver highlighted.

Many restaurants let you choose normal or contactless delivery. With a normal delivery, the driver rings the doorbell and hands you your food. With contactless delivery, the driver places the food on your doorstep and texts you that it's there, so there's no human contact involved. You make this choice when you're placing your order.

Ordering Groceries Online

Many grocery stores also offer online ordering and home delivery. The process works much like ordering meal delivery from a restaurant but with many more options.

In most instances, you place your order directly from the grocer's website. Most grocery stores offer the same selection online as they do in their stores, including fresh meats, vegetables, bakery goods, and dry goods. You may be prompted to specify options in case your first choice of brand or size isn't available, but it's pretty much like ordering from a big menu of available grocery items.

Many larger grocery chains handle their own deliveries, but others use third-party delivery services such as Instacart (www.instacart.com) or Shipt (www.shipt.com). You'll probably have to pay a delivery fee and perhaps specify a tip for the delivery driver. Because many grocery items need to stay refrigerated, most stores let you specify a delivery time so you can be sure that you're home to receive the delivery.

Buying and Selling on Online Marketplaces

Traditional retailers aren't the only places to buy merchandise online. You can also buy goods from individuals selling to other individuals through a number of online marketplaces. These marketplaces also let you sell things yourself, which is a good way to move things you no longer use, much like an online garage sale.

Craigslist

Craigslist (www.craigslist.org), shown in Figure 12.2, works like an online version of traditional newspaper classified ads. Individuals list items for sale, and you contact those sellers (via Craigslist) to arrange purchases.

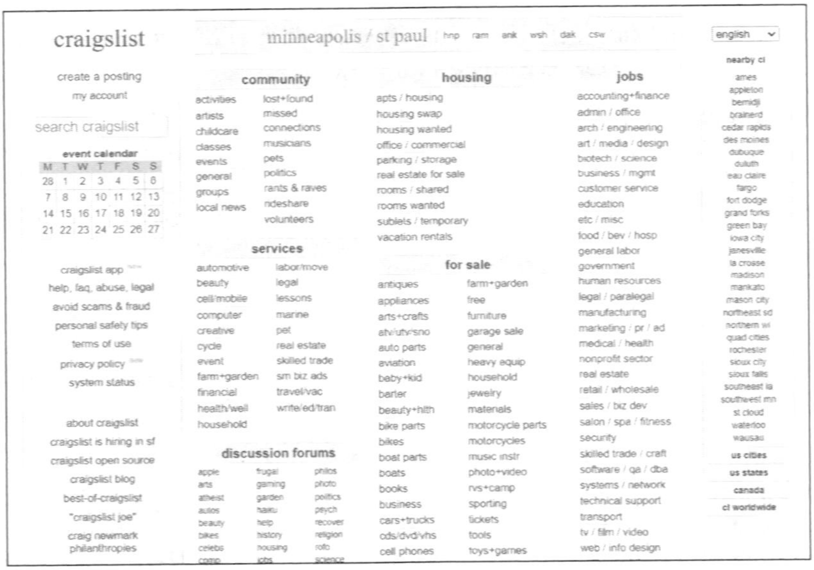

FIGURE 12.2

Buying and selling on Craigslist.

Craigslist only does ad listings, so you have to arrange payment directly to the seller. (Most sellers accept cash only.) Unlike some online marketplaces, Craigslist is best for buying and selling locally, where you can pick up the items you buy directly from the sellers; it's not really for buying or selling items that need to be shipped.

Craigslist also lets you place listings for items you have for sale. In most categories, listings are free.

CAUTION   Just as with traditional classified ads, Craigslist offers no buyer protections. Before handing over any money, plug in anything electric or electronic and test its capabilities, thoroughly inspect items in good lighting and from all angles, and make sure the product is exactly what you want. You should also arrange to pick up any items you buy in a public space and take a friend with you, for extra protection.

 CAUTION   Under no circumstances should you accept payment via personal check. It's far too easy for a shady buyer to write you a check and take off with the merchandise, only for you to discover a few days later that the check bounced. If you *must* accept a personal check, hold onto the merchandise for a full 10 working days to make sure the check clears; it's probably easier for all involved for the buyer to just get the cash.

eBay

eBay (www.ebay.com), shown in Figure 12.3, started out as an online auction site but today offers a mixture of items for auction or for sale at a fixed price. In an online auction, you bid for a given item, and the buyer with the highest bid at the end of the auction period wins the item. Fixed-price sales are just like buying an item from normal online retailers.

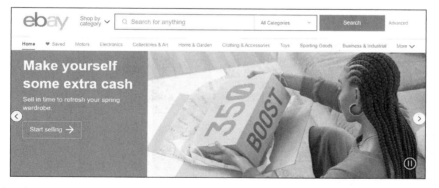

FIGURE 12.3

Buying and selling on eBay.

When you purchase from an eBay seller, you make your payments through eBay and are covered by eBay's buyer protection plan. Note, however, that when you're buying from individual sellers, it's not always as smooth or as safe as buying from normal retailers. (Many individuals selling on eBay don't accept returns, for example.)

Unlike Craigslist, which is mainly for local sales, eBay sellers sell and ship items across the United States and around the world. In addition to individual sellers, many traditional retailers and online retailers offer products for sale on the eBay marketplace.

You can also sell items on eBay, either for auction or for a fixed-price. You pay eBay a fee to list the item and another fee when the item sells.

Etsy

Etsy (www.etsy.com), shown in Figure 12.4, is a marketplace for handmade and vintage items such as artwork, clothing, collectibles, crafts, jewelry, and such. Sellers are often individuals who make their own goods and sell them online via Etsy. You pay via the Etsy site using credit card, debit card, or PayPal.

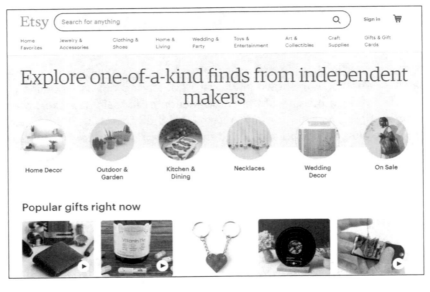

FIGURE 12.4

Buying and selling on Etsy.

Etsy is a great site to sell items that you make yourself. Like eBay, you pay a listing fee to list an item for sale and a transaction fee when the item sells.

Facebook Marketplace

If you're a Facebook member, you can buy and sell items on the Facebook Marketplace (www.facebook.com/marketplace), shown in Figure 12.5. The Facebook Marketplace is a lot like Craigslist in that it's really just a series of item listings. You don't buy and sell through Facebook; you just use Facebook to list items for sale.

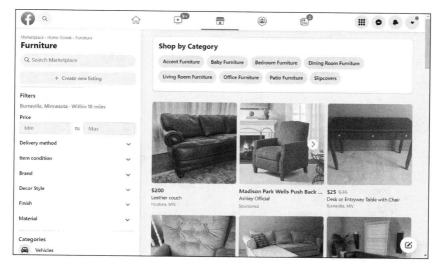

FIGURE 12.5

Buying and selling on the Facebook Marketplace.

If you want to buy an item, you contact the seller (another Facebook member) directly and arrange payment and pickup with them. (Cash is king on the Facebook Marketplace.) As with Craigslist, buying something listed on the Facebook Marketplace is strictly buyer beware.

Selling on the Facebook Marketplace means creating a listing for the item you want to sell. There are no fees involved.

 NOTE   Facebook is a social network you can use to connect with family and friends. Learn more about Facebook in Chapter 15, "Social Networking with Facebook, Twitter, and Other Social Media."

Reverb

Reverb (www.reverb.com), shown in Figure 12.6, is an online marketplace for new, used, and vintage musical instruments, DJ gear, and recording and sound reinforcement equipment. It's the go-to site for musicians and anyone working with them.

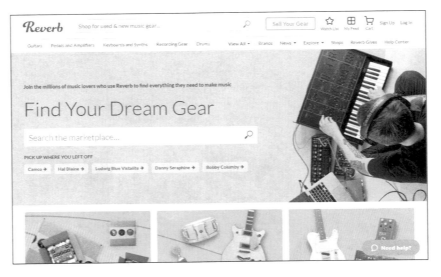

FIGURE 12.6

Buying and selling musical instruments on Reverb.

You can find gear from both individual sellers and music stores on Reverb. You pay through Reverb via credit/debit card, PayPal, or Reverb Payments, the site's proprietary payment system; there's also financing available through Affirm. The site offers a buyer protection plan, although buying from individual sellers can sometimes be problematic if you end up with a defective item or something not as described.

Reverb is a pretty good place for selling used musical instruments and gear because you have a targeted audience. Although Reverb doesn't charge listing fees, you do pay a 5% fee when you sell an item, along with a 2.5% to 2.7% payment processing fee.

THE ABSOLUTE MINIMUM

Here are the key points to remember from this chapter:

- You can find just about any type of item you want for sale somewhere on the Internet.

- Shopping online is a lot like shopping in a traditional store; you find the product you want, go through the checkout system, and make your payment.

- Internet shopping is very safe, especially if you buy from a major merchant that offers a secure server and a good returns policy.

- You can also use the Internet to order food and groceries for delivery.

- Several online marketplaces let you both buy and sell items; the most popular include Craigslist, eBay, Etsy, Facebook Marketplace, and Reverb.

PART V

COMMUNICATING ONLINE

SENDING AND RECEIVING EMAIL

Email is a quick and efficient way to communicate with friends, family, and colleagues. An email message is like an old-school letter, except it's composed electronically and delivered almost immediately via the Internet.

You can use a dedicated email program, such as Microsoft Outlook or the Mail app included with Windows 11, to send and receive email from your personal computer. If you prefer, you can use a web mail service such as Gmail or Yahoo! Mail to manage all your email from any web browser on any computer. Either approach is good and enables you to create, send, and read email messages from all your friends, family, and colleagues.

How Email Works

Email—short for "electronic mail"—is like traditional postal mail, except that you compose messages that are delivered electronically via the Internet. When you send an email message to another Internet user, that message travels from your PC to your recipient's PC through a series of Internet connections and servers, almost instantaneously. Email messages can be of any length and can include file attachments of various types.

To make sure your message goes to the right recipient, you have to use your recipient's *email address*. Each email address is unique and has three parts:

- The user's name
- The @ sign
- The user's domain name (usually the name of the Internet service provider, or ISP)

As an example, if you use Comcast as your Internet provider (with the domain name comcast.net) and your login name is jimbo, your email address is jimbo@comcast.net.

POP/IMAP Email

There are two different ways to send and receive email via the Internet.

The traditional way to send and receive email uses a protocol called the *Post Office Protocol (POP)*. POP email requires use of a dedicated email software program and—at the ISP level—separate email servers to send and receive messages.

Internet Message Access Protocol (IMAP) is a newer type of email. It works just like POP email through your ISP but offers a few more options for synchronizing messages between different devices.

To use POP/IMAP email, you have to use a special email program, such as Microsoft Outlook (part of the Microsoft Office suite) or the Mail app included with Windows 11. That email program has to be configured to send email to your ISP's outgoing mail server (called an *SMTP server*) and to receive email from your ISP's incoming mail server (called a POP3 or IMAP server). If you want to access your email account from another computer, you have to use a similar email program and go through the entire configuration process all over again on the second computer.

Web-Based Email

You're not limited to using the "hard-wired" POP/IMAP email offered by your ISP; you also can send and receive email from web mail services, such as Google's Gmail and Yahoo! Mail. These web mail services enable you to access your email from any computer, using any web browser.

If you use a PC in multiple locations—in the office, at home, or on the road—web mail is a convenient way to check your email at any time of day, no matter where you are. You also can use web mail to check your email from your smartphone or tablet; the device you use doesn't matter.

With web mail, you don't have to go through the same sort of complicated configuration routine that you use with POP/IMAP email. All you have to do is go to the email service's website and enter your user ID and password, and you're ready to send and receive messages.

 TIP Most ISPs offer web-based access to their traditional POP/IMAP email, which is convenient when you're away from home and need to check your email. Many traditional POP/IMAP email services, such as Microsoft Outlook, also offer web-based access.

Most web mail services are completely free to use. Some services offer both free versions and paid versions, with paid subscriptions offering additional message storage and functionality.

The largest web mail services include the following:

- Gmail (mail.google.com)
- iCloud (www.icloud.com/mail)
- Mail.com (www.mail.com)
- Outlook.com (www.outlook.com)
- ProtonMail (www.protonmail.com)
- Yahoo! Mail (mail.yahoo.com)

Using the Windows Mail App

Windows 11 includes a built-in Mail app for sending and receiving email messages. You open the Mail app from the Start screen.

By default, the Mail app manages email from the Outlook email account linked to your Microsoft account. This means you see Outlook messages in your Mail Inbox, and you can easily send emails from your Outlook account. You also can set up the Mail app to send and receive messages from a Gmail account.

Navigating the Mail App

The Mail app, at its default size, displays three panes, as shown in Figure 13.1. The small far-left pane displays all the email accounts installed in the app and folders from the selected account. Select a folder, such as your Inbox, and all the messages from that folder display in the middle pane. Select a message, and it displays in the right-hand pane.

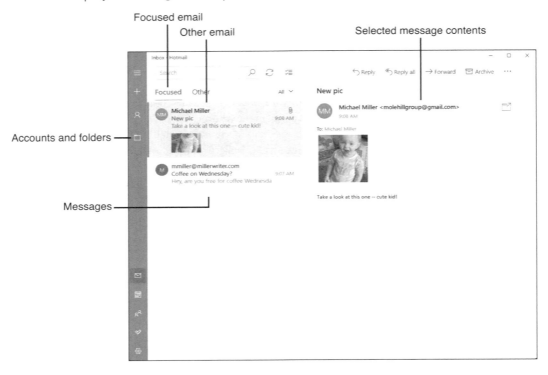

FIGURE 13.1

Viewing messages in the Mail app.

You can choose to display focused messages or all other messages by selecting the appropriate tab at the top of the message pane. Focused messages are those that Mail thinks you're most interested in. (And it's right most of the time.) Other messages are pretty much everything else—advertising messages, notifications from social media and other apps, and so forth.

Adding Another Email Account

By default, the Mail app sends and receives messages from the email account associated with your Microsoft account. You can, however, configure Mail to work with other email accounts, if you have them. Follow these steps:

1. Click or tap the Settings (gear) icon at the bottom of the navigation pane.

2. When the Settings pane appears, click or tap Manage Accounts.

3. When the Accounts pane appears, click or tap Add Account.

4. When the Add an Account window appears, select the type of account you want to add.

5. When the next pane appears, enter the email address and password for that account, and then click or tap the Sign In or Connect button.

The Mail app lets you add Outlook.com (including Hotmail, Live.com, and MSN Mail accounts), Office 365 (including Microsoft Exchange), Gmail (Google), Yahoo! Mail, iCloud, and other POP/IMAP email accounts. To view the Inbox of another email account, click or tap the name of that account in the left pane in the Mail app.

Reading and Replying to Messages

To read a message, all you have to do is click or tap it. The message content displays in the full app window, as shown in Figure 13.2.

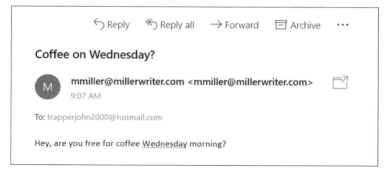

FIGURE 13.2

Reading an email message.

To reply to a message, follow these steps:

1. From an open message, click or tap Reply at the top of screen. (If you want to respond to all recipients of a multirecipient message, click or tap Reply All instead.)

2. The content pane changes to a reply message pane, as shown in Figure 13.3. Enter your reply at the top of the message; the bottom of the message "quotes" the original message.

3. Click or tap Send when you're ready to send the message.

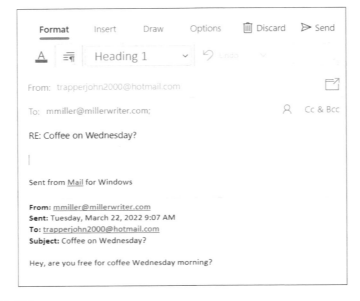

FIGURE 13.3

Replying to a message.

Viewing Attachments

Some messages come with files attached—pictures, documents, you name it. If the attachment is a picture file, you typically see a thumbnail version of the picture within the body of the message.

To view an attachment, just click or tap it. To save the attached file to your computer, right-click it and select Save.

 CAUTION Email file attachments are some of the biggest sources of computer viruses and spyware infections. Malicious users attach viruses and spyware to email messages, oftentimes disguised as legitimate files; when a user clicks or taps to open the file, his computer is infected with the virus or spyware. You should avoid opening any file sent to you from a user you don't know, or even from people you do know if you weren't expecting them. If you receive an email from a complete stranger with an unknown file attached, that's almost definitely a malicious file that you shouldn't open. Instead, delete the entire message. Learn more about computer viruses and spyware in Chapter 21, "Protecting Your PC from Computer Attacks, Malware, Spam, and More."

Sending a New Message

It's equally easy to create and send a new email message. Follow these steps:

1. Click or tap New Mail in the navigation pane to display the new message pane, shown in Figure 13.4.

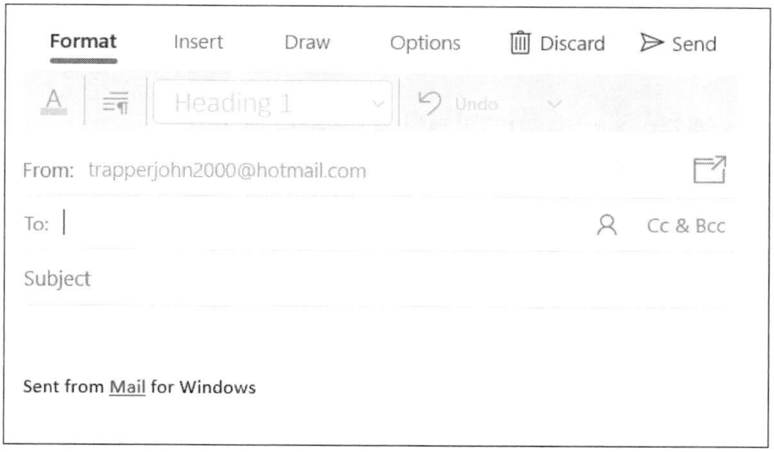

FIGURE 13.4

Creating a new email message.

2. Click or tap within the To: field and begin entering the name or email address of the message's recipient. Mail displays a list of matching names from your contact list; select the person you want to email.

3. Click or tap the Subject field and type a subject for this message.

4. To attach a file to this message, click or tap the Insert tab and then click or tap Attach. When the Open dialog box appears, navigate to and select the file you want to attach; then click or tap the Open button.

5. When you're ready to send the email, click or tap Send.

That's it. Windows sends your message using your default email account.

Attaching a File

Sometimes you may want to send a picture or other type of file to a friend via email. It's easy to do in the Mail app:

1. Create a new email as normal.

2. Click or tap the Insert tab (see Figure 13.5).

Format	**Insert**	Draw	Options	🗑 Discard	➤ Send
📎 Files	⊞ Table	🖼 Pictures	ⓒ Link	😊 Emoji	

FIGURE 13.5

Attaching a file to a message.

3. Click or tap Files to open the Open dialog box.

4. Navigate to and select the file you want to attach.

5. Click or tap Open; the selected file is added to your message.

6. Complete the email as necessary and then click or tap Send.

 NOTE When attaching a picture file, click or tap the Files button, not the Pictures button. Only use the Pictures button if you want to insert the picture within the body of the email message.

Using Web-Based Email

Web-based email has become increasingly popular because it's easy to set up and use. You can access your email from any computer, mobile phone, or tablet with a web browser and an Internet connection.

The two most popular web-based email services today are Microsoft's Outlook Online and Google's Gmail.

Using Outlook Online

If you have an Outlook email address, you easily can use Outlook Online to send and receive email messages from any computer or connected device. Use any web browser to go to outlook.live.com, log into your account with your email address and password, and all your messages are automatically displayed.

As you can see in Figure 13.6, the Outlook Online window has three panes. The left pane displays your accounts and folders; the center displays messages in the selected folder; and the right pane displays the contents of the selected message. Action buttons for the selected message are in the toolbar and above any open message.

Accounts and folders   Selected message contents

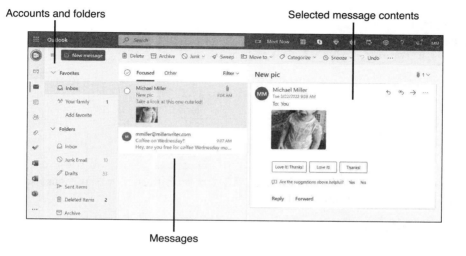

Messages

FIGURE 13.6

Viewing messages in Outlook Online.

To reply to a message, open the message and click or tap the Reply button. To create a new message, click or tap + New Message in the left pane. To send a message, click or tap the Send button.

Using Gmail

Gmail is the largest web mail service in use today. You access Gmail at mail.google.com. If you don't yet have a Google account, you're prompted to sign up for one.

The Gmail interface consists of two panes, as shown in Figure 13.7. The left pane lists all your folders, including the Inbox. The right pane displays all messages in the selected folder. (There are three tabs in this pane, to display Primary emails, Social media emails, and Promotions.)

FIGURE 13.7

Viewing messages in Gmail.

To view a message, click or tap it in the messages pane. You see the contents of that message, as shown in Figure 13.8. Action buttons for that message are to the top right of the message.

FIGURE 13.8

Reading and replying to a Gmail message.

To reply to a message, open the message and click or tap the Reply (curved left arrow) button above the message. To create a new message, click or tap the + Compose button in the left pane (refer to Figure 13.7). To send a message, click or tap the Send button.

THE ABSOLUTE MINIMUM

Here are the key points to remember from this chapter:

- Email is a fast and easy way to send electronic letters over the Internet.

- There are two types of email: POP/IMAP email, which requires a separate email program, and web mail, which can be sent and received from any web browser.

- You can use the Windows Mail app to send and receive email from your default email account; the app also consolidates messages from other services you've connected to your account.

- The most popular web mail services include Google's Gmail and Microsoft's Outlook Online.

- Don't open unexpected files attached to incoming email messages; they might contain computer viruses!

14

VIDEO CHATTING WITH FRIENDS AND FAMILY

Email is a good way to communicate, but it's not immediate, and it certainly isn't personal. When you want to talk to someone face-to-face, it's time to start video chatting with Zoom or Microsoft Teams. All you need is a webcam built into or connected to your PC and a good Internet connection, and you can participate in one-on-one video chats or group video meetings with friends, family, and coworkers.

Video Chatting with Zoom

Emailing is one thing. Talking face to face is another—which is what video chat is all about.

Video chat has been popular for a number of years, but it became virtually ubiquitous during the COVID-19 pandemic, when everyone was stuck at home. Almost overnight, people had to learn to use video chat for remote work, remote school, and just keeping in touch with others remotely.

Fortunately, video chatting is easy to do. To participate in a video chat, both you and the person you want to talk to must have webcams built into or connected to your PCs. In addition, you both must be connected to the Internet for the duration of the call and be subscribed to the same video chat service. After that, it's a simple matter of clicking a few onscreen buttons and smiling into the camera.

 NOTE   Learn more about Zoom, Microsoft Teams, and other video chat services in my book, *My Video Chat for Seniors*. It's available wherever good books are sold.

 NOTE   Most notebook PCs have webcams built in, which you can use to video chat on Zoom and other services. If your PC doesn't have a built-in webcam or if you just want to upgrade for better quality, you can purchase and connect an external webcam to make video calls. Webcams are manufactured and sold by Logitech and other companies and connect to your PC via USB. They're inexpensive (as low as $30 USD or so) and sit on top of your monitor.

Getting to Know Zoom

There are a number of video chat services available today, of which the most popular is Zoom. Zoom offers both free and paid versions; the paid version is primarily for businesses and large organizations, whereas the free version is perfect for personal use.

You can use Zoom from the company's website, in any web browser, or in the Zoom app. Functionality is similar between the two, although the app may be a little easier to use. (I use the app throughout this chapter.)

The first time you use Zoom (from Zoom's website), you're prompted to download and install the Zoom app. You can also install it before you start using Zoom, from Zoom's website, if you want. Learn more (and download the app) at www.zoom.us.

Zoom calls its video chats Zoom meetings—whether you're chatting one on one or in a large group. You can have up to 100 participants in a Zoom meeting, and each meeting can last up to 40 minutes. (If you need more time, you can easily launch or schedule a second chat immediately following the first one.)

NOTE   Zoom and Microsoft Teams, discussed later in this chapter, are just two of several consumer-oriented video-calling services you can use on your Windows 11 PC. Other popular services include Facebook Messenger (for Facebook members only), Google Meet (meet.google.com), Skype (www.skype.com), and, if you have Apple computers and devices, FaceTime (support.apple.com/facetime).

Accepting a Meeting Invitation

When someone else is hosting a Zoom meeting, that person sends out invitations, typically via email, to all participants. This is true of both instant meetings (those being held immediately) and those scheduled for a future time.

Joining a meeting from an invitation is relatively easy. Follow these steps:

1. From within the email, click the link for the Zoom meeting.

2. If you're prompted to use your device's audio and/or video, do so.

3. You may be placed in a virtual waiting room until admitted by the meeting leader. This is particularly the case if you join a scheduled meeting a few minutes early. Just sit back and cool your heels.

4. Once you're admitted to the meeting, you're ready to go. You see a large image of the meeting leader in the window and a smaller thumbnail of you, as shown in Figure 14.1. Other participants may appear in similar thumbnails, or you may all appear in a grid.

5. Click or mouse over the screen to display the chat controls.

6. Click the Mute Audio icon to mute your microphone. Click this icon again to unmute your mic.

7. Click the Stop Video icon to turn off your computer's camera. Click this icon again to turn your camera back on.

8. Click the red Leave button to leave the meeting.

Other participant   Your thumbnail

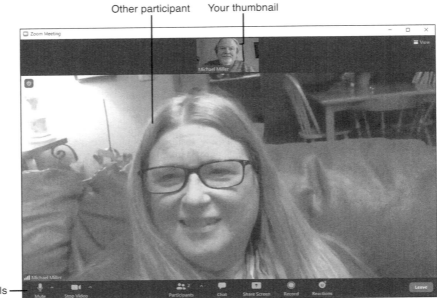

Chat controls

FIGURE 14.1

Participating in a Zoom meeting.

Joining a Meeting Manually

Clicking or tapping a link is the easiest way to join a Zoom meeting, but it's not the only way. When you receive an invitation via email or text, that invitation typically includes a meeting ID and optional passcode that you can enter manually into the Zoom app. This is particularly useful if you receive a text invitation on your phone but want to Zoom using another device, such as your tablet or computer.

Follow these steps:

1. When it's time for the meeting, launch the Zoom app on your computer. Sign in, if necessary, and then select the Home tab.

2. Click or tap the Join icon.

3. Enter the meeting ID into the Meeting ID field, as shown in Figure 14.2.

4. Accept or change your name.

5. Click or tap Join.

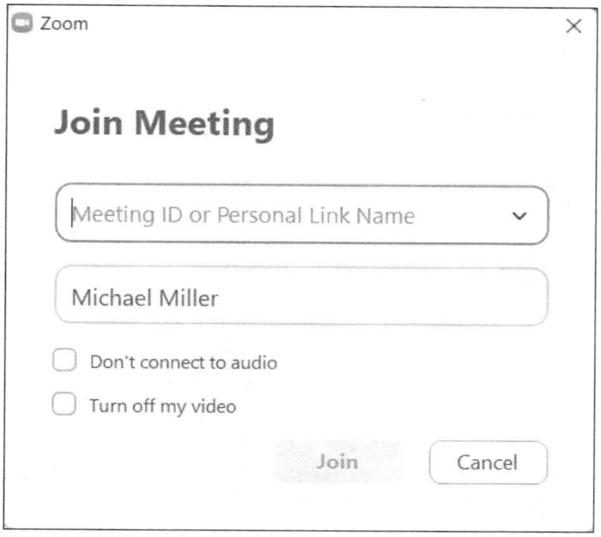

FIGURE 14.2

Joining a Zoom meeting manually.

6. If prompted for a passcode or password, enter it and then click or tap Join Meeting.

7. If prompted, click or tap Join with Video.

8. If you're placed in a virtual waiting room, wait to be admitted.

9. Once you're admitted to the meeting, you're ready to go.

Switching Views

When you're in a Zoom meeting, you have the choice of viewing the other participants in one of two views. You switch between views by clicking the View button and selecting the view you want.

Speaker View puts the person currently speaking in the large video window, with up to three other participants in smaller thumbnails. In this view, the person in the large window is constantly changing, depending on who's talking.

Gallery View displays many participants (up to 49 at a time) in a grid layout. The person currently speaking is highlighted with a green border. If there are more participants than can fit on screen, you can scroll through additional participants by clicking the right or left arrows on your keyboard.

Applying a Virtual Background

The virtual background option is one of the most fun options Zoom offers, and it's the one I'm asked about the most. Instead of the other participants looking at the room or blank wall beyond you, you can add a virtual background that makes it appear as if you're somewhere else, like the one in Figure 14.3. It's easy to do—and you can choose from Zoom's stock backgrounds or any image stored on your computer. You can even download other backgrounds from the Internet!

FIGURE 14.3

The author with a virtual background in a Zoom meeting—I'm really sitting in my cluttered home office, not in front of the Golden Gate Bridge!

 NOTE   Zoom's virtual backgrounds work best if you're sitting in front of a solid-color background. They work even better if the background is green. (This is the fabled "green screen effect.") For best effect, you can set up an actual green screen, in the form of a green cloth or paper backdrop, which you can find online or at your local photography store.

Here's how to change your background during a Zoom meeting:

1. Click or tap the up arrow next to the Stop Video button.

2. Click or tap Choose Virtual Background. This displays the Settings window with the Virtual Background tab selected.

3. Select the Video Backgrounds tab. Zoom's built-in backgrounds are displayed. You'll also see any other backgrounds you've recently selected.

4. Click or tap one of these backgrounds to use it. (Click or tap Blur if you simply want a blurred background.) You see a preview of the virtual background.

5. If you have a green screen background, check the I Have a Green Screen option.

6. Check Mirror My Video to view the virtual background as others see it.

7. Return to your normal background by selecting None.

8. Close the Settings window when you're done.

Leaving a Meeting

When a meeting officially ends, you and all other participants are automatically disconnected from it. You can, however, leave a meeting before it officially ends, which is common.

To leave a Zoom meeting, all you have to do is display the chat controls and then click or tap the red Leave icon. When prompted, select Leave Meeting, and Zoom hangs up for you.

Starting a New Instant Meeting

Starting your own Zoom meeting—with one or more other participants—is equally easy. You can schedule meetings in advance (which I get to next) or start what Zoom calls an instant meeting. Here's how to do it:

1. From within the Zoom app, select the Home tab and then click or tap New Meeting, as shown in Figure 14.4.

2. If you're prompted to connect or use your device's audio and/or video, do so.

3. Your meeting is now live, with you as the only participant until you invite others to your meeting. Click or tap Participants to open the Participants panel.

4. Click or tap the up arrow on the Participants button; then click or tap Invite.

5. Click or tap to select the Email tab.

6. Select your email client. (In most cases, you should select Default Email.)

7. You see a new email message with the meeting information already entered. Enter the email address(es) of your desired participant(s) and click or tap to send the invitation.

FIGURE 14.4

Starting a new Zoom meeting.

Scheduling a Meeting in Advance

What if you want to Zoom with your siblings on Thursday at 7:00 p.m. or have a regularly scheduled virtual book club meeting over Zoom every Wednesday morning at 8:00 a.m.? Fortunately, Zoom lets you schedule meetings in advance so others can plan to attend:

1. From the Home tab, click or tap Schedule. The Schedule Meeting window opens.

2. Enter a name or topic for the meeting.

3. Enter the start date and time.

4. Enter the length or duration of the meeting—up to a maximum of 40 minutes on a free account.

5. If it's a recurring meeting (one that happens on the same day every week or month, or the same time every day), click or tap Recurring Meeting and select how often it repeats.

6. Select whether you want Zoom to generate an automatic meeting ID or use your personal meeting ID. (In most instances, let Zoom generate the ID automatically for better security.)

7. Make sure Waiting Room is checked.

8. Select whether you want the host video (your video) on or off. (You can change this during the meeting if you want.)

9. Select whether you want participants' video on or off. (You can also change this during the meeting.)

10. Select if you want this meeting added to a specific calendar app.

11. Click Save. Your upcoming Zoom meeting is now scheduled.

Starting and Ending a Meeting

There are a few tasks you need to undertake to both start and end a meeting.

When you launch a new meeting, participants who log in are ushered into a virtual waiting room, where they stay until you admit them into the meeting. As each participant enters, click or tap Admit to admit them into the meeting. (This is only if you have the waiting room option enabled; otherwise, participants are immediately admitted to the meeting.)

Ending a Zoom meeting is even easier. To end a meeting, click or tap the red End button—and, when prompted, select End Meeting for All.

Video Chatting with Microsoft Teams

Zoom isn't the only video chat service out there. Microsoft offers a chat service that's integrated into Windows 11: Microsoft Teams. Teams is tied into your Microsoft account by default and launches when you click the Chat button on the Windows taskbar.

Unlike Zoom and most other video chat services, Microsoft Teams is a full-featured collaborative communication platform, originally targeted at businesses, that includes a robust video meeting component. During the COVID-19 crisis, Microsoft revamped the video chat in Teams to be more user-friendly and appealing to individual consumers.

Like Zoom, Microsoft offers both paid and free versions of Microsoft Teams. The paid version of Teams is part of the Microsoft 365 suite of applications targeted primarily at businesses and large organizations on a subscription basis. The free version, which you'll be using, is targeted at regular consumers and offers a limited feature set. This free version focuses on video chatting but also offers text chat and real-time collaboration via Microsoft Office apps.

Accepting a Meeting Invitation

Like Zoom, Microsoft Teams calls a video chat a meeting. A Teams meeting can include up to 100 people. When someone invites you to join a Teams meeting, you receive an invitation within Windows or via email.

To accept an invitation and join a Teams meeting, follow these steps:

1. Click or tap Accept in the invitation.

2. If you're prompted to turn on your camera and microphone, do so.

3. Click or tap Join Now.

4. You are placed in a waiting room (called the Lobby) until the host admits you to the meeting.

5. When you join the meeting, you see the current speaker onscreen, and your image in a live thumbnail, as shown in Figure 14.5. If there are more than just the two of you in the meeting, you see the other speakers in a grid.

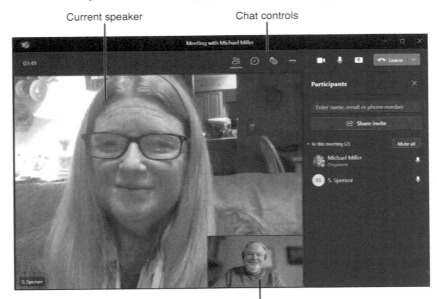

FIGURE 14.5

Joining a Microsoft Teams meeting.

6. Click or tap the Mute button to mute your microphone. Click or tap the button again to unmute your mic.

7. Click or tap the Turn Camera Off button to turn off your camera. Click or tap this button again to turn your camera back on.

8. Click or tap the Leave button to leave the meeting.

Blurring Your Background

Microsoft Teams lets you blur the background behind you on the screen. This is good if don't want to show the other participants a messy room behind you or just want to make things look a little more interesting.

Here's how to do it:

1. From within a meeting, click or tap the More Actions (three-dot) button.

2. Select Apply Background Effects to open the Background Settings panel.

3. Click or tap Blur.

4. Click or tap Preview to see what the effect looks like.

5. Click or tap Apply to apply the effect.

6. Click the X to close the Background Settings panel.

Launching a New Teams Meeting

When you want to host your own Microsoft Teams meeting, you can invite any of your contacts in the People app or other people via their email addresses:

1. Click or tap the Chat icon in the Windows taskbar to display the Teams panel, shown in Figure 14.6.

2. Recent actions are listed here. Click or tap one of these to resume that meeting or text chat. *Or...*

3. Click or tap Meeting to start a new meeting.

4. Make sure your camera and microphone are turned on.

5. Click or tap Background Filters if you want to blur your onscreen background.

6. Click or tap Join Now to start the meeting.

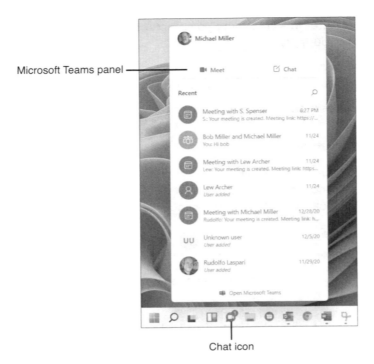

Microsoft Teams panel

Chat icon

FIGURE 14.6

Starting a new Microsoft Teams meeting.

7. You're prompted to invite other people to the meeting. Click or tap Share via Default Email.

NOTE You can also paste a link to the meeting into other mail or messaging programs or social media messages. Just click or tap Copy Meeting Link and then paste that link into the other app.

8. Your default email app opens with a new message created. Enter the email addresses of the people you want to invite to the meeting and then send the message.

9. Close the Invite People to Join You window and return to the main meeting window.

10. When a recipient clicks the link in the invitation you sent, they're placed in the virtual Lobby, and you see an onscreen message. Click or tap Admit to let them into the meeting.

11. You see the other people in your meeting. Your live picture appears in a thumbnail in the corner.

12. The other participants are listed in the Participants panel on the right side of the window. Click or tap Share Invite to invite other people to the meeting.

13. Click or tap the Leave button to leave the meeting but leave it up and running for other participants. *Or...*

14. Click or tap the down arrow next to the Leave button and then click or tap End Meeting to end the meeting for all participants.

15. When prompted to end the meeting, click or tap End.

 NOTE Microsoft Teams also lets you participate in text chats with people in your contacts list. Just open the Microsoft Teams panel and click or tap the Chat button. Enter the name, phone number, or email address of a contact into the To field, and then type your message into the Type a New Message field. Press Enter and your message is sent. (It appears on the right side of the window; messages from other participants appear on the left side of the window.)

THE ABSOLUTE MINIMUM

Here are the key points to remember from this chapter:

- If you have a webcam built into or connected to your PC, you can use Zoom or Microsoft Teams to video chat with friends and family members over the Internet.

- Two of the most popular video chat services are Zoom and Microsoft Teams.

- Teams is integrated into Windows 11 and launches when you click the Chat icon in the Windows taskbar.

- Both Zoom and Teams offer free versions for consumer use and let you chat with one or more participants in group meetings.

SOCIAL NETWORKING WITH FACEBOOK, TWITTER, AND OTHER SOCIAL MEDIA

Want to find out what your friends, family, and colleagues are up to? Want to let them know what you're doing today? Then you need to hop onboard the social networking train; it's how savvy online users connect today.

Social networking enables people to share experiences and opinions with each other via community-based websites. Whether you use Facebook, Twitter, Pinterest, or some other social networking site, it's a great way to keep up to date on what your friends and family are doing.

Using Facebook

No question about it, the number-one social network today is Facebook (www.facebook.com). Facebook has more than two billion active users each month worldwide; chances are, most of your friends and family are already on Facebook, just waiting for you to join in the fun.

Signing Up with and Signing In to Facebook

You can access Facebook using Microsoft Edge, Google Chrome, or any web browser, at www.facebook.com.

If you're new to Facebook, use this page to create a new account for yourself. Click Create New Account and then enter your first and last name, email address or phone number, desired password, and birthday; then click Sign Up. Follow the rest of the steps to create your account and get started.

After you sign up for Facebook, you can log in to your account by going to the same page and entering your email address and password into the boxes at the top of the page. Click the Log In button to proceed.

Getting to Know Facebook

You navigate the Facebook website from the navigation sidebar on the left side of the page. The middle of the screen displays the selected page or content, and the right column displays a variety of different content, including upcoming friend birthdays, marketplace listings, and the like.

 NOTE Like most websites, Facebook constantly upgrades its feature set, so what you see might differ somewhat from what I describe here.

The default selection in the navigation sidebar is your Feed, and for good reason; as you can see in Figure 15.1, this is where all the status updates from your friends display. Scroll down the page to view more updates.

You can navigate the Facebook website from the toolbar at the top of the page. In addition to the big Search box, which you use to search for people and things on the Facebook site, the toolbar enables you to click or tap to see friend requests, private messages, and notifications.

FIGURE 15.1

The Facebook Home page—complete with the Feed of your friends' status updates.

Searching for Friends

Social networking is all about keeping in touch with friends, and the easiest way to find friends on Facebook is to let Facebook find them for you—based on the information you provided for your personal profile. The more Facebook knows about you, especially in terms of where you've worked and gone to school, the more friends it can find.

The easiest way to find friends on Facebook is to search for a particular person:

1. Click or tap the Search icon on the tool bar. This expands the icon into a Search box.

2. Enter the person's name into the Search box and then press Enter.

3. On the search results page, click the People option in the Filters pane. This displays only people who meet your search criteria, as shown in Figure 15.2.

4. Fine-tune your search by using the controls in the Filters pane. For example, you can filter the results by city, education (schools attended), and work.

5. If your friend is listed, click the Add Friend button to send that person a friend request.

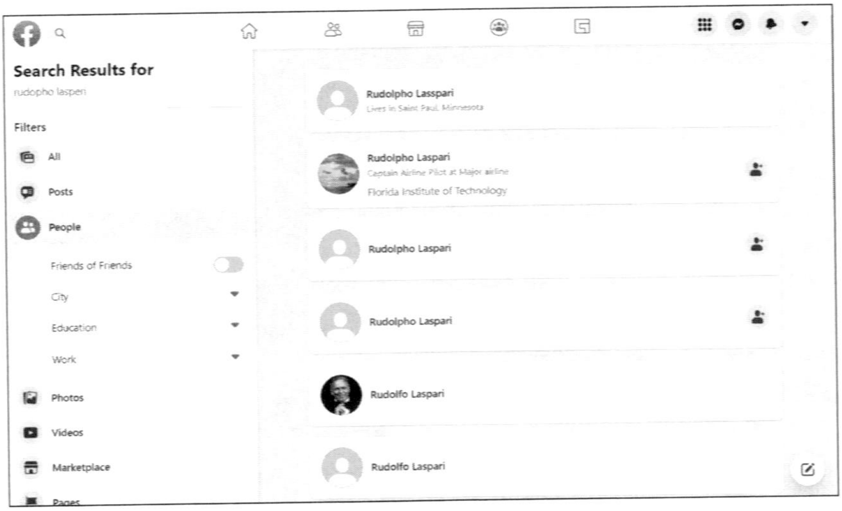

FIGURE 15.2

Searching for friends on the Facebook website.

 NOTE   Facebook doesn't automatically add a person to your friends list. Instead, the person receives an invitation to be your friend; they can accept or reject the invitation. To accept or reject any friend requests you've received, click the Friend Request button on the Facebook toolbar. (And don't worry; if you reject a request, that person won't be notified.)

Viewing a Friend's Profile Page

After you add some folks to your Facebook friends list, you can easily see what they've been up to by visiting their profile pages. A profile page, like the one shown in Figure 15.3, displays all that person's status updates and activities on the Facebook site, in the form of a timeline. But that's not all that's there.

To view detailed personal information about your friend, click the About tab. To view the pictures this person has uploaded, click Photos, and to see a list of this person's friends, click Friends.

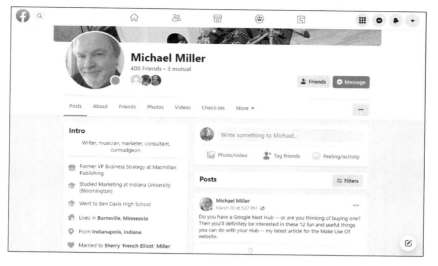

FIGURE 15.3

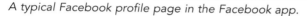

A typical Facebook profile page in the Facebook app.

Posting Status Updates

We've talked a lot about Facebook being the perfect place to update your friends and family on what you're up to—things you're doing, thoughts you're thinking, accomplishments you're accomplishing, you name it. The easiest way to let people know what's what is to post what Facebook calls a *status update*.

Every status update you make is broadcast to everyone on your friends list, displayed in the Feed on their Home pages. This way, everyone who cares enough about you to make you a friend knows everything you post about. And that can be quite a lot—from simple text posts to photos and videos and even links to other web pages.

Facebook makes it extremely easy to post a status update. Here's how you do it:

1. Click Home in the Facebook toolbar to display the Feed.

2. Go to the Create Post box at the top of the page and type your message into the What's On Your Mind? field. The Create Post box expands to display a series of option buttons at the bottom, as shown in Figure 15.4.

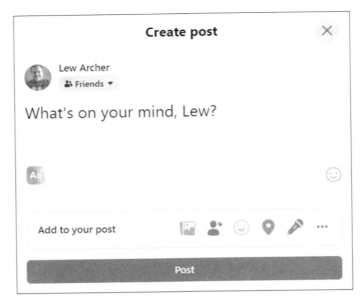

FIGURE 15.4

Posting a new status update.

3. To include a photograph in your status update, click or tap the Photo/Video button beneath the Create Post box; this opens the Choose File to Upload or Open dialog box. (Which dialog box displays depends on which web browser you use.) Navigate to and select the photo(s) you want to upload; then click or tap the Open button.

4. To include a link to a web page, enter the URL (web address) for that page into the Create Post box. Facebook should recognize the link and display a thumbnail image from the page.

5. To include your location in this status update, click or tap the Check In button. (You may need to click or tap the More—three-dot—button to display this and other buttons.) If Facebook can tell your location automatically, it displays a list of options. Otherwise, start entering your location manually; as you type, Facebook displays a list of suggested locations, along with a map of the current selection. Click or tap the correct location from the resulting list.

CAUTION   You might not want to identify your location on every post you make. If you post while you're away from home, you're letting potential burglars know that your house is empty. You're also telling potential stalkers where they can find you. For these reasons, use caution when posting your location in your status updates.

6. To "tag" a friend in your status update, click or tap the Tag Friends button beneath the Create Post box. Enter the name of the person you want to tag. As you type, Facebook displays a drop-down list with matching names from your Facebook friends list. Select the friend from the list.

7. Click or tap the Share button to post your status update to the Facebook site.

Determine Who Can—or Can't—See a Status Update

By default, everyone on Facebook can read every post you make. If you'd rather send a given post to a more select group of people, you can change the privacy settings for any individual post. This enables only selected people to see that post; other people on your friends list won't see it at all.

Here's how to do it:

1. Enter the text of your status update, or any photos you want to upload, into the Create Post box as normal.

2. Click or tap the Privacy button to display a list of privacy options, as shown in Figure 15.5.

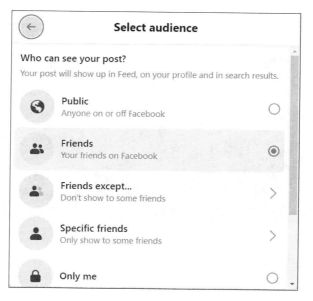

FIGURE 15.5

Selecting privacy options for a status update.

3. Click or tap Public to let everyone on Facebook see the post.

4. Select Friends to make a post visible only to people on your friends list.

5. Click or tap Friends Except to specify which of your friends you don't want to see this post.

6. Click or tap More Options to view more privacy options, including sending to specific friends lists you've created.

7. With the privacy settings selected, click or tap the Share button to send this status update to those people you've selected.

Viewing Friends' Updates in Your Feed

The posts you make display in your friends' Feeds. Conversely, your Feed displays all the status updates posted by people on your friends list.

Here's how to read, like, and comment on posts in the Feed:

1. Click or tap Feed in the navigation sidebar to display your Feed.

2. Your friends' posts display in the Feed in the middle of the page. The newest posts are at the top; scroll down through the list to read older posts. (Figure 15.6 shows a typical post with photo.)

FIGURE 15.6

A typical Facebook post.

3. To leave a comment about a post, click or tap Comment and then enter your text into the resulting Write a Comment box.

4. To "like" a post, click or tap Like. Or mouse over the Like button and select from one of the available emoji options (Like, Love, Haha, Wow, Sad, or Angry).

5. If a post includes one or more photos, click or tap the photo to view a larger version of that photo.

6. If a post includes a video, playback (without sound) should begin automatically. To turn on the sound, click or tap the Mute button. To pause playback, click or tap the Pause button.

7. If a post includes a link to another web page, that link appears beneath the post, along with a brief description of the page. Click or tap link to open the other page in your web browser.

Managing Your Privacy on Facebook

Facebook is all about connecting users to one another. That's how the site functions, after all, by encouraging "friends" and all sorts of public sharing of information.

The problem is that Facebook, by default, shares all your information with just about everybody. Not just your friends or friends of your friends, but the entire membership of the site. And not just with Facebook members, either; Facebook also shares your information with third-party applications and games and with other sites on the Web.

Fortunately, you can configure Facebook to be much less public than it is by default. If you value your privacy, this might be worth doing.

With that in mind, here's how to perform a privacy checkup on Facebook:

1. Click the Account (down arrow) button on the Facebook toolbar to display the pull-down menu.

2. Click Settings and Privacy.

3. Click Privacy Checkup.

4. Follow the onscreen instructions to configure your privacy settings and make Facebook safer to use.

Using Twitter

Facebook might be the biggest social network on the Web today, but it's not the only one. There are several other social networks that help you keep in touch with friends and family—and, in some cases, focus on specific types of users or interests.

We'll start our examination of these other social networks by looking at Twitter. Unlike Facebook, Twitter isn't a fully featured social network per se. Instead, Twitter is a kind of microblogging service that enables you to create short (up to 280 characters) text posts—called *tweets*—that your followers receive and read. Tweets can be text only or include images, videos, and links to other web pages.

 NOTE   Most people use Twitter to follow other users rather than to tweet themselves. The most popular tweeters include celebrities, politicians, companies and brands, and news organizations and reporters.

Joining Twitter

You access Twitter from the Twitter website (www.twitter.com), using Microsoft Edge or another web browser. When you first access the site, you're prompted to either sign in or sign up.

If you're new to Twitter, go to the Sign Up pane and choose to sign up with an existing Google or Apple account or with your own email address or phone number. If you choose that last option, you need to enter your name, email address, desired password, and birthday. Click or tap the Sign Up for Twitter button to complete the process.

If you're already a Twitter user, go to the Log In pane, enter your email address or Twitter username, enter your password, and then click or tap the Log In button.

Navigating Twitter

After you register and sign in, you see the Twitter Home page, shown in Figure 15.7.

The left side of the page displays icons that, when clicked, take you to specific pages on the site. The Home page is displayed by default; to return to this page at any time, click the Home icon.

The middle of the page displays your Twitter feed, tweets from the users you're following, newest first. You can click any links in a tweet to go to the mentioned web page or view an embedded photo.

The right side of the page displays trending tweets and tweets in which you may be interested. There's also a Search box at the top of the column you can use to search for topics of interest and other users.

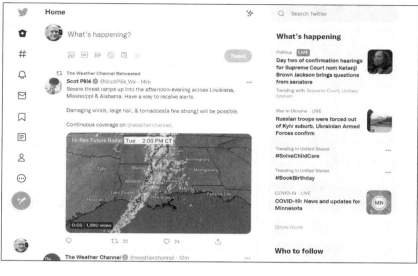

FIGURE 15.7

Twitter's home page.

Tweeting with Twitter

To compose and send a tweet, start by clicking the Home button to open the Home page. The What's Happening box, at the top of the middle column, is where you enter new tweets.

Click or tap within this box, shown in Figure 15.8, to enter your text—up to 280 characters. (Spaces count as characters, by the way.) You can include a photo by clicking or tapping the Add Photo button at the bottom on the far left. When you finish, click or tap the Tweet button to send your message on its way.

FIGURE 15.8

Composing a new tweet.

TIP Because space is limited, many tweeters use abbreviations in their tweets. You can mention a hot topic (and make the term searchable) by preceding it with a hashtag (#), like this: #*HotTopic*. To mention a given user in a tweet, put an @ sign in front of their username, like this: @*username*.

Following Other Users

If friends or family members are on Twitter, you can follow their activities by "following" their tweets.

The easiest way to do this is to use Twitter's Search function. Enter the person's name, Twitter username, or email address into the Search box at the top of the Home page, and then press Enter.

If the person you want is listed in the search results, click that person's name to display their profile page. Click the Follow button, and all tweets from that user start appearing on your Twitter home page.

 CAUTION Some users protect their profiles so that strangers can't follow them without their permission. When you click or tap the Follow button for these users, they have to register their approval before you can follow them.

Customizing Your Profile

As you've just seen, every Twitter user has a profile page on the site. To view your profile page, click or tap Profile on the menu strip on the left side of the page.

From there, click or tap the Edit Profile button to begin editing. You can edit any of the information on this page, and you can change the profile picture that others see.

Using Pinterest

Pinterest is kind of a visual version of Facebook that's become increasingly popular among average, nontechnical users. The user base includes a fairly large number of women aged 30 and older who like to share pictures of clothing, DIY projects, recipes, and the like.

What Pinterest Is and What It Does

Unlike Facebook, which lets you post text-based status updates, Pinterest is all about images. The site consists of a collection of virtual online "pinboards" that people use to share pictures they find interesting. Users "pin" photos and other images to their personal boards and then share their pins with online friends.

Here's how it works. You start by finding an image on a web page that you like and want to share. You then "pin" or save that image to one of your boards, which are like old-fashioned corkboards, except online.

A Pinterest board becomes a place where you can create and share collections of those things you like or find interesting. You can have as many boards as you like, organized by category or topic.

Friends who follow you see the images you pin, and you see the ones they pin. You can "like" other people's pins and repin their items to your boards, thus repeating the original pin. It's a visual way to share things you like online.

Joining Pinterest is free; in fact, you can sign up using your Facebook username and password. (Or with your email address, of course.) Go to www.pinterest.com to get started.

Navigating the Pinterest Site

Pinterest is a relatively easy website to get around. After you log on, it's a simple matter of displaying certain types of pins from certain users and then knowing how to get back to the main page.

The Pinterest home page, shown in Figure 15.9, consists of a toolbar of sorts at the top, with individual pins filling the bulk of the page beneath that. You use the toolbar to navigate the site.

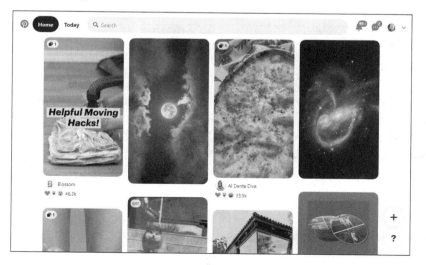

FIGURE 15.9

Pinterest's home page.

To search for pins about a particular topic, enter your query into the Search box and press Enter. You can typically fine-tune your search results by clicking a topic panel at the top of the results page.

Viewing Boards and Pins

A user's presence on Pinterest is defined by that person's boards and the pins posted there. To view a friend's board and its contents, all you have to do is click or tap that friend's name anywhere on the Pinterest site and your friend's personal Pinterest page displays with thumbnails of their boards, as shown in Figure 15.10.

FIGURE 15.10

Viewing a Pinterest profile page.

To open a board, just click or tap it. This displays all the pins for the selected board. Each pin consists of the pinned image, descriptive text (supplied by the user who pinned the item), and the URL for the website where this image was found. To view the web page where the image originally appeared, click or tap the pin.

Following Other Users

When you find someone who posts a lot of things you're interested in, you can follow that person on Pinterest. When you follow a person, that person's new pins display on your Pinterest home page.

You can find people to follow by using Pinterest's Search box to search by name or interest. After you locate a person you want to follow, just go to that person's personal Pinterest page, and click or tap the Follow button.

You also can opt to follow a specific board rather than all of that person's pins. From the person's personal page, click or tap the Follow button for the board you want to follow.

Repinning Existing Items

As you find items you like on the Pinterest site, you can "repin" those items to your boards. To repin an item from its thumbnail image, follow these steps:

1. Mouse over the item you want to repin to display the action controls shown in Figure 15.11.

FIGURE 15.11

Repinning an item.

2. Pinterest suggests a board for this item. If that's the board you want, click or tap Save.

3. If you want to pin to a different board, click or tap the down arrow next to the suggested board. This displays a list of all your boards, top suggestions first.

4. Select the board you want to pin this item to. This automatically saves the pin to that board.

Pinning Items from the Web

Pinterest is all about pinning items of interest—hence the name, a combination of "pin" and "interest." To fully participate in the Pinterest community, you have to learn how to pin items to your boards. There are several ways to do this.

The simplest way to create a pin is from the Pinterest site. To do this, you first need to know the address (URL) of the web page you want to pin. With that URL in hand, follow these steps:

1. Click or tap the + button in the lower-right corner of the Pinterest window, and then select Create a Pin.

2. On the next page, click or tap Save from Website.

3. Enter the URL of the page you want to pin in the text box and press Enter.

4. Pinterest displays all the images from that web page, as shown in Figure 15.12. Click or tap the image you want to pin and click or tap the red Add to Pin button.

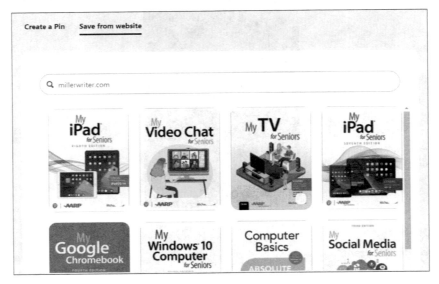

FIGURE 15.12

Selecting an image to pin.

5. On the next page, shown in Figure 15.13, select the board you want to pin to or click or tap Create Board to create a new board for this pin.

FIGURE 15.13

Creating a new pin.

Creating New Boards

You can create as many different boards as you like, each focusing on a specific topic. Create individual boards to match your interests and hobbies.

To create a new board, follow these steps:

1. Click or tap your name at the top-right corner of any page to open your profile page.

2. Click or tap the + button.

3. Click or tap Create Board.

4. When the Create a Board dialog box appears, enter a name for this board in the Name box.

5. Make sure the Keep It a Secret option is turned off. (Turn it on if you want to create a private board that no one but you can see.)

6. Click or tap the Create button.

Pinterest creates the board and displays the page for this board. (It's currently empty.) You can start pinning items to the board!

Using LinkedIn

LinkedIn is a different kind of social network—not necessarily in how it works but in whom it appeals to. Whereas Facebook, Twitter, and Pinterest are aimed at a general audience, LinkedIn is targeted at business professionals. As such, you can use LinkedIn to network with others in your industry or profession or even to hunt for a new position at another firm. (Figure 15.14 shows the LinkedIn home page—with its definite business slant.)

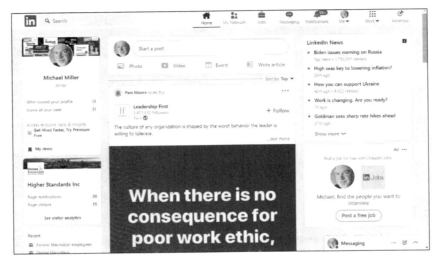

FIGURE 15.14

The LinkedIn home page.

LinkedIn membership is free. To join, go to www.linkedin.com and choose to continue either with an existing Google account or with your email address or phone number. If you choose the latter option, enter your first and last names, email address, and desired password. Click or tap the Join Now button, and you're prompted to enter information to complete your personal profile—employment status, company, title, and so forth. Follow the onscreen instructions to complete the process.

 TIP Use the menu bar at the top of each page to find your way around the LinkedIn site. The menu bar contains links to the LinkedIn home page, your personal profile, your LinkedIn contacts, groups you belong to, LinkedIn's job search features, and your message Inbox.

Personalizing Your Profile

Each LinkedIn member has a profile page. This profile page is what other Linked-In users see when they search for you on the site; it's where you make your initial impression to potential employers and people with whom you want to make contact.

Because your profile page serves as your *de facto* résumé on the LinkedIn site, you want to control the information you display to others. Presenting only selected information can help you present yourself in the best possible light.

Fortunately, your LinkedIn profile is fully customizable; you can select which content others see. This content can include a snapshot of your personal information (shown in Figure 15.15), your contact info, summaries of your professional experience and education, recommendations from other users, and more.

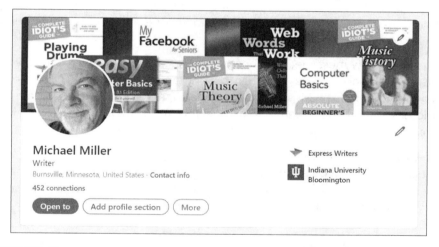

FIGURE 15.15

Snapshot information on a LinkedIn profile page.

To view your profile page, click your name or picture on the menu bar. To edit any section of the page, click the Edit (pencil) button for that section.

Finding New Connections

LinkedIn's equivalent to Facebook friends is called *connections*. These are business or professional contacts you know and trust. Anyone on the LinkedIn site can become a connection; you can also invite people who are not yet LinkedIn members to join your connections list.

You can search for LinkedIn members in your email contacts list. (LinkedIn searches AOL Mail, Gmail, Outlook, Yahoo! Mail, and other email programs and services.) In addition, LinkedIn can search for members who've gone to the same schools or worked for the same employers that you have. You can also invite non-LinkedIn members to be new connections.

To add new connections, click My Network in the toolbar. You see suggested connections from LinkedIn, or you can click Connections to add connections from your email contacts lists, invite others to join your LinkedIn network, and see who LinkedIn recommends as connections.

Contacting Other LinkedIn Members

Networking on LinkedIn involves a lot of personal contact, using LinkedIn's internal email system. This system enables you to send messages to and receive messages from people on your connections list and anyone else who is a member of the LinkedIn site.

To send a new message, click or tap the Messaging button on the toolbar to display your Inbox page, and then click or tap the Compose a New Message icon. When the New Message page appears, enter the recipient's name or email address in the Type a Name box. Type your message into the Write a Message box, and then click or tap the Send button when done.

To view messages you've received, click or tap the Messaging button on the toolbar. This displays all messages you've received in the left pane. The newest messages are listed first; unread messages are in bold. To read a message, all you have to do is click or tap the message header.

Using Social Networks—Smartly and Safely

Social networking puts your whole life out there in front of your friends and family—and, in some cases, just about anyone perusing a network's profiles. With so much personal information displayed publicly, how do you protect yourself against those who might want to do harm to you or your children?

Protecting Your Children

Given that social networks are so popular among teenagers and preteens, many parents worry about their children being cyberstalked on these sites. That worry is not ill founded, especially given the amount of personal information that most users post on their social networking profiles.

It's important to note that all social networking sites try to police themselves, typically by limiting access for younger users. In addition, sites such as Facebook work hard to keep known sex offenders off their sites by monitoring lists of known sex offenders and culling those users from their sites.

That said, the best way to protect your children on social networking sites is to monitor what they do on those sites. As such, you need to become "friends" with your children on Facebook, follow their Twitter feeds, and visit their profile pages on a regular basis. You might be surprised what you find there.

It's an unfortunate fact that not all teens and preteens are wise about what they put online. It's not unusual to find provocative pictures posted on their social networking profiles; you probably don't want your children exposing themselves in this fashion.

You also need to warn your kids that not everyone on Facebook or Twitter is truly a "friend." They should be circumspect about the information they make public and with whom they communicate. It's also worth noting that kids shouldn't arrange to meet in person strangers who they're "friends" with online; it's not unheard of for unsavory adults to use social networks as a stalking ground.

In other words, teach your kids to be careful. Hanging out on a site like Facebook is normally no more dangerous than hanging out at the mall, but even malls aren't completely safe. Caution and common sense are always called for.

Protecting Yourself

The advice you give to your children regarding social networks also applies to yourself. Think twice before posting personal information or incriminating photographs, and don't broadcast your every move on your profile page. Also, don't automatically accept friend requests from people you don't know.

Most important, don't view Facebook and similar sites as online dating services. Yes, you might meet new friends on these social networks, but use caution about transferring online friendships into the physical world. If you decide to meet an online friend offline, do so in a public place and perhaps with another friend along. Don't put yourself at risk when meeting strangers—and remember that until you get to know them in person, anyone you correspond with online remains a stranger.

THE ABSOLUTE MINIMUM

Here are the key points to remember from this chapter:

- Social networking sites enable you to keep in touch with what your friends and family are doing.

- The largest social networking site today is Facebook, with more than two billion monthly users.

- On Facebook, view your friends' activity in the Feed and let others know what you're doing by posting your own status updates.

- Twitter is a way to broadcast short text messages and photos to your followers—and to follow others who tweet.

- Pinterest is a popular social network—a way to share interesting images with friends.

- LinkedIn is a social network for business professionals.

- Whichever social networking sites you use, be smart about the information you post; some personal information is best not made public.

PART VI

GETTING PRODUCTIVE

INSTALLING AND USING DESKTOP APPLICATIONS

When you want to do something on your computer, you need to use the appropriate applications. *Applications*—more commonly called *apps*—are software programs that perform one or more functions. Some apps are work-related; others provide useful information; still others are more entertaining in nature. But whatever it is you want to do, you need to launch the right app.

Finding and Installing New Apps

Your new computer system probably came with a bunch of programs preinstalled on its hard disk. Some of these apps are part of Windows, some might be preview or limited-use versions provided by the PC manufacturer (included in the hope you'll purchase the full version if you like what you see), and some are real, honest-to-goodness fully functional applications.

As useful as some of these programs might be, at some point you're going to want to add something new. Maybe you want to install the full version of Microsoft Office or purchase a full-featured photo-editing program, such as Adobe Photoshop Elements. Maybe you want to add some educational apps for the kids or a productivity program for yourself. Maybe you just want to play some new computer games.

Whatever type of app you're considering, installing it on your computer system is easy. In fact, you might find just what you're looking for in the online Microsoft Store. Wherever you find a new app, however, installing it on your system is relatively easy, as you'll soon discover.

Downloading Apps from the Microsoft Store

You can find all sorts of apps from many different companies online in the Microsoft Store. You search or browse the app store for the apps you want and then purchase and download them directly to your computer.

Many of the apps in the Microsoft Store are free, and others only cost a few dollars. You access the Microsoft Store from its own app, which you'll find on the Windows Start menu. (It's the shopping bag icon.)

As you can see in Figure 16.1, the Microsoft Store offers all manner of free and paid apps, as well as games you can play on your PC. The Home screen displays a selection of featured deals, picks for you, popular apps, and more. Scroll down to see more categories or scroll right within a category to view more items within.

To view only apps, click or tap the Apps tab in the left-hand sidebar. To view only games, click or tap Gaming. To view movies and TV shows for purchase, click or tap Movies & TV. You can then browse from there.

If you know the app you're looking for, an easier approach is to use the Store's search function. Just click or tap within the Search box at the top of any screen and then enter the name or description of the app and press Enter. The app you're looking for should be somewhere on the search results screen.

FIGURE 16.1

Browsing for apps in the Microsoft Store.

When you find an app you want, click or tap it to view the app's page in the Store, like the one shown in Figure 16.2. Scroll down to read more about the app, as well as view consumer reviews.

CorelDRAW Graphics Suite

ⓘ Provided and updated by **Corel Corporation**

| 2.9 ★ | 51 | E ESRB | EVERYONE |
| Average | Ratings | | In-App Purchases, Users Interact |

Install

Creativity meets productivity in this complete suite of professional graphics applications for vector illustration, page layout, photo editing, typography,...

Multimedia design

FIGURE 16.2

Getting ready to download and install a new app from the Microsoft Store.

If it's a free app, click the Install button to download it to your computer. If it's a paid app, click the price button to purchase it. You'll be prompted for your payment information; then you're good to go.

NOTE Many paid apps offer a free trial, at the end of which you can opt to purchase the app. Look for the Free Trial button in the app description.

Your new app is automatically downloaded and installed to your PC. You see a notification pop up when the installation is complete, and many apps launch automatically after this initial install. Otherwise, look for your new app in the All Apps section of the Start menu.

Purchasing Apps from Your Local Retailer

If you're looking for more traditional productivity apps, you may have to buy them in a box from a local retailer. You can find Windows-compatible software programs at many consumer electronics, office, and computer stores. For that matter, mass merchants such as Target and Walmart still carry a selection of computer software. Traditional software programs run the gamut from rather generic apps that cost less than $10 USD to more sophisticated productivity apps that cost several hundred dollars or more.

Some software programs today come on either a CD-ROM or a DVD disc; these disks typically come with their own built-in installation utilities. All you have to do is insert the program's disc into your computer's CD/DVD drive, if it has one. The installation utility should run automatically. Follow the onscreen instructions to install the program.

That said, it's becoming increasingly common for the software you buy in a store to *not* come with a CD or DVD disc because most PCs sold today lack those drives. Instead, inside the box, you find a license key and instructions for downloading and installing that app from the manufacturer's website. (You use the key—a series of numbers and letters—to "unlock" and register the downloaded software.)

Finding and Installing Apps Online

The age of physical software distribution is rapidly coming to an end. Nowadays, most software publishers make their products available via download from the Internet. This lets you get your new apps immediately without having to make a trip to the store. (And it gets around the whole physical installation issue if your computer doesn't have a CD/DVD drive.)

When you download a program from a major software publisher, the process is generally easy to follow. You probably have to read a page of dos and don'ts, agree to the publisher's licensing agreements, and then click a button to start the download. If you purchase a commercial program online, you also need to provide your credit card information, of course. Then, after you specify where (which folder on your hard disk) you want to save the downloaded file, the download begins.

When the download is complete, you should be notified via an onscreen dialog box. When prompted, choose to run the program you just downloaded. Follow the onscreen instructions from there.

 CAUTION   Limit your software downloads to reputable download sites and software publisher sites. Programs you download from unofficial sites might contain computer viruses or spyware, which can damage your computer. Learn more in Chapter 21, "Protecting Your PC from Computer Attacks, Malware, Spam, and More."

Understanding Web-Based Apps

Another type of app is becoming increasingly popular. You don't actually install this type of app on your computer; instead, it runs over the Web from what we call the *cloud*.

In essence, the cloud is that nebulous assemblage of computers and servers on the Internet. Cloud-based computing involves storing your files on and running apps from the cloud. The apps aren't located on your PC; they're located in the cloud, and you run them from within Microsoft Edge, Google Chrome, or a similar web browser.

Because of this, cloud apps are sometimes called web-based apps. They're just like traditional software-based apps, except they run over the Internet.

One of the chief advantages of web-based apps is that they can run on any computer at any location, and they don't take up hard disk space. This is especially important if you have a device without traditional hard disk storage, such as a tablet, ultrabook, or smartphone—or if you need to access your apps and documents from a variety of computers or other devices. Just point your web browser on any given device to the web-based app and start running—no installation required.

What types of cloud apps are available? Some of the more popular apps are traditional office apps in the cloud, such as Google Docs, Sheets, and Slides (docs.google.com), and similar apps from Zoho (www.zoho.com). For that matter, Microsoft Office Online (www.office.com) offers free web-based versions of Microsoft's popular Office applications (Word, Excel, PowerPoint, and the like).

Of course, there's a lot more than that out there. So if you're into universal document access and online collaboration, keep an eye open!

Managing Your Apps

Whatever type of app you install on your computer, you need to learn how to use it. The first thing you need to learn is where to find your apps—and how to launch them.

Finding Your Installed Apps

Each new application you install on your computer should automatically place a reference to itself on the Start menu. To browse through all installed apps, all you do is click or tap the Start button to open the Start menu. The top half of the Start menu lists apps you've pinned there. To view all your apps, click or tap See All.

As you can see in Figure 16.3, the Start menu now lists all your apps in alphabetical order. Scroll to and click an app to open it.

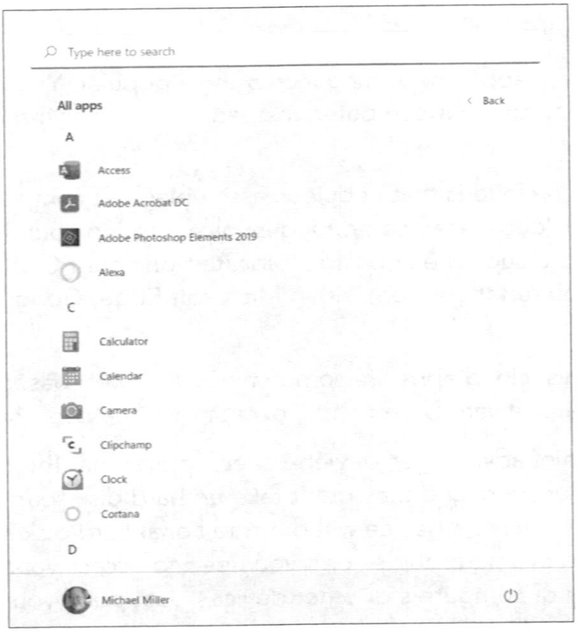

FIGURE 16.3

Browsing through all installed apps on the Start menu.

If you have a lot of apps installed on your PC, scrolling through the list on your Start menu might be cumbersome. You can instead search for specific apps, using the Search function on the taskbar. Just click the Search icon on the taskbar to display the Search panel, shown in Figure 16.4. Start typing the name of the app you're looking for into the Type Here to Search field at the top and, as you type, Windows suggests apps (and other items) that match your query. If the app you want is listed here, click it to launch it.

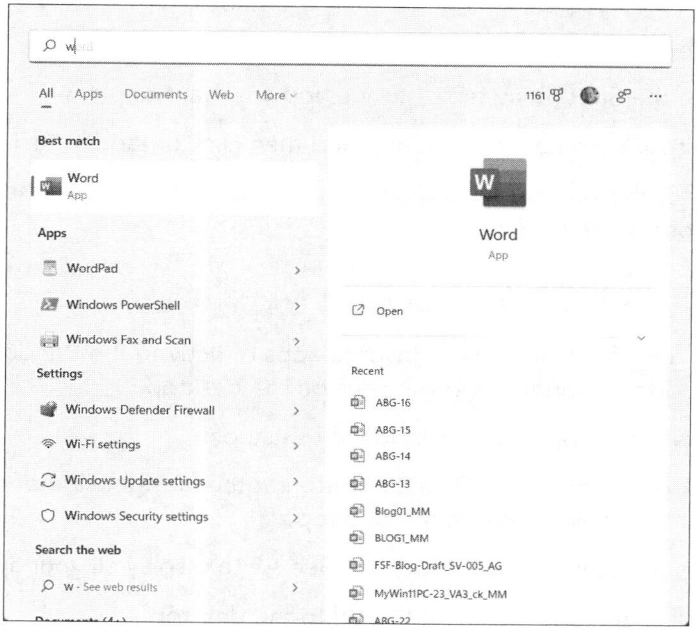

FIGURE 16.4

Searching for apps in Windows 11.

Pinning Apps to the Start Menu

You might find that it's easier to launch a frequently used app by adding it to the Windows Start menu—what's known as "pinning" the app. When you pin an app to the Start menu, you create a tile for the app; you can click or tap the tile to launch the app.

To pin an app to the Start menu, follow these steps:

1. From the Start menu, click or tap All Apps to display all your apps.

2. Scroll to the app you want to pin.

3. Right-click the app and then select Pin to Start.

Pinning Apps to the Taskbar

You also can pin your favorite apps to the Windows taskbar. This way, you can easily access them no matter what you're doing on the desktop.

Follow these steps:

1. From the Start menu, scroll to the app you want to pin.

2. Right-click the name of the app and then click or tap Pin to Taskbar.

An icon for the selected app is added to the taskbar. You can then drag it to a different position, if you like.

Adding App Shortcuts to the Desktop

You can add shortcuts to your favorite apps directly to the Windows desktop. These shortcuts appear as small icons on the desktop.

To create a desktop shortcut, follow these steps:

1. Click or tap the Show Desktop button at the far-right side of the taskbar to minimize all windows on the desktop.

2. From the Start menu, click or tap See All to display all your apps.

3. Scroll to the app you want to add to the desktop.

4. Click and drag the app from the Start menu onto the desktop.

The menu item remains on the Start menu, but a shortcut to that item is placed on the desktop. (This shortcut may be labeled Shortcut or Copy, or just have the name of the app.) You can drag the shortcut to whatever position you want on the desktop.

Working with Applications

Most apps today work in much the same fashion. Modern apps share many onscreen elements, so if you know how to use one program, you can probably use others. In the following sections, I describe the more common elements.

Using Toolbars and Ribbons

Most newer apps put their most frequently used operations on one or more *toolbars* or *ribbons*, typically located just below the menu bar. (Figure 16.5 shows a typical toolbar; Figure 16.6 shows a ribbon.) Both toolbars and ribbons display a row of buttons with either an icon or descriptive text (or sometimes both) relevant to the task at hand; some ribbons have different *tabs* that contain different, related sets of commands. You activate the associated command or operation by clicking the button with your mouse.

FIGURE 16.5

A typical toolbar in the QuickBooks app.

FIGURE 16.6

A ribbon with tabs for different types of operations in Microsoft Excel.

 TIP   If the toolbar or ribbon is too long to display fully on your screen, you see a right arrow at the far-right side. Click this arrow to display the buttons that aren't currently visible.

TIP   If you're not sure which button does what on a toolbar or ribbon, you can mouse over the button to display a ToolTip. A *ToolTip* is a small text box that displays the button's label or other useful information.

Using Menus

Many older pieces of software use a set of pull-down *menus* to store all the commands and operations you can perform. The menus are aligned across the top of the window, just below the title bar, in what is called a *menu bar*.

You open (or pull down) a menu by clicking the menu's name with your mouse. The full menu appears just below the menu bar, as shown in Figure 16.7. You activate a command or select a menu item by clicking it with your mouse.

Some menu items have a little black arrow to the right of the label. This indicates that additional choices are available, displayed on a *submenu*. Click the menu item or the arrow to display the submenu.

FIGURE 16.7

Navigating the menu system in the Notepad app.

TIP   If an item in a menu, toolbar, or dialog box is dimmed (or grayed), that means it isn't available for the current task.

Other menu items have three little dots (called an ellipsis) to the right of the label. This indicates that additional choices are available. Click the menu item to display a dialog box of those choices.

Closing an Open App

When you're working with a desktop app, you should close it when you're done. The easiest way to do this is to click the X at the top-right corner of the window. You might also pull down the app's File menu and select Exit or click or tap the File tab and click or tap Exit from there.

THE ABSOLUTE MINIMUM

Here are the key points to remember from this chapter:

- An application, or app, is a software program that performs a specific function.

- You can purchase, download, and install free and low-priced apps from the online Microsoft Store.

- Some apps can be purchased physically, on either CD or DVD, and install automatically when you insert the installation disc into your computer's CD/DVD drive.

- A more common way to purchase apps today is over the Internet, just by clicking a button on a website (and providing your credit card number if asked).

- Web-based or cloud apps don't install on your PC; instead, they run over the Internet within your web browser.

- Browse all apps installed on your computer from the Start menu.

- You can search for apps from the Search box on the Windows taskbar.

- You can pin apps to the Start menu or taskbar, or you can create shortcuts for the desktop.

- Most apps use some combination of pull-down menus, toolbars, and ribbons.

17

DOING OFFICE WORK

To do office work—writing letters and reports, crunching budgets, and creating presentations—you need a particular type of app called an *office suite*. An office suite is a combination of different programs, each designed to perform a specific task.

The most common office suite components are a *word processor* (for writing letters and memos), a *spreadsheet* (for crunching your numbers), and a *presentation program* (for creating and giving presentations to small and large groups). With these office apps installed on your computer, you're ready to do just about anything you might be asked to do in the workplace.

Doing office work requires you to stay organized. The best way to do this is with a dedicated calendar app that lets you track appointments, manage your to-do list, and such.

So you need a suite of office apps and a complementary calendar app. Read on to learn more.

Getting to Know Microsoft Office

The most popular office suite today is Microsoft Office, which comes to you from the same folks who produce Microsoft Windows. Microsoft Office is available as traditional desktop software for purchase, as desktop software available on a subscription plan (kind of like leasing it), and as web-based apps. The web-based version is available for free but isn't as full-featured as the desktop versions. (There are also versions of Office available for smartphone and tablets, but this book doesn't deal with those.)

Microsoft Office contains several productivity applications; which apps are included depends on the version of Office you have. All versions include Word (word processing), Excel (spreadsheet), and PowerPoint (presentations). Some versions also include Outlook (email), Access (database), and Publisher (desktop publishing).

You can learn more about Office at products.office.com. You can even purchase and subscribe to Office there.

Using Office on the Desktop

The version of Office that reigns supreme is the traditional desktop software version—whether purchased outright or leased on a subscription basis. This is a software program—actually, a group of programs—that you install on your computer, either from a physical installation DVD or over the Internet. (The online installation is definitely the most convenient.)

There are several different editions of the Microsoft Office suite, each containing a unique bundle of programs. Which Office programs you get depends on the edition of Office you have. Table 17.1 details the different editions and plans currently available.

TABLE 17.1 Microsoft Office Editions

Edition	Applications Included	OneDrive Cloud Storage Included	Number of Users	Description	Price
Microsoft 365 Personal	Access Excel OneNote Outlook PowerPoint Publisher Teams Word	1TB	1	Subscription model, apps installed on your PC but downloaded and continuously updated over the Internet	$69.99 USD/year or $6.99 USD/month

Microsoft 365 Family	Access Excel OneNote Outlook PowerPoint Publisher Teams Word	1TB	6	Subscription model, apps installed on your PC but downloaded and continuously updated over the Internet	$99.99 USD/ year or $9.99 USD/month
Office Home and Student 2021	Word Excel PowerPoint	None	1	Traditional one-time software purchase with no online updates; for casual home and student users	$149.99 USD
Office Home and Business 2021	Excel Outlook PowerPoint Word	None	1	Traditional software one-time purchase with no online updates; similar to Home and Student but with Outlook added	$249.99 USD

Microsoft is really pushing the Microsoft 365 subscriptions, and I think they're the best deal going. You spend less money upfront, get 1TB (terabyte) of online storage, and end up with software that constantly calls into the mothership to keep itself continuously updated. If you have just a single PC in your house, go with the Microsoft 365 Personal version at $69.99 USD per year. If you have more than one PC, you can't beat the Microsoft 365 Family version, which enables you to install the software on up to six PCs for just $99.99 USD per year.

 NOTE   Many new PCs come with a trial version of Office installed. You can use this version for 90 days at no charge; at that point, you have the option of purchasing the software or having the trial version deactivated.

Using Office on the Web

If you don't want to go to all the trouble of purchasing and installing an expensive piece of software, you can still use Microsoft Office on the Web. The web-based version of Microsoft Office can run on any computer over the Internet.

Microsoft Office on the Web is free, which is always appealing. The individual apps, however, don't come with all the sophisticated functionality of the software versions, so there's a trade-off. Bottom line: If you're not a power user, you might get by with the free apps in the online version of Office instead of purchasing and installing the traditional software version of Office.

You access Office on the Web from within Microsoft Edge, Google Chrome, or any other web browser. Launch your web browser and go to www.office.com. Click an app icon in the sidebar to launch that online app.

The home page for each app lists your most recently created files in the navigation pane on the left, as shown in Figure 17.1. You can open an existing file or click the appropriate tile to create a new file.

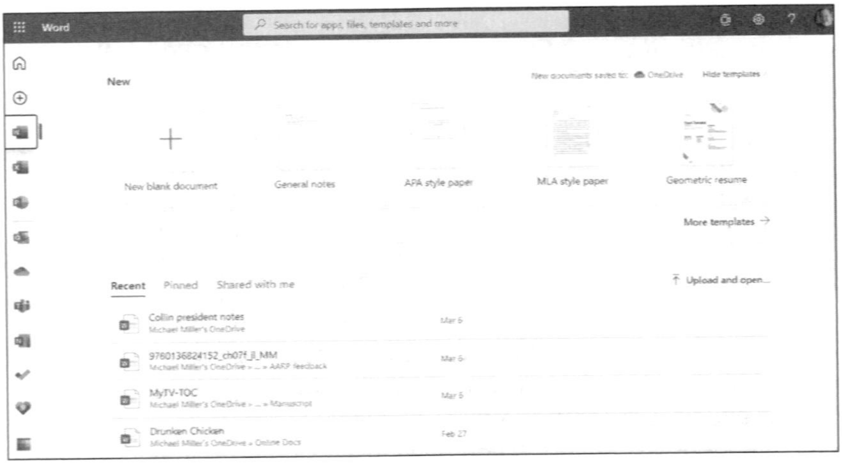

FIGURE 17.1

Using Microsoft Word Online.

TIP You also can open and edit existing documents from Microsoft OneDrive. Go to www.onedrive.com to view your online files; click a file to open it in the corresponding online app.

Which Version of Office Should You Use?

Given the choice of a free web-based version of Microsoft Office or a somewhat expensive desktop version, many users choose the web-based version of Office. There's a good argument for that—free is always more attractive than paid.

Although Office on the Web is more basic than the full-featured Office you can buy in a store, for many users, it offers all the features they need. It's great for doing simple letters and memos, home budgets and planning, and even basic presentations. There's the added plus that you can run the online version of Office on any Windows-based PC or tablet without having to install anything. Getting up and running is as quick and easy as clicking a few buttons.

If your needs are more sophisticated, however, a paid desktop version of Office is the way to go. There are so many advanced functions in the Office software that it's unlikely you'll ever use them all. But if your work involves creating brochures or newsletters, fancy comparison spreadsheets, or sophisticated presentations with animations and such, you have to go the Office software route; you just can't do some of this stuff in the web-based version.

Word Processing with Microsoft Word

When you want to write a letter, fire off a quick memo, create a report, or create a newsletter, you use a word processing app. For most computer users, that means Microsoft Word, the most popular word processing program of the past decade.

 NOTE The next sections examine the online versions of Word, Excel, and PowerPoint. The desktop versions differ slightly in terms of layout and functionality.

Exploring the Word Workspace

Let's take a quick tour of the Word workspace—so you know what's what and what's where.

If you use the web-based version of Word, you see the screen shown in Figure 17.2. At the top of the screen is the ribbon, which provides all the buttons and controls you need to create and edit a document. Different tabs on the ribbon display different collections of functions; click a tab, such as File, Home, Insert, or View, to access commands associated with that particular operation.

Beneath the ribbon is the document itself. Begin typing at the cursor.

Click a tab on the ribbon to access all the related commands. For example, the File tab contains basic file opening and saving operations; the Home tab contains most of the editing and formatting functions you use on a daily basis; the Insert tab contains commands to add images and tables to a document; and the View tab contains commands that enable you to change how a document is viewed or displayed.

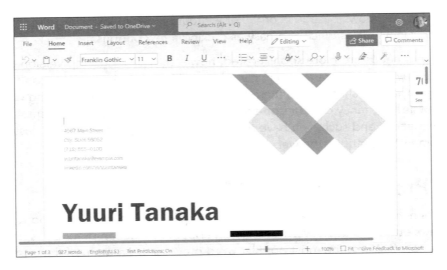

FIGURE 17.2

The Word workspace on the web—all functions are on the ribbon.

TIP If you're not sure just what a button on a ribbon or toolbar does, you're not alone—those little graphics are sometimes difficult to decipher. To display the name of any specific button, just hover your cursor over the button until the descriptive *ScreenTIP* appears.

Working with Documents

Anything you create with Word is called a *document*. A document is nothing more than a computer file that can be copied, moved, and deleted—or edited—from within Word.

To create a new document with Word Online, go to the main Word page and click one of the templates on the right for the type of document you want to create. If you don't want to use one of these templates, click New Blank Document.

Word opens a new blank document, ready for editing. Give this document a name by clicking the File tab and then clicking Save As.

Opening an existing document is just as easy. Just go to the main Word page, scroll through the list of recent documents on the left, and then click the one you want to open.

After you make changes to a document, you'll want to save those changes. With the desktop versions of Word, you have to save your changes manually. (Click File,

Save.) With Word Online, however, the app automatically saves your work in the cloud. You don't have to manually save a thing.

Entering Text

You enter text in a Word document at the *insertion point*, which appears onscreen as a blinking cursor. When you start typing on your keyboard, the new text is added at the insertion point.

You move the insertion point with your mouse by clicking a new position in your text. You move the insertion point with your keyboard by using your keyboard's arrow keys.

Editing Text

After you enter your text, it's time to edit. With Word, you can delete, cut, copy, and paste text—or graphics—to and from anywhere in your document or between documents.

Before you can edit text, though, you have to *select* the text to edit. The easiest way to select text is with your mouse; just hold down your mouse button and drag the cursor over the text you want to select. You also can select text using your keyboard; use the Shift key—in combination with other keys—to highlight blocks of text. For example, Shift+left arrow selects one character to the left; Shift+End selects all text to the end of the current line.

Any text you select appears as white text against a black highlight. After you select a block of text, you can then edit it in a number of ways, as detailed in Table 17.2.

TABLE 17.2 Word Editing Operations

Operation	Keystroke
Delete	Del
Copy	Ctrl+Ins or Ctrl+C
Cut	Shift+Del or Ctrl+X
Paste	Shift+Ins or Ctrl+V

Formatting Text

After your text is entered and edited, you can use Word's numerous formatting options to add some pizzazz to your document. Fortunately, formatting text is easy.

When you want to format your text, select the Home tab on the ribbon. This tab includes buttons for bold, italic, and underline, as well as font, font size, and font color. To format a block of text, highlight the text, and then click the desired format button.

Checking Spelling and Grammar

If you're not a great speller, you'll appreciate Word's automatic spell checking. You can see it right onscreen; just deliberately misspell a word, and you see a squiggly red line under the misspelling. That's Word telling you you've made a spelling error.

When you see that squiggly red line, position your cursor on top of the misspelled word, and then right-click your mouse. Word displays a pop-up menu with its suggestions for spelling corrections. You can choose a replacement word from the list or return to your document and manually change the misspelling.

Sometimes Word encounters a word it doesn't recognize, even though the word is spelled correctly. In these instances, you can add the new word to Word's spelling dictionary by right-clicking the word and selecting Add from the pop-up menu.

Printing Your Document

When you finish editing your document, you can instruct Word to send a copy to your printer. To print a document, select the File tab, click Print, and then click the Print button. You now see the Print page or dialog box for your web browser; select the printer you want to use and then click the Print button.

Number Crunching with Microsoft Excel

When you're on your computer and want to crunch some numbers, you use a program called a *spreadsheet*. Microsoft Excel is the spreadsheet program in the Microsoft Office suite, and it's available in both web-based and traditional desktop versions.

Exploring the Excel Workspace

A spreadsheet is nothing more than a giant list. Your list can contain just about any type of data you can think of—text, numbers, and even dates. You can take any of the numbers on your list and use them to calculate new numbers. You can sort the items on your list, pretty them up, and print the important points in a report. You can even graph your numbers in a pie, line, or bar chart!

In a spreadsheet, everything is stored in little boxes called *cells*. Your spreadsheet is divided into a lot of these cells, each located in a specific location on a giant grid made of *rows* and *columns*. Each cell represents the intersection of a particular row and column.

As you can see in Figure 17.3, each column has an alphabetic label (A, B, C, and so on). Each row, however, has a numeric label (1, 2, 3, and so on). The location of each cell is the combination of its column and row locations. For example, the cell in the upper-left corner of the spreadsheet is in column A and row 1; therefore, its location is signified as A1. The cell to the right of it is B1, and the cell below A1 is A2.

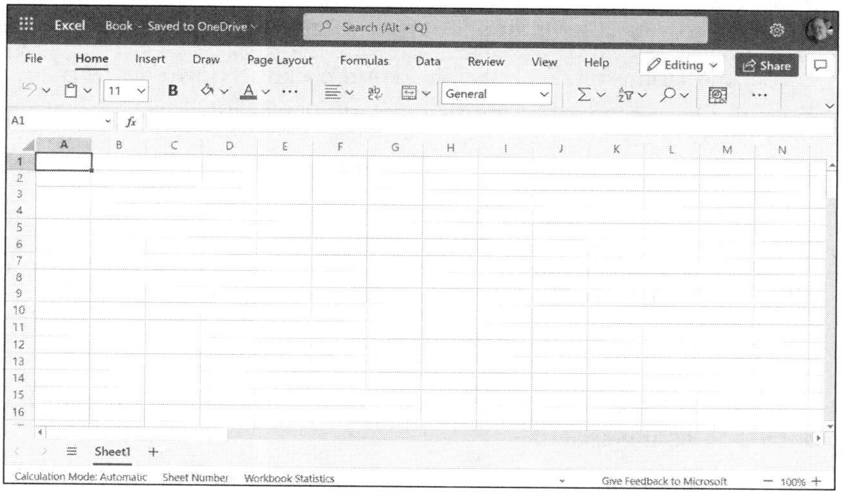

FIGURE 17.3

An Excel spreadsheet—divided into many rows and columns.

Entering Data

Entering text or numbers into a spreadsheet is easy. Just remember that data is entered into each cell individually—you can fill up a spreadsheet with hundreds or thousands of cells filled with their own data.

To enter data into a specific cell, follow these steps:

1. Select the cell you want to enter data into.

2. Type your text or numbers into the cell; what you type is echoed in the Formula bar at the top of the screen.

3. When you finish typing data into the cell, press Enter.

TIP You can enter numbers and text directly into the selected cell or into the Formula bar at the top of the spreadsheet. The Formula bar echoes the contents of the active cell.

Inserting and Deleting Rows and Columns

Sometimes you need to go back to an existing spreadsheet and insert some new information.

To insert a new row or column in the middle of your spreadsheet, follow these steps:

1. Click the row or column header *after* where you want to make the insertion.

2. Select the Home tab on the ribbon and click the down arrow below the Insert button; then select either Insert Rows or Insert Columns.

Excel inserts a new row or column either above or to the left of the row or column you selected.

To delete an existing row or column, follow these steps:

1. Click the header for the row or column you want to delete.

2. Select the Home tab on the ribbon and click the Delete button.

The row or column you selected is deleted, and all other rows or columns move up or over to fill the space.

Adjusting Column Width

If the data you enter into a cell is too long, you see only the first part of that data—there'll be a bit to the right that looks cut off. It's not cut off, of course; it just can't be seen because it's longer than the current column is wide.

You can fix this problem by adjusting the column width. Wider columns allow more data to be shown; with narrow columns, you can display more columns per page.

To change the column width, move your cursor to the column header, and position it on the dividing line on the right side of the column you want to adjust. When the cursor changes shape, click the left button on your mouse and drag the column divider to the right (to make a wider column) or to the left (to make a smaller column). Release the mouse button when the column is the desired width.

TIP   To make a column the exact width for the longest amount of data entered, position your cursor over the dividing line to the right of the column header and double-click your mouse. This makes the column width automatically "fit" your current data.

Calculating with Formulas

Excel enables you to enter just about any type of algebraic formula into any cell. You can use these formulas to add, subtract, multiply, divide, and perform any nested combination of those operations.

Excel knows that you're entering a formula when you type an equal sign (=) into any cell. You start your formula with the equal sign and enter your operations *after* the equal sign.

For example, if you want to add 1 plus 2, enter this formula into a cell: **=1+2**. When you press Enter, the formula disappears from the cell—and the result, or *value*, displays.

Table 17.3 shows the algebraic operators you can use in Excel formulas.

TABLE 17.3   Excel Operators

Operation	Operator
Add	+
Subtract	−
Multiply	*
Divide	/

So if you want to multiply 10 by 5, enter **=10*5**. If you want to divide 10 by 5, enter **=10/5**.

Including Other Cells in a Formula

If all you're doing is adding and subtracting numbers, you might as well use a calculator. Where a spreadsheet becomes truly useful is when you use it to perform operations based on the contents of specific cells.

To perform calculations using values from cells in your spreadsheet, you enter the cell location into the formula. For example, if you want to add cells A1 and A2, enter this formula: **=A1+A2**. If the numbers in either cell A1 or A2 change, the total automatically changes, as well.

An even easier way to perform operations involving spreadsheet cells is to select them with your mouse while you're entering the formula. To do this, follow these steps:

1. Select the cell that will contain the formula.

2. Type =.

3. Click the first cell you want to include in your formula; that cell location is automatically entered in your formula.

4. Type an algebraic operator, such as +, −, *, or /.

5. Click the second cell you want to include in your formula.

6. Repeat steps 4 and 5 to include other cells in your formula.

7. Press Enter when your formula is complete.

Quick Addition with AutoSum

The most common operation in any spreadsheet is the addition of a group of numbers. Excel makes summing up a row or column of numbers easy via the AutoSum function.

All you have to do is follow these steps:

1. Select the cell at the end of a row or column of numbers, where you want the total to appear.

2. Select the Home tab on the ribbon and click the AutoSum button.

Excel automatically sums all the preceding numbers and places the total in the selected cell.

Excel's AutoSum also includes a few other automatic calculations. When you click the down arrow on the bottom of the AutoSum button, you can perform the following operations:

- **Sum**, which totals the values in the selected cells

- **Average**, which calculates the average of the selected cells

- **Count Numbers**, which counts the number of selected cells

- **Max**, which returns the largest value in the selected cells

- **Min**, which returns the smallest value in the selected cells

TIP When you reference consecutive cells in a formula, you can just enter the first and last number of the series separated by a colon. For example, you can enter cells A1 through A4 as A1:A4.

Using Functions

In addition to the basic algebraic operators previously discussed, Excel includes a variety of *functions* that replace the complex steps present in many formulas. For example, if you want to total all the cells in column A, you could enter the formula **=A1+A2+A3+A4**. Or you could use the SUM function, which enables you to sum a column or row of numbers without having to type every cell into the formula. (And when you use AutoSum, it's simply applying the SUM function.)

In short, a function is a type of prebuilt formula.

You enter a function in the following format: *=function(argument)*, where *function* is the name of the function and *argument* is the range of cells or other data you want to calculate. Using the last example, to sum cells A1 through A4, you'd use the following function-based formula: **=sum(A1,A2,A3,A4)**.

Excel includes hundreds of functions. You can access and insert any of Excel's functions by following these steps:

1. Select the cell where you want to insert the function.

2. Select the Home tab on the ribbon. Then click the down arrow beneath the AutoSum button and select More Functions.

3. When the Insert Function dialog box appears, pull down the Select a Category list to display the functions of a particular type.

4. Click the function you want to insert.

5. If the function has related arguments, a Function Arguments dialog box displays; enter the arguments and click OK.

6. The function you selected is inserted into the current cell. You can manually enter the cells or numbers into the function's argument.

 TIP In the desktop version of Excel, you can access more functions directly from the Formula tab on the ribbon.

Formatting Your Spreadsheet

You don't have to settle for boring-looking spreadsheets. You can format the way the data appears in your spreadsheet—including the format of any numbers you enter.

When you enter a number into a cell, Excel applies what it calls a "general" format to the number—it just displays the number, right-aligned, with no commas or dollar signs. You can, however, select a specific number format to apply to any cells in your spreadsheet that contain numbers.

All of Excel's number formatting options are in the Number section of the Home tab. Click the Dollar Sign button to choose an accounting format, the Percent button to choose a percentage format, the Comma button to choose a comma format, or the General button to choose from all available formats. You can also click the Increase Decimal and Decrease Decimal buttons to move the decimal point left or right.

In addition, you can apply a variety of other formatting options to the contents of your cells. You can make your text bold or italic, change the font type or size, or even add shading or borders to selected cells.

These formatting options are found in the Font and Alignment sections of the Home tab. Just select the cell(s) you want to format; then click the appropriate formatting button.

Creating a Chart

Numbers are fine, but sometimes the story behind the numbers can be better told with a picture. The way you take a picture of numbers is with a *chart*, such as the one shown in Figure 17.4.

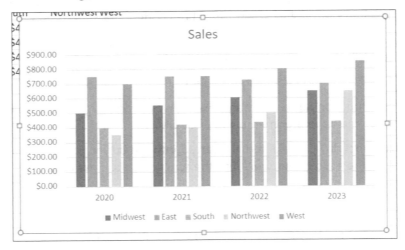

FIGURE 17.4

Some numbers are better represented via a chart.

You create a chart based on numbers you've previously entered into your Excel spreadsheet. It works like this:

1. Select the range of cells you want to include in your chart. (If the range has a header row or column, include that row or column when selecting the cells.)

2. Select the Insert tab on the ribbon.

3. In the Charts section of the Insert tab, click the button for the type of chart you want to create.

4. Excel displays a variety of charts within that general category. Select the type of chart you want.

5. When the chart appears in your worksheet, select the Design tab on the ribbon to edit the chart's type, layout, and style.

Giving Presentations with Microsoft PowerPoint

When you need to present information to a group of people, the hip way to do it is with a PowerPoint presentation. Microsoft PowerPoint is a presentation program—that is, an app you can use to both create and give presentations.

If you work in an office, you probably see at least one PowerPoint presentation a week—if not one per day. Teachers use PowerPoint to present lesson materials in class. Kids even use PowerPoint to prepare what used to be oral reports.

So get with the program—and learn how to create your own great-looking presentations with PowerPoint!

Exploring the PowerPoint Workspace

As you can see in Figure 17.5, PowerPoint on the web looks a lot like the other Office apps. The workspace is dominated by the ribbon at the top of the screen, with the current slide displayed in the middle.

On the left side of the workspace is something unique to PowerPoint—the Slides pane, which displays all the slides in your presentation, one after another. Below the current slide is a Notes pane, which enables you to enter presentation notes.

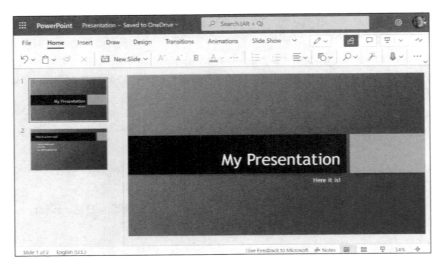

FIGURE 17.5

The PowerPoint workspace.

Applying a Theme

You don't have to reinvent the wheel to design the look of your presentation. PowerPoint includes a number of slide *themes* that you can apply to any presentation, blank or otherwise. A theme specifies the color scheme, fonts, layout, and background for each slide you create in your presentation.

To apply a new theme to your current presentation, select the Design tab on the ribbon. Available themes display in the Themes section; click a theme to apply it to your presentation.

It's that simple. All the colors, fonts, and everything else from the theme are automatically applied to all the slides in your presentation—and every new slide you add carries the selected design.

 NOTE Don't confuse the slide *layout*, which defines which elements appear on the slide, with the slide *template*, which defines the colors and fonts used.

Inserting New Slides

When you create a new presentation, PowerPoint starts with a single slide—the *title slide*. Naturally, you need to insert additional slides to create a complete presentation. PowerPoint enables you to insert different types of slides, with different types of layouts for different types of information.

To insert a new slide, all you have to do is select the Home tab on the ribbon and click the New Slide button. This displays the New Slide dialog box; select the slide layout you want and then click the Add Slide button.

Adding and Formatting Text

You can enter text for a slide directly into that slide. When PowerPoint creates a new slide, the areas for text entry are designated with boilerplate text—"Click to add title" (for the slide's title) or "Click to add text" (for regular text or bullet points). Adding text is as easy as clicking the boilerplate text and then entering your own words and numbers. Press Enter to move to a new line or bullet. To enter a subbullet, press the Tab key first; to back up a level, press Shift+Tab.

Formatting text on a slide is just like formatting text in a word processing document. Select the text you want to format and then click the appropriate button in the Font section of the Home tab.

 TIP You can add transitions between slides and animate objects on a slide. Use the Transitions tab on the ribbon to apply transitions and the Animations tab to apply animation effects.

Start the Show!

To run your slideshow, select the View tab and click the Slide Show button. To move from one slide to the next, all you have to do is click your mouse.

Exploring Google Docs

Microsoft Office isn't the only productivity software out there. Many schools and offices are using a web-based alternative from Google, called Google Docs.

Like Office Online, Google Docs runs in any web browser on any connected device—computer, smartphone, tablet, you name it. It's free and great for collaboration; multiple users can work on the same document at the same time.

Google Docs consists of four separate web apps:

- Docs (word processor, like Word)
- Sheets (spreadsheet, like Excel)

- Slides (presentations, like PowerPoint)
- Forms (online forms)

You access all these apps by pointing your web browser to docs.google.com. As you can see in Figure 17.6, this opens a dashboard to all your online documents, with your word processing documents front and center. To switch to documents from another app, click the Menu (three-line) button at the top left and select Sheets, Slides, or Forms.

≡ 🗎 Docs	🔍 Search		
Start a new document		Template gallery ⌄ ⋮	
Blank	Letter Spearmint	Project proposal Tropic	Resume Serif	Resume Coral

Previous 7 days		Owned by anyone ▾	Last modified ⊞ A̲Z 🗀
🗎 Using Work.Expresswriters.com		Support (... Mar 15, 2022	⋮
🗎 EW Writer's Policy and Welcome		Support (... Mar 15, 2022	⋮
Previous 30 days			
🗎 Performance Analysis		David Sca... Mar 10, 2022	⋮

FIGURE 17.6

The Google Docs dashboard.

NOTE All your Google Docs documents are stored online in Google Drive, Google's cloud-based storage service. You also can access your documents by going directly to Google Drive at drive.google.com.

To open an existing document, simply click its thumbnail. To create a new document of any type, first switch to the dashboard page for that app, and then click either the template you want to use or Blank to create a document without a template. This opens a new untitled document of the chosen type. To give this document a name, click the Untitled box at the top of the page, and enter a new name. You don't have to do any further saving; Google saves all your changes online, automatically.

Using Google Docs Word Processor

Google Docs is the name of Google's productivity suite and the name of the word processing app in the suite. Docs works pretty much like Microsoft Word, and you use it for similar tasks—creating memos, letters, newsletters, and the like.

As you can see in Figure 17.7, the Google Docs workspace consists of the document you're working on, with a toolbar and series of pull-down menus above that. Start typing at the cursor, and then use the controls on the toolbar (or the appropriate pull-down menu) to edit and format your text. Click the Print button to print your work.

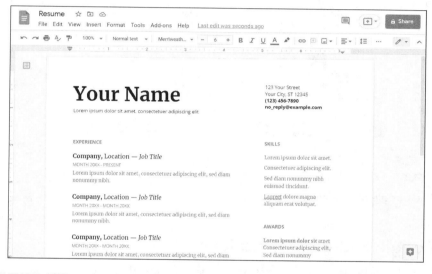

FIGURE 17.7

The Google Docs workspace.

Google Docs offers much of the same functionality as Microsoft Word. About the only major thing missing is the lack of styles and features for more scholarly documents. Beyond that, Docs does a great job with your day-to-day word processing tasks.

Using Google Sheets Spreadsheet

Google Sheets is the spreadsheet app in the Google suite. It offers most of the features and functionality of Microsoft Excel, including charts, formulas, and a full complement of functions.

Figure 17.8 shows the Google Sheets workspace. The spreadsheet takes up the bulk of the workspace, with a toolbar and pull-down menus above that. You access individual sheets within the main sheet via tabs at the bottom of the window.

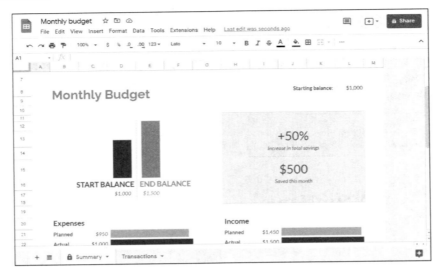

FIGURE 17.8

The Google Sheets workspace.

Using Google Slides Presentations

Google Slides is the presentation app in the Google suite. It compares with PowerPoint in its capability for you to create and give professional-looking presentations.

Figure 17.9 shows the Google Slides workspace. The slide sorter is on the left, the current slide is big in the middle, and a notes pane is underneath the current slide. You access all functions from the toolbar and pull-down menus; when you're ready to give a presentation, click the Present button above the toolbar.

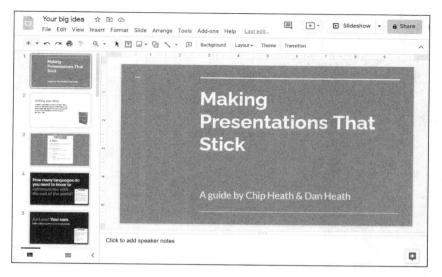

FIGURE 17.9

The Google Slides workspace.

Using the Windows Calendar App

In today's hectic world, you need to stay organized. Fortunately, you can use your new computer to help you plan and manage your schedule. Just turn to the Calendar app that comes with Windows 11. It's both useful and easy to use.

Displaying Different Views

As you can see in Figure 17.10, the left side of the Calendar app displays a mini monthly calendar, a list of the various calendars available to display, and navigational icons at the bottom. On the right side of the app, you see the current calendar in the selected view.

By default, the Calendar app displays a traditional monthly calendar (the Month view). To display a different view—Day, Work Week, or Week—click or tap that option above the calendar. (To view in Work Week mode, click the down arrow next to the Week option and then select Work Week.) To move from month to month (or week to week), click or tap the up or down arrows above the calendar. To center the calendar on the current day, click or tap Today.

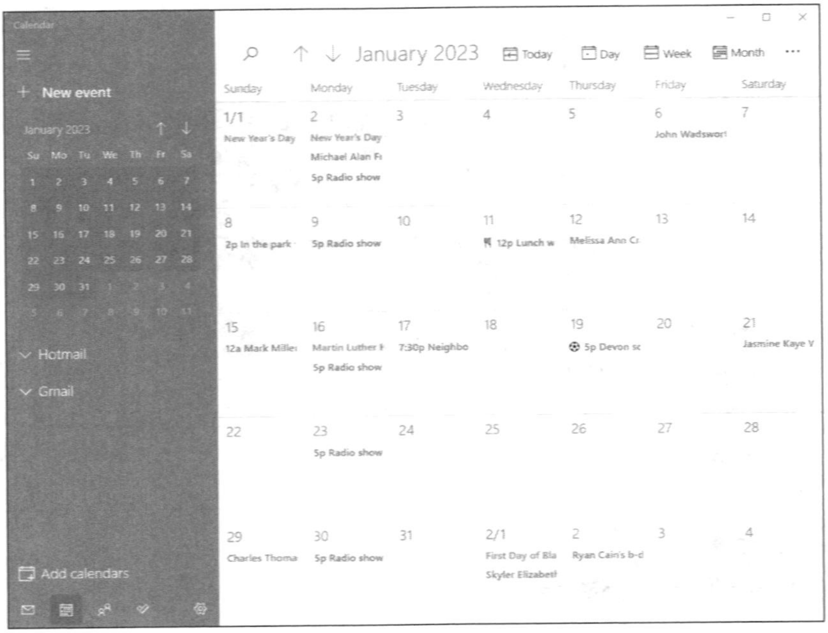

FIGURE 17.10

The Calendar app in monthly view.

You can also display your calendar in other views. Click or tap the Show (three-dot) button at the top right and select the desired view—Day, Week, Month, or Year.

To view more details about an appointment (what Calendar calls an *event*), click or tap the item. The appointment screen opens; you can then edit anything about the appointment. Click or tap the Save button to save your changes.

Creating a New Event

To create a new event on your calendar, click or tap + New Event in the left column to display the new event pane, shown in Figure 17.11. In this pane, enter the name of the event into the Event Name field and the location in the Location field. Enter starting and ending dates and times—unless it's an all-day event, in which instance, you check the All Day option.

You also can use this window to create a recurring event, as well as invite others to this event. To keep this event private, check the Private (lock) button.

When you finish entering information about this event, click or tap Save.

Home

Save | Delete | Online meeting | Busy | 15 minutes

Details

People

● ∨ Event name ● ∨

Invite someone

Sort by Original order ∨

Location

Me
trapperjohn2000@hotmail.com

Start: January 01, 2023   8:00 AM ∨   All day

End: January 01, 2023   8:30 AM ∨

FIGURE 17.11

Creating a new event.

THE ABSOLUTE MINIMUM

Here are the key points to remember from this chapter:

- To perform common work-related tasks, you need the individual apps that make up an office suite.

- The most popular office suite today is Microsoft Office, which is available in either web-based or traditional desktop software versions.

- Microsoft Word is the word processor in Microsoft Office, used to write letters and reports.

- Microsoft Excel is Office's spreadsheet program, used for budgets and other number crunching.

- Microsoft PowerPoint is for creating and giving presentations.

- Google Docs is a web-based office suite that competes directly with Microsoft Office. It's free.

- Use the Windows Calendar app to keep track of your appointments.

18

WORKING WITH DIGITAL PHOTOS

In the old days, if you wanted to share your photos with friends and family, you had to have extra prints made at the Fotomat and then hand them out personally or mail them off in a big envelope. This approach was not only time-consuming, but it was costly; you had to pay real money for each extra print you made.

In today's age of digital photography, it's a lot easier to view and share your photos by using your computer and the Internet. In fact, you can even edit your digital photos to eliminate red-eye and such before you share them. It's a whole new digital world out there. All you need is some sort of digital camera (like the one in your smartphone) and a computer.

Transferring Pictures from Your Camera, Smartphone, or Tablet

If you want to edit or print your digital photos, you need to connect your digital camera or smartphone or tablet to your PC—which is relatively easy to do. You can download photos from a photo storage site, transfer digital photos directly from your camera or camera's memory card, or even scan existing photo prints.

Downloading from the Internet

If you take photos with the camera in your smartphone or tablet, chances are you're storing those photos on some online storage site. If you have an Android device, you can configure it to upload every photo you take to Google Photos. If you have an Apple iPhone or iPad, it's set to upload all your photos to Apple's iCloud. Those uploads to the cloud happen automatically.

Once your photos are online, it's a simple matter to download them to your computer. Whether you're using Google Photos or iCloud, all you have to do is use your computer's web browser to access the site and sign into your account. Now you can navigate to the photo(s) you want to download and click the appropriate Download button. Your photos are downloaded over the Internet to your computer.

Transferring Photos from a Smartphone or Tablet via USB

You can also manually transfer photos from your smartphone or tablet to your PC, using a standard USB cable. Follow these general steps:

1. Connect the phone or tablet to your computer using the appropriate USB cable.

2. If you're prompted to "choose what happens with this device," opt to open files with File Explorer. If you don't see this prompt, proceed to step 3.

3. Launch File Explorer on your PC.

4. Click or tap the This PC icon in the Navigation pane.

5. Select the icon for your phone or tablet.

6. Navigate through the folders on your device until you come to the one that contains your device's photos (typically in the DCIM folder).

7. Hold down the Ctrl key and click each photo you want to transfer.

8. Select the Home tab, click or tap the Move To button, and then click or tap Pictures.

All the photos you've selected will be moved from your iPhone or iPad to the Pictures folder on your PC.

Transferring Pictures from a Digital Camera via USB

If you have a standalone digital camera, you can use the same method to transfer photos from your camera to your PC. Just connect your camera to your computer via USB and follow the previous steps to navigate to and copy the pictures on your camera.

Know that some digital cameras come with their own proprietary picture management programs. If you've installed such a program on your PC, this program may launch when you connect your camera to your computer. If so, and this program asks to download the pictures from your camera, follow the onscreen instructions to proceed.

You might also have installed a third-party photo-editing program, such as Adobe Photoshop Elements. If so, this program might launch when you connect your camera to your PC. Again, just follow the onscreen instructions to proceed.

 CAUTION   Depending on the apps you have installed on your system, you might get multiple prompts to download photos when you connect your camera. If this happens, pick the program you'd prefer to work with and close the other dialog boxes.

Transferring Pictures from a Memory Card

Another way to get photos from your digital camera to your computer is to use your PC's memory card reader. Most computers today have memory card readers built in; if yours doesn't, you can always add a low-cost external memory reader via USB. You then insert the memory card from your digital camera into the memory card reader, and your PC recognizes the card as if it were another hard disk.

In many cases, Windows automatically recognizes a memory card full of photos and asks whether you want to download them. If not, you can use File Explorer to copy files from the memory card to your computer. Just open File Explorer and click the drive icon for the memory card. This displays the card's contents, typically in a subfolder labeled DCIM. You can then move, copy, and delete the photos stored on the card as you would with any other type of file in Windows.

Scanning a Picture

If your photos are of the old-fashioned printed variety, you can turn them into digital files using a flatbed scanner. (Many home printers have scanners built-in.) The scanning starts automatically when you press the Scan button on your scanner. Your print photo is saved as a digital file for future use.

Note that some third-party software programs, such as Adobe Photoshop Elements, enable you to scan photos from the program. In most instances, scanning via one of these programs offers more options than scanning via Windows; you can change the resolution (in dots per inch) of the scanned image, crop the image, and even adjust brightness and contrast if you want. If you're scanning a lot of old, washed-out prints, this approach might produce better results.

 NOTE   By default, Windows stores all your pictures in the Pictures folder, which you can access from File Explorer. This folder includes a number of features specific to the management of picture files, as well as all the normal file-related tasks, such as copying, moving, or even deleting your photos.

Viewing Your Photos with the Windows Photos App

Viewing photos in Windows 11 is a snap. All you have to do is open the Photos app included with Windows 11. You can use the Photos app to both view and edit your digital photos.

As you can see in Figure 18.1, the Photos app displays all the photos and folders stored on your computer. Select the Collection tab to see your photos displayed by date. Select the Albums tab, and the app organizes your pictures into folder-like photo albums. You also can sort your photos by people (using facial recognition technology) or the original folders on your PC.

FIGURE 18.1

Viewing your photo collection in the Photos app.

Click through the albums or folders until you find a photo you want to view and then click that photo to view it in the full window, as shown in Figure 18.2. To move to the next picture in the folder or group, click the right arrow onscreen or press the right arrow key on your keyboard. To return to the previous picture, click the left arrow onscreen or press the left arrow key on your keyboard.

FIGURE 18.2

Viewing a single photo.

To view the picture fullscreen, click the Fullscreen button at the lower-right corner of the screen. To return to the normal Photos window, either click or tap the Exit Fullscreen button or press Esc on your computer keyboard.

To delete a photo, open the picture and then click or tap the Delete (trash can) icon in the toolbar. Alternatively, press the Del key on your computer keyboard.

 TIP To use the current picture as the image on the Windows Lock screen, display the photo full screen, click or tap the See More (three-dot) button at the top right, click Set As, and then click Set as Lock Screen. (You also can set a photo as the desktop background by selecting Set as Background.)

Editing Your Photos with the Photos App

Not all the digital photos you take turn out perfectly. Some pictures are too light, whereas others are too dark. Some have bad color, and some need to be cropped to highlight the important area.

Fortunately, the Photos app enables you to do this sort of basic photo editing. A better-looking photo is only a click or tap away!

Opening Editing Mode

To edit a photo in the Photo app, you have to open the app's editing mode. All you have to do is navigate to and display the photo you want to edit; then click or tap the Edit Image button on the toolbar. The photo is now displayed in the Photo app's editor.

Cropping or Rotating a Photo

Is your picture sideways? Do you want to zoom into just part of the picture? Then you want to use the Crop and Rotate controls. Follow these steps:

1. Open editing mode for the photo.

2. Select the Crop tab, shown in Figure 18.3.

3. To rotate the photo 90 degrees clockwise or counterclockwise, click or tap the appropriate Rotate button underneath the photo. (Click or tap again to further rotate the photo.)

4. To crop the photo, drag the corners of the white border until the picture appears as you like.

5. Click or tap Save as Copy when done.

FIGURE 18.3

The Photo app's Crop and Rotate controls.

NOTE   To crop to a specific aspect ratio, click the Aspect Ratio button and make a selection.

Applying Filters

The Photos app includes several built-in filters you can apply to your pictures. Use these filters to apply interesting effects quickly and easily to a photo:

1. Open editing mode for the photo.

2. Select the Filter tab, shown in Figure 18.4.

3. Click a filter to apply it to your photo.

4. Drag the Filter Intensity slider to apply more or less of the selected filter.

5. Click Save as Copy when done.

FIGURE 18.4

Applying a filter in the Photos app.

Adjusting Brightness

When a photo is too dark or too light, use the Photos app's Light controls. There are six controls available, as shown in Figure 18.5:

• **Brightness** makes a picture lighter or darker.

• **Exposure** increases or decreases the picture's exposure, effectively making it lighter or darker.

- **Contrast** increases or decreases the difference between the photo's darkest and lightest areas.

- **Highlights** brings out or hides detail in too-bright highlights.

- **Shadows** brings out or hides detail in too-dark shadows.

- **Vignette** applies a light or dark effect around the edge of the picture.

To use these controls, open editing mode for the photo, select the Adjustment tab, and go to the Light section on the right.

FIGURE 18.5

Adjusting a photo's Light levels.

 NOTE   If, when you edit a photo, you decide you don't want to keep the changes you make, simply click or tap the Cancel Changes (X) button at the top of the window.

Adjusting Color

The Photos app also lets you adjust various color-related settings. There are three controls available, as shown in Figure 18.6:

- **Saturation** adjusts the amount of color in the image.

- **Warmth** adjusts the color temperature, from warmer (more orange) to cooler (more blue).

- **Tint** adjusts the shade of colors in the image.

You adjust an image's color by opening editing mode for that photo, selecting the Adjustment tab, and going to the Colour section on the right side.

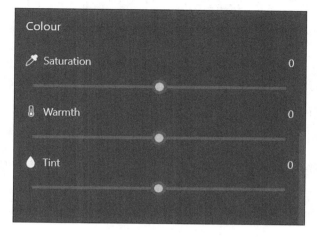

FIGURE 18.6

Adjusting a photo's color levels.

Printing and Sharing Your Photos

After you touch up (or otherwise manipulate) your photos, it's time to print or share them.

Choosing the Right Printer and Paper

If you have a color printer, you can make good-quality prints of your image files. Even a low-priced color inkjet can make surprisingly good prints, although the better your printer, the better the results.

Some manufacturers sell printers specifically designed for photographic prints. These printers use special photo print paper and output prints that are almost indistinguishable from those you get from a professional photo processor. If you take a lot of digital photos, one of these printers might be a good investment.

The quality of your prints is also affected by the type of paper you use. Printing on standard laser or inkjet paper is okay for making proofs, but you'll want to use a thicker, waxier paper for those prints you want to keep. Check with your printer's manufacturer to see what type of paper it recommends for the best-quality photo prints.

Making the Print

You can print photos directly from the Photos app. Here's how to do it:

1. From within the Photos app, navigate to and display the photo you want to print.

2. Click or tap the See More (three-dot) button on the toolbar.

3. Click or tap Print.

4. When the Print window appears, select the printer you want to use.

5. Select how many copies to print.

6. Pull down the Orientation list and select either Portrait (vertical) or Landscape (horizontal).

7. Click or tap the Print button to print the photo.

Printing Photos Professionally

If you don't have your own photo-quality printer, you can use a professional photo-processing service to print your photos. You can create prints from your digital photos in two primary ways:

- Copy your image files to a memory card or USB drive and deliver the device by hand to your local photo finisher.

- Go to the website of an online photo-finishing service and transfer your image files over the Internet.

The first option is convenient for many people, especially because numerous drugstores, supermarkets, and discount stores (including Target and Walmart) offer onsite photo-printing services. Often the printing service is via a self-serve kiosk; just insert your storage device, follow the onscreen instructions, and come back one-half hour later for your finished prints.

The second option is also convenient. With most services, you have the option of having your prints mailed to you or having them printed and ready at a local drugstore or discount store.

There are a number of photo-printing services online, including the following:

- dotPhoto (www.dotphoto.com)

- Mpix (www.mpix.com)

- Nations Photo Lab (www.nationsphotolab.com)

- Shutterfly (www.shutterfly.com)
- Snapfish (www.snapfish.com)

Sharing Your Photos

The Windows Photos app makes it easy to share your photos with other users online. You can share via OneDrive or Skype, or via email.

To share a photo, follow these steps:

1. Open the photo you want to share.

2. Click or tap the See More (three-dot) button in the toolbar.

3. Click or tap Share.

4. Select how you want to share.

5. If you opt to share via email, enter the recipient's email address, message subject, and any optional message text when prompted; then click or tap Send.

THE ABSOLUTE MINIMUM

Here are the key points to remember from this chapter:

- You can transfer photos to your PC via USB connection or, if you have a digital camera, from the camera's memory card.

- If your photos are on your phone or tablet, you can download your photos from Google Photos or Apple's iCloud.

- The Windows Photos app enables you to view, edit, print, and share digital photos stored on your computer.

- You can order photo prints from a variety of online printing services or from your local drugstore, supermarket, or department store.

PART VII

EXPLORING ONLINE ENTERTAINMENT

WATCHING MOVIES AND TV SHOWS ONLINE

How people watch TV shows and movies is changing. In the old days, your living room TV was tethered to your cable company's cable and you watched whatever it was they had available. Or maybe you stuck a DVD into your DVD player to watch movies on your TV set.

Today, more and more people are cutting the cable cord and ditching their DVD players to watch streaming video over the Internet—in their living rooms and on their personal computers. The Internet is home to Amazon Prime Video, Disney+, Hulu, Netflix, and other streaming video services that enable you to watch pretty much whatever movies and TV shows you want, at your convenience. Why bother with cable at all when a whole world of viewing is available online?

Online streaming video will change your viewing habits. Just fire up your PC, connect to the Internet, and watch that episode of *NCIS* or *Chopped* that you missed last week. You could go on a binge and watch every single season of *Friends* or *Schitt's Creek* in a single (long) sitting. Maybe you want to watch the latest made-for-streaming series, such as *Ted Lasso* or *Stranger Things*. Or perhaps you're in the mood to purchase or rent the latest fresh-from-the-theaters blockbuster and watch it at your convenience in your own home.

It's all a matter of knowing where to look for the videos you want—and launching the right app for viewing them.

Watching Streaming Video Services

There's a ton of programming on the Web that you don't have to purchase or download separately to your computer. This programming is available via a technology called *streaming video*. The movie or TV show you pick is streamed over the Internet in real time to your computer. You watch the programming in your web browser or in a dedicated app. Assuming you have a fast enough Internet connection, you can find tens of thousands of TV shows and movies to watch at dozens of different websites.

The most popular streaming video services today are Amazon Prime Video, Apple TV+, Discovery+, Disney+, HBO Max, Hulu, Netflix, Paramount+, and Peacock. All of these offer some sort of free trial period, so you can try them out before you commit.

 NOTE   You can view all the streaming video services discussed in this chapter from their individual websites via any web browser. Some also have their own Windows apps, available for free in the online Microsoft Store.

Watching Amazon Prime Video

Amazon Prime Video, shown in Figure 19.1, is an extension of Amazon's Prime service, which gives you free two-day shipping on selected Amazon purchases. If you're a Prime member, your subscription to Amazon Prime Video is free.

FIGURE 19.1

Amazon Prime Video.

Amazon Prime Video offers a wide selection of new and older movies and TV series, although this selection is weighted toward newer items. Amazon also offers a lot of original programming, called Prime Originals; these programs include *The Boys, Bosch, Good Omens, The Man in the High Castle, The Marvelous Mrs. Maisel, Tom Clancy's Jack Ryan,* and *The Wheel of Time.* You'll also find a variety of movies and TV shows for purchase or rental; once you've paid for an item, you can stream it for viewing on your PC.

You get to Amazon Prime Video by going to www.amazon.com, pulling down the menu, and selecting Prime Video. Look for items that are labeled as Included with Prime. (Amazon also offers programming for purchase or rental, which I discuss later in this chapter.)

 NOTE The Amazon Prime shipping membership costs $139 USD per year and includes Amazon Prime Video. If you're not a full Prime member, you can subscribe to Prime Video only for $8.99 USD per month. Given the minimal difference in the total yearly price, most people are better off getting the whole Prime membership (with Prime Video thrown in free) than paying for Prime Video separately.

Watching Apple TV+

Apple TV+, shown in Figure 19.2, is Apple's streaming video service. It offers a selection of original series—including *For All Mankind, The Morning Show, Ted Lasso, Schmigadoon!,* and *Severance*—as well as some theatrical movies.

FIGURE 19.2

Apple TV+.

You watch Apple TV+ in your web browser on Apple's website (www.apple.com/apple-tv-plus/). It costs $4.99 USD per month.

Watching Discovery+

Discovery+, shown in Figure 19.3, is the streaming home for reality and do-it-yourself programming from A&E, Animal Planet, Discovery, DIY Network, Food Network, HGTV, History Channel, Lifetime, Magnolia Network, OWN, Science Channel, TLC, and the Travel Channel. You watch Discovery+ in your web browser on the Discovery+ website (www.discoveryplus.com). A subscription runs $4.99 USD per month.

FIGURE 19.3

Discovery+.

NOTE Discovery Networks acquired AT&T's media properties in April of 2022, all of which are included in the current HBO Max streaming service. Discovery plans on combining Discovery+ and HBO Max into a single service at some point in time, so look for big things to happen later in 2022.

Watching Disney+

Disney+, shown in Figure 19.4, offers streaming content from properties owned by the Walt Disney media conglomerate—specifically movies and television series from Disney, Marvel, National Geographic, Pixar, and 20th Century Fox. This includes all the Marvel superhero movies, programming from the Disney Channel and Disney Jr., classic and current Disney movies, and all the *Star Wars* movies and series.

FIGURE 19.4

Disney+.

That's a lot of content, which makes it a favorite service for many, especially when there are younger viewers, comic book fans, or *Star Wars* followers in the household. Original Disney+ programming includes *The Beatles: Get Back*, *The Book of Boba Fett*, *The Falcon and the Winter Soldier*, *Hawkeye*, *Loki*, *The Mandalorian*, *The Mighty Ducks: Game Changers*, and *WandaVision*.

You watch Disney+ in your web browser on the Disney+ website (www.disneyplus.com). A subscription costs $7.99 USD per month or $79.99 USD per year.

Watching HBO Max

HBO Max, shown in Figure 19.5, offers content from all WarnerMedia properties, including Cartoon Network, CNN, The CW, DC Comics, HBO, New Line Cinema, Turner Classic Movies (TCM), and the Warner Bros. film studio. Despite the HBO name, HBO Max is designed to be a full-service streaming service, much like Netflix, with a mix of existing and original programming.

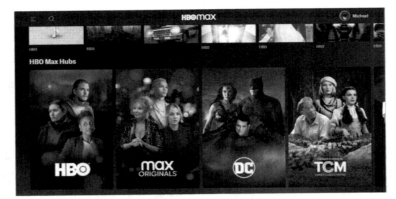

FIGURE 19.5

HBO Max.

Some of the more popular HBO Max originals include *The Flight Attendant, Game of Thrones, Mare of Easttown, Peacemaker, Succession,* and *Titans.* HBO Max is also home of the *Sex and the City* revival, *And Just Like That....*

You watch HBO Max in your web browser on the HBO Max website (www.hbomax.com). A monthly subscription runs $9.99 USD with commercials or $14.99 USD without commercials, although you may get a discount if you also subscribe to HBO through your cable provider.

Watching Hulu

Hulu, shown in Figure 19.6, is a streaming service that offers a mix of movies, television shows, and original programming. It is particularly known for its selection of current episodes from the major TV networks; it's a great place for catching up on any recent shows you've missed.

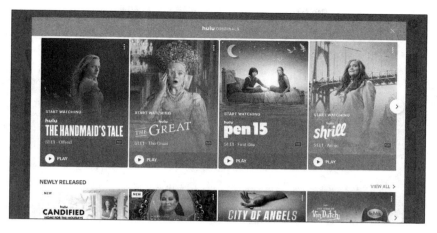

FIGURE 19.6

Hulu.

Original programming available on Hulu includes *American Horror Story, Dopesick, The Great, The Handmaid's Tale, Letterkenny, Only Murders in the Building,* and *Reservation Dogs.* Hulu is also a good place to find a variety of vintage television programs.

Hulu offers two subscription plans, with and (sort of) without commercials. The basic Hulu plan runs $6.99 USD per month and inserts commercials into the programs you watch. If you want to minimize the number of commercials you see, sign up for the $12.99 USD No Ads plan—but know that you'll still see commercials on some programs, but there will be fewer of them.

You watch Hulu in your web browser on the Hulu website (www.hulu.com).

 NOTE Hulu is majority owned by Disney, which also has the Disney+ and ESPN+ streaming services. As such, they offer a subscription package that bundles all three services—Disney+, ESPN+, and Hulu—for just $13.99 USD per month, or $19.99 USD per month for the No Ads version. If you watch just two of these three services, it's a pretty good deal.

Watching Netflix

Netflix, shown in Figure 19.7, is arguably the most popular streaming service today, with more than 150 million subscribers worldwide. It started out offering mainly movies but has shifted over the years to add a variety of newer and classic TV shows, plus a plethora of original programming.

FIGURE 19.7

Netflix.

In terms of programming, Netflix has become a fairly well-rounded service. It still offers a good selection of movies (although not nearly as many as it used to), but it also provides a large number of recent and (some) older TV series.

Netflix is the streaming leader, however, in original programming, both series and movies. Its original series are well-known and well-respected, and include *Bridgerton, Cobra Kai, The Crown, Euphoria, Fuller House, Grace and Frankie, The Kominsky Method, Ozark, Squid Game, Stranger Things, Tiger King, The Umbrella Academy*, and *The Witcher*.

You find the Netflix service at www.netflix.com. Netflix offers three different subscription plans: Basic ($9.99 USD per month), Standard ($15.49 USD per month), and Premium ($19.99 USD per month). The big difference is how many users can watch at the same time, from just one (Basic) to two (Standard) to four (Premium).

Watching Paramount+

Paramount+, shown in Figure 19.8, offers content from the CBS television network (including CBS news and sports), as well as BET, Comedy Central, MTV, Nickelodeon, Paramount Pictures, and the Smithsonian Channel. (All channels are owned by the Paramount Global conglomerate, formerly known as ViacomCBS.)

Paramount+ is also the home for a variety of original programming, including *The Good Fight, Mayor of Kingstown, Seal Team, The Stand,* and all the new *Star Trek* shows (including *Star Trek: Discovery, Star Trek: Picard,* and *Star Trek: Strange New Worlds*).

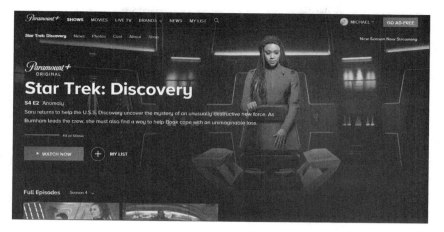

FIGURE 19.8

Paramount+.

There are two monthly subscription plans. The Essential plan runs $4.99 USD per month or $49.99 USD per year. If you want to excise advertisements and livestream your local CBS station, go with the Premium plan for $9.99 USD per month or $99.99 USD per year.

As with all of these streaming services, you watch Paramount+ in your web browser on the Paramount+ website (www.paramountplus.com).

Watching Peacock

Peacock, shown in Figure 19.9, is NBCUniveral's streaming video service, with programming from the NBC, Syfy, and USA networks, as well as movies from Universal Pictures. Peacock also offers a variety of original programming, including shows like *Bel-Air, Girls5Eva, Joe vs. Carole, Killing It, MacGruber, Rutherford Falls, Saved by the Bell, The Thing About Pam,* and *Yellowstone.*

You watch Peacock in your web browser on the Peacock website (www.peacocktv.com). As for subscriptions, Peacock offers a free version with commercials and limited programming; a Premium version with all the service's programming and all the ads, for $4.99 USD per month; and a Premium Plus version with no ads for $9.99 USD per month.

 NOTE Because Peacock and NBCUniversal are owned by Comcast, if you get your cable or Internet service from Comcast/Xfinity, you may be able to get a discount on the Peacock service.

FIGURE 19.9

Peacock.

Watching Other Streaming Video Services

That's a lot of movies and TV shows to watch, but it's not all that's available. There are literally dozens of other streaming video services available for viewing over the Internet on your Windows 11 PC. Table 19.1 details some of the more popular ones.

TABLE 19.1 Other Streaming Video Services

Service	URL	Description	Monthly Subscription (USD)
Acorn TV	www.acorn.tv	Programming from the UK, Canada, and New Zealand	$5.99
BET+	www.bet.plus	Programming from Black creators for Black audiences	$9.99
BritBox	www.britbox.com	Programming from the BBC and ITV	$6.99
BroadwayHD	www.broadwayhd.com	Broadway shows and concerts	$8.99
Crackle	www.crackle.com	Older movies and TV shows	Free
Criterion Channel	www.criterionchannel.com	Classic films from the Criterion Collection	$10.99
ESPN+	plus.espn.com	Live sporting events from various ESPN channels	$6.99
FilmRise	www.filmrise.com	Movies, '80s and '90s TV shows	Free

Freevee	www.amazon.com/freevee	Older movies and TV shows plus some originals (including *Bosch: Legacy*)	Free
Plex	www.plex.tv	Older movies and TV shows	Free
Pluto TV	www.pluto.tv	Older TV shows, movies, and children's programming	Free
Popcornflix	www.popcornflix.com	Older movies, reality TV shows, children's programming	Free
The Roku Channel	therokuchannel.roku.com	Older movies and TV shows, news, sports	Free
Shout Factory TV	www.shoutfactorytv.com	Classic and cult TV shows and movies (including *Mystery Science Theater 3000*)	Free
Tubi	www.tubitv.com	Older movies and TV shows, reality TV shows	Free
Xumo	www.xumo.tv	Older movies and TV shows	Free

Watching Live TV Online

Streaming movies and series is great, but it doesn't let you watch network programming in real time. In the past, if you wanted to watch TV shows live, you needed either an over-the-air (OTA) antenna (not always easy or practical) or a cable or satellite subscription (pricey). Now, however, there's another alternative: live TV streaming services.

A live streaming video service does just what the description implies—it lets you watch live TV, from both local channels and cable/satellite channels, over the Internet. This type of service displays a program guide, like the kind from a cable or satellite provider, with available channels listed by time of day. (Figure 19.10 shows the program guide for Hulu + Live TV, one of the more popular of these live TV streaming services.)

Channels are streamed in real time, as they're broadcast, for playback on your Windows PC or other device. None of these services are free, however; all have a monthly subscription fee.

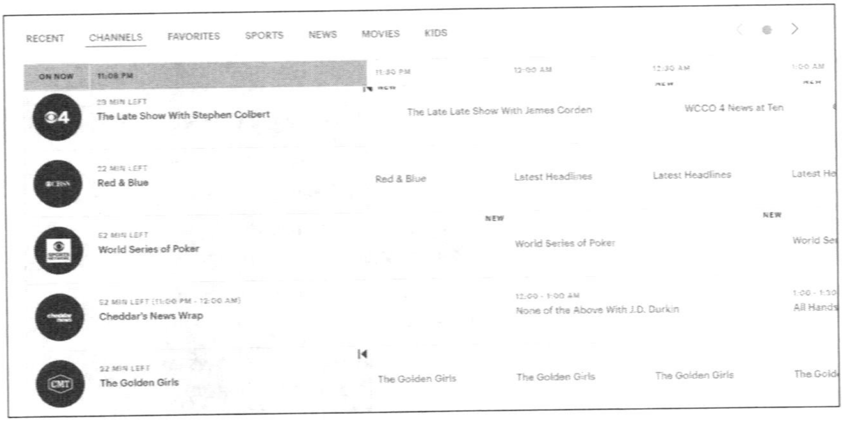

FIGURE 19.10

The program guide for Hulu + Live TV.

NOTE   Most live streaming services offer a variety of local TV stations, but not always all the stations available in your area. If you live in a large metropolitan area, chances are most of your local stations will be available on most live streaming services, but it isn't guaranteed. There are many cities where one or more local stations simply aren't available on a given live streaming service. This is something you need to check for specifically before you sign up for a service.

Table 19.2 details the major live streaming services available for viewing online. Note that cable channel lineups and local station availability differ significantly from service to service. In addition, each service offers different subscription levels; the more you pay, the more channels you get.

TABLE 19.2   Live Streaming Video Services

Service	URL	Monthly Subscription (USD)
DirecTV Stream	www.directv.com/stream/	$69.99+
fuboTV	www.fubto.tv	$69.99+
Hulu + Live TV	www.hulu.com/live-tv	$69.99+ (includes Disney+ and ESPN+)
Philo	www.philo.com	$25.00
Sling TV	www.sling.com	$35.00+
YouTube TV	tv.youtube.com	$64.99+

NOTE   Don't confuse the regular Hulu service, discussed previously, with the Hulu + Live TV service; the latter offers full live streaming, complete with local and cable channels. Likewise, don't confuse YouTube TV with regular YouTube, which I discuss later in this chapter; in this instance, the former is the live streaming service.

Buying and Renting Movies Online

All these streaming video services are great, but they don't always offer the most recent hit movies. (You wouldn't expect them to, at their low monthly subscription prices.) If you want to see a flick fresh from the movie theater, you need to purchase it or rent it—which you can do from various online video stores.

You'll pay anywhere from a buck up to $20 USD to watch these programs, and they stream just like the content available from other streaming services. You just have to pay for them, one at a time.

The most popular online video stores include the following:

- Amazon Prime Video (www.amazon.com)

- Google Play (play.google.com)

- Vudu (www.vudu.com)

Watching Videos on YouTube

Then there's YouTube (www.youtube.com), which is the biggest video site on the Web. What's cool about YouTube is that other users upload the majority of the videos, so you get a real mix of professional quality and amateur clips, as you can see in Figure 19.11.

Anyone can upload a video to YouTube, and at times it seems like practically everyone has. There are tons of how-to and self-improvement videos on YouTube, as well as pranks, funny animals and funny humans, videogame play-throughs, product reviews—you name it. There are also tons of old television programs uploaded by users, as well as old and new music videos, movie trailers, and the like. And, best of all, YouTube is all free—no monthly subscription required.

 NOTE   You're not limited to watching streaming video on your computer screen. You can connect your computer to your living room or bedroom TV via HDMI cable or wirelessly mirror your computer screen on your TV screen. Learn more in Chapter 6, "Connecting Printers and Other Devices to Your PC."

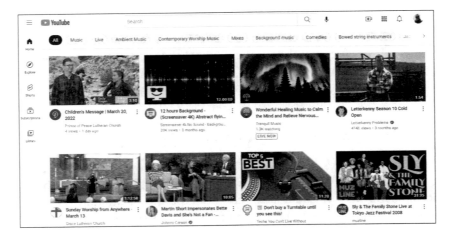

FIGURE 19.11

View professional and user-uploaded videos at YouTube.

THE ABSOLUTE MINIMUM

Here are the key points to remember from this chapter:

- Streaming video services let you watch movies, TV shows, and other videos on your computer, over the Internet.

- All streaming video services let you watch from their websites, in your web browser. Some have Windows apps available for free from the online Microsoft Store.

- The most popular streaming video services today are Amazon Prime Video, Apple TV+, Discovery+, Disney+, HBO Max, Hulu, Netflix, Paramount+, and Peacock.

- To watch live broadcast and cable programming, subscribe to a live streaming TV service, such as Hulu + Live TV or YouTube TV.

- If you want to watch recent Hollywood movies, you need to purchase or rent from an online video store, such as Amazon, the Google Play store, or Vudu.

- If you want to watch videos uploaded by other users, or even upload your own videos for others to watch, check out YouTube.

LISTENING TO MUSIC AND PODCASTS ONLINE

Your personal computer is a full-featured digital music machine. Not only can you watch TV shows and movies online, as you learned in the last chapter, but you can also use your PC to stream music from Pandora, Spotify, and other online services. There's a whole world of great music ahead!

Listening to Streaming Music Online

The music industry has changed a lot in the past few decades. In the late 1990s, everybody was listening to music on compact discs—which had supplanted vinyl records and cassettes in the 1980s. In the early 2000s, however, we all learned to love digital music downloads from the Internet, first from unauthorized download sites, such as Napster, and later from legal online music stores, such as Apple's iTunes Store.

Digital downloading (and ripping digital music from purchased CDs) was the big thing for a while, but within the past few years, we've seen another significant change in the way we get our music. We're now in the age of streaming music, where we listen to music online, often for free, without purchasing a single song. It's kind of like a highly personalized type of radio, delivered to our computers (and smartphones and tablets) over the Internet.

These online music services don't download music files to your computer or other device; instead, music is streamed in real time, just the way Hulu and Netflix stream video. You need an Internet connection to stream music in this fashion, of course, but there always seems to be some sort of connection nearby. (If there isn't, you can't listen to your streaming music.)

There are two primary types of delivery services for streaming audio online. The first model is like traditional radio in that you can't dial up specific tunes; you have to listen to whatever the service beams out, but in the form of personalized playlists or virtual radio stations. These services are typically free but include advertising. The second model, called *on-demand services*, lets you specify which songs you want to listen to. You typically have to pay a monthly subscription fee for these services.

Today, most streaming audio services offer both types of delivery. Pandora, for example, offers a free service that plays personalized "stations" but no on-demand listening, as well as a paid service that lets you dial up specific songs, albums, and artists. You can pick the type of streaming music service that best fits your needs.

Listening to Pandora

Pandora, shown in Figure 20.1, was one of the first and remains one of the most popular streaming music services. You can access Pandora from any web browser, at www.pandora.com or from Pandora's Windows app, available in the online Microsoft Store. Pandora claims to have more than 40 million tracks in its music library.

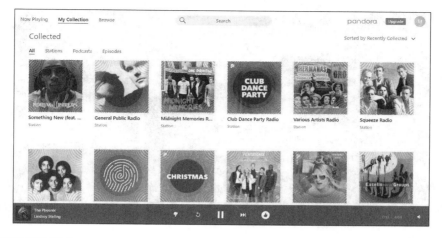

FIGURE 20.1

Viewing user-created "stations" on Pandora.

Pandora offers three different subscription plans.

The basic plan is free but requires that you sign up and sign in. The free plan is much like traditional AM or FM radio; you listen to the songs Pandora selects for you, along with accompanying commercials. It's a little more personalized than traditional radio, however, in that you create your personalized stations (up to 100). All you have to do is choose a song or artist; Pandora then creates a station with other songs like the one you picked. This plan is ad-supported, so you'll be subjected to commercials every handful of songs—just like traditional radio.

Pandora Plus is just like the free plan but cuts out the commercials. For this, you pay $4.99 USD per month.

Pandora Premium, at $9.99 USD per month (or $14.99 USD per month for the Family plan, which includes up to six accounts), is a bit different. In addition to the personalized stations, you also get on-demand playback. That is, you can search for and play any song in the Pandora library. You can also create your personalized playlists of songs you select.

Listening to Spotify

Another big streaming music service is Spotify, shown in Figure 20.2, which lets you choose specific tracks to listen to on demand—as well as create your personalized playlists. Spotify has a bigger library than Pandora, with more than 82 million individual tracks. There is a free Spotify Windows app available in the Microsoft Store or you can listen from any web browser at www.spotify.com.

FIGURE 20.2

Listening to music on demand with Spotify.

Spotify's basic membership is free, but you're subjected to commercials every few songs. If you want to get rid of the commercials and get unlimited skips, sign up for the $9.99 USD per month Spotify Premium plan (or $14.99 USD per month for the Family plan, which includes up to six accounts).

Listening to Other Streaming Music Services

Pandora and Spotify are the most popular streaming music services today, but they're not the only ones. Table 20.1 details some of the other big streaming music services, all of which you can access over the Internet.

TABLE 20.1   On-Demand Streaming Music Services

Service	URL	Price (USD)	Selection
Amazon Music Unlimited	www.amazon.com	Subscription ($7.99/month for Prime members; $9.99/month for non-Prime members)	90 million tracks
Apple Music	www.apple.com/apple-music/	Subscription ($9.99/month)	90 million tracks
Napster	www.napster.com	Premier ($9.99/month) Family ($14.99/month)	60 million tracks
Tidal	www.tidal.com	Premium ($9.99/month) HiFi ($19.99/month)	80 million tracks
YouTube Music	music.youtube.com	Basic (free) Premium ($9.99/month)	80 million tracks

Listening to Traditional Radio Stations Online

In addition to all the personalized stations you can create with Pandora and similar services, you can listen to traditional AM and FM radio over your computer. You don't need to have a radio handy to listen to your favorite stations; just tune in over the Internet using your web browser. (These services are great if you want to listen to your hometown radio stations when you're on vacation, or if you've moved away.)

There are three main services for listening to AM/FM radio online, as detailed in Table 20.2. All of these services are free, and all let you browse or search for local stations by location and genre. Note, however, that there is little overlap between the three services; you'll need to choose among them to listen to specific stations. (Figure 20.3 shows TuneIn Radio.)

TABLE 20.2   Streaming Radio Online

Service	URL	Selection
Audacy	www.audacy.om	500+ stations
iHeartRadio	www.iheart.com	1,000+ stations
TuneIn Radio	www.tunein.com	120,000+ stations

FIGURE 20.3

Listening to a local FM station with TuneIn Radio.

NOTE   If you listen to SiriusXM satellite radio in your car, you can listen to Sirius/XM Radio online, for free, at www.siriusxm.com/player/. SiriusXM offers more than 200 channels of music, news, and talk—including several web-only channels that aren't available via normal satellite radio.

Purchasing and Downloading Digital Music

Streaming music services enable you to listen to all the music you want, which is great. The only bad thing about this is that you don't actually own any of this music; you have to be connected to the Internet and the service to get access to the music they offer.

If you're of a certain age, you're more used to compiling your own personal music collection. Although CDs are fast becoming old tech, you can still create your own music library—via digital music you purchase and download from the Internet.

Examining Online Music Stores

There are a number of digital music stores online, all offering tens of millions of tracks and albums in digital format, for prices starting at less than $1 a track. All you need to order is a web browser and a credit card; then you can browse and search for the music you want.

Table 20.3 details the most popular of these online music stores.

TABLE 20.3 Online Music Stores

Store	URL	Selection
Amazon Digital Music Store	www.amazon.com/mp3/	50 million tracks
Apple iTunes Store	www.apple.com/itunes/music/	50 million tracks
Google Play Music	play.google.com/music/	40 million tracks

 TIP The iTunes Store is the store of choice if you have an Apple iPhone or iPad; it fits in seamlessly with the Apple infrastructure and offers music in Apple's popular AAC file format. The Amazon and Google stores are more universal (and preferred if you have an Android smartphone or tablet), offering music in the ubiquitous MP3 file format.

Playing Downloaded Music on Your PC

To play the digital music you download, you need a digital music player app.

If you're buying from Apple's iTunes Store, you'll use Apple's iTunes app to both purchase and play your music. It's available free from Apple's website.

Other online music stores offer their web-based music players, which work just fine. You also can use third-party music player apps, including the Media Player app included with Windows 11. As shown in Figure 20.4, Windows Media Player lets you play both music and videos stored on your computer.

FIGURE 20.4

Listening to downloaded music with the Windows Media Player app.

Listening to Podcasts Online

In addition to listening to music, you can also use your Windows 11 PC to listen to podcasts online. A podcast is like a traditional radio program, but it streams over the Internet. There are all types of podcasts available—music podcasts, true crime podcasts, political podcasts, you name it.

Most podcasts are free and available from major streaming music services, such as Spotify and TuneIn Radio. You can also find podcasts on dedicated podcast websites, such as Audible (www.audible.com) and Google Podcasts (podcasts.google. com), shown in Figure 20.5.

Listening to a podcast in your web browser is just like listening to your favorite music. Browse or search for a given podcast and then click the specific episode to which you want to listen. You can then pause and restart, skip forward or back, and (on some sites) listen at a faster speed so you get through the podcast quicker. Most sites also let you subscribe to individual podcasts, which means you'll be notified when new episodes post.

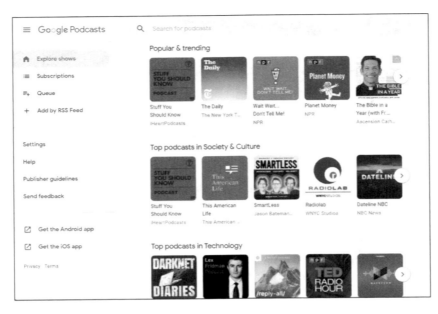

FIGURE 20.5

Browsing for podcasts on Google Podcasts.

THE ABSOLUTE MINIMUM

Here are the key points to remember from this chapter:

- You can listen to music over the Internet with streaming music services such as Pandora and Spotify.

- Many radio stations are available for online listening from Audacy, iHeartRadio, and TuneIn Radio.

- You can purchase and download individual tracks and complete albums from online music stores such as the Amazon MP3 Store, Apple's iTunes Store, and Google Play Music.

- Use the Windows Media Player app to listen to music you've downloaded online.

- Find and listen to podcasts online from most streaming music sites or from Audible or Google Podcasts.

PART VIII

KEEPING YOUR SYSTEM UP AND RUNNING

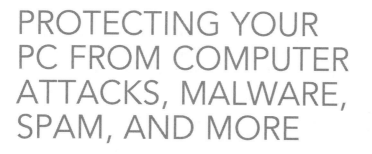

PROTECTING YOUR PC FROM COMPUTER ATTACKS, MALWARE, SPAM, AND MORE

As you've seen, a lot of what you'll do on your computer revolves around the Internet. Unfortunately, when you connect your computer to the Internet, you open a whole new can of worms—literally. Computer worms, viruses, spyware, spam, and the like can attack your computer and cause it to run slowly or not at all. In addition to these malicious software programs (called *malware*) that can infect your computer, you're likely to come across all manner of inappropriate content that you'd probably rather avoid. It can be a nasty world online.

Fortunately, it's easy to protect your computer and your family from these dangers. All you need are a few software utilities—and a lot of common sense!

Safeguarding Your System from Computer Viruses

A *computer virus* is a malicious software program designed to do damage to your computer system by deleting files or even taking over your PC to launch attacks on other systems. A virus attacks your computer when you launch an infected software program, launching a "payload" that oftentimes is catastrophic.

Watching for Signs of Infection

How do you know whether your computer system has been infected with a virus?

In general, whenever your computer starts acting different from normal, it's possible that you have a virus. You might see strange messages or graphics displayed on your computer screen or find that normally well-behaved programs are acting erratically. You might discover that certain files have gone missing from your hard disk or that your system is acting sluggish—or failing to start at all. You might even find that your friends are receiving emails from you (that you never sent) that have suspicious files attached.

If your computer exhibits one or more of these symptoms—especially if you've just downloaded a file from the Internet or received a suspicious email message—the prognosis is not good. Your computer is probably infected.

 NOTE Many computer attacks today are executed using personal computers compromised by a computer virus. These so-called *zombie computers* are operated via remote control in an ad hoc attack network called a *botnet*. A firewall program protects against incoming attacks and botnet controllers.

Catching a Virus

Whenever you share data with another computer or computer user (which you do all the time when you're connected to the Internet), you risk exposing your computer to potential viruses. There are many ways you can share data and transmit a virus:

- Opening an infected file attached to an email message or instant message sent to you from within a social network
- Launching an infected program file downloaded from the Internet
- Sharing a USB memory drive or data CD/DVD that contains an infected file
- Sharing over a network a computer file that contains an infection

Of all these methods, the common means of virus infection is via email. Whenever you open a file attached to an email message, you stand a good chance of infecting your computer system with a virus—even if the file was sent by someone you know and trust. That's because many viruses "spoof" the sender's name, thus making you think the file is from a friend or colleague. The bottom line is that no email or instant message attachment is safe unless you were expressly expecting it.

Practicing Safe Computing

Because you're not going to completely quit doing any of these activities (how can you live without email!), you'll never be 100% safe from the threat of computer viruses. There are, however, some steps you can take to reduce your risk:

- Don't open email attachments from people you don't know—or even from people you do know, if you aren't expecting them. That's because some viruses can hijack the address book on an infected PC, thus sending out infected email that the owner isn't even aware of. Just looking at an email message won't harm anything; the damage comes when you open a file attached to the email. A good rule of thumb is that if you weren't expecting the file, don't open it.

- Don't accept files sent to you via instant messaging or social networking chat; like email attachments, files sent via messaging and chat can be easily infected with viruses and spyware.

- Download files only from reliable file archive websites, such as Download.com (www.download.com) and Softpedia (www.softpedia.com), or from legitimate online stores, such as the Microsoft Store.

- Don't execute programs you find posted to web message boards or blogs.

- Don't click links sent to you from strangers via instant messaging or in a chat room.

- Share USB drives, CDs, DVDs, and files only with users you know and trust.

- Use antivirus software—and keep it up-to-date with the most recent virus definitions.

These precautions—especially the first one about not opening email attachments—should provide good insurance against the threat of computer viruses.

 CAUTION If you remember nothing else from this chapter, remember this: Never open an unexpected file attachment. Period!

Disinfecting Your System with Antivirus Software

Antivirus software programs can detect known viruses and protect your system against new, unknown viruses. These programs check your system for viruses each time your system is booted, and you can configure them to check any programs you download from the Internet. They're also used to disinfect your system if it becomes infected with a virus.

Fortunately, Windows 11 comes with its own built-in antivirus utility. It's called Windows Security, and here's how you open it:

1. From the Start menu, click or tap the Settings icon to open the Settings app.

2. Click or tap Privacy & Security.

3. Click or tap Windows Security.

4. Click or tap Open Windows Security.

 NOTE Windows Security may or may not be activated on your new PC. Some computer manufacturers prefer to include third-party antivirus software and thus disable Windows Security by default.

As you can see in Figure 20.1, Windows Security runs in the background, monitoring your computer against all sorts of malware, including both viruses and spyware. In fact, if all you see are green check marks, there's nothing much you need to do.

Windows Security	− □ ✕

Security at a glance

See what's happening with the security and health of your device and take any actions needed.

- ⌂ Home
- ○ Virus & threat protection
- ⎙ Account protection
- (ꙮ) Firewall & network protection
- ▭ App & browser control
- ⌷ Device security
- ♡ Device performance & health
- 👪 Family options
- ↺ Protection history

Virus & threat protection
No action needed

Account protection
No action needed

Firewall & network protection
No action needed

App & browser control
No action needed

Device security
View status and manage hardware security features.

Device performance & health
No action needed

⚙ Settings

FIGURE 20.1

Windows Security—the built-in antimalware utility for Windows.

Of course, you're not locked into using Microsoft's antimalware solution. There are a lot of third-party antivirus programs available, including the following:

- AVG Internet Security (www.avg.com)

- Avira Antivirus (www.avira.com)

- Bitdefender Total Security (www.bitdefender.com)

- IObit Malware Fighter (www.iobit.com)

- Malwarebytes for Windows (www.malwarebytes.org)

- McAfee Total Protection (www.mcafee.com)

- Norton 360 (http://us.norton.com)

- Trend Micro Antivirus + Security (www.trendmicro.com)

 CAUTION Kaspersky Anti-Virus is another antimalware program popular in some circles. However, the U.S. government has issued warnings that Kaspersky Lab, a Russian company, has close ties to Russian intelligence organizations. As such, I cannot recommend Kaspersky to my readers.

Whichever antivirus program you choose, you need to configure it to go online periodically to update the virus definition database the program uses to look for known virus files. Because new viruses are created every week, this file of known viruses must be updated accordingly.

Hunting Down Spyware

Even more pernicious than computer viruses is the proliferation of *spyware*. A spyware program installs itself on your computer and then surreptitiously sends information about the way you use your PC to some interested third party.

Spyware typically gets installed in the background when you're installing another program. Peer-to-peer file-trading networks (*not* legitimate online stores, such as Amazon or the iTunes Store) are one of the biggest sources of spyware; when you install the file-trading software, the spyware is also installed. Also bad are fly-by-night file download sites, which often trick you into installing spyware as part of the software download process.

Having spyware on your system is nasty—almost as bad as being infected with a computer virus. Some spyware programs even hijack your computer and launch pop-up windows and advertisements when you visit certain web pages. If there's spyware on your computer, you definitely want to get rid of it.

While pure antivirus programs won't catch spyware (because spyware isn't a virus), most fully featured antimalware programs include antispyware tools. Check the feature set of whatever antivirus program you're using to ensure it offers anti-spyware protection.

 NOTE Windows Security, included free in Windows 11, guards against both viruses and spyware.

Fighting Email Spam

If you're like most users, you get a fair amount of unsolicited, unauthorized, and unwanted email messages in your inbox—in other words, *spam*. These spam messages are the online equivalent of the junk mail you receive in your postal mailbox and are a huge problem.

Although it's probably impossible to do away with 100% of the spam you receive (you can't completely stop junk mail, either), there are steps you can take to reduce the amount of spam you have to deal with. The heavier your spam load, the more steps you can take.

Protecting Your Email Address

Spammers accumulate email addresses via a variety of methods. Some use high-tech methods to harvest email addresses listed on public web pages and message board postings. Others use the tried-and-true approach of buying names from list brokers. Still others automatically generate addresses using a "dictionary" of common names and email domains.

One way to reduce the amount of spam you receive is to limit the public use of your email address. It's a simple fact: The more you expose your email address, the more likely it is that a spammer will find it—and use it.

To this end, you should avoid putting your email address on your blog or web page, or on your company's web page. You should also avoid including your email address in postings you make to web-based message boards or comments sections. In addition, you should most definitely not include your email address in any of the conversations you have in chat rooms or via instant messaging.

Another strategy is to actually use *two* email addresses. Take your main email address (the one you get from your ISP) and hand it out only to a close circle of friends and family; do *not* use this address to post public messages or to register at websites. Then obtain a second email address (you can get a free one at Outlook.com or Gmail) and use that one for all your public activity. When you post on a message board or newsgroup, use the second address. When you order something from an online merchant, use the second address. When you register for website access, use the second address. Over time, the second address will attract the spam; your first email address will remain private and relatively spam-free.

TIP   If you do have to leave your email address in a public forum, you can insert a spamblock into your address—an unexpected word or phrase that, although easily removed, will confuse the software spammers use to harvest addresses. For example, if your email address is johnjones@myisp.com, you might change the address to read johnSPAMBLOCKjones@myisp.com. Other users will know to remove the SPAMBLOCK from the address before emailing you, but the spam harvesting software will be foiled.

Blocking Spammers in Your Email Programs

Most email software and web-based email services include some sort of spam filtering. You should always enable the antispam features in your email program or service. Doing so should block most of the unwanted messages you might otherwise receive.

TIP   It's a good idea to review messages in your spam folder periodically to make sure no legitimate messages have been accidentally sent there.

Resisting Phishing Scams

Phishing is a technique used by online scam artists to steal your identity by tricking you into disclosing valuable personal information, such as passwords, credit card numbers, and other financial data. If you're not careful, you can mistake a phishing email for a real one—and open yourself up to identity theft.

A phishing scam typically starts with a phony email message that appears to be from a legitimate source, such as your bank, eBay, PayPal, or another official institution. When you click the link in the phishing email, you're taken to a fake website masquerading as the real site, complete with logos and official-looking text. You're encouraged to enter your personal information into the forms on the web page; when you do so, your information is sent to the scammer, and you're now a victim of identity theft. When your data falls into the hands of criminals, it can be used to hack into your online accounts, make unauthorized charges on your credit card, and maybe even drain your bank account.

Until recently, the only guard against phishing scams was common sense. That is, you were advised never to click through a link in an email message that asks for any type of personal information—whether that be your bank account number or eBay password. Even if the email *looks* official, it probably isn't; legitimate institutions and websites never include this kind of link in their official messages. Instead, access your personal information only by using your web browser to go directly to the website in question. Don't link there!

Fortunately, Windows now offers some protection against phishing scams, in the form of a SmartScreen Filter in the Microsoft Edge web browser that alerts you to potential phishing sites. When you attempt to visit a known or suspected phishing site, the browser displays a warning message. Do not enter information into these suspected phishing sites—return to your home page instead!

If you use the Google Chrome browser instead of Edge, Google offers similar antiphishing protection called Google Safe Browsing. When you attempt to enter a suspicious or known malicious website, the browser pops up a warning to that effect. If you see such a warning, don't proceed.

Even with these protections, you still need to use your head. Don't click through suspicious email links, and don't give out your personal information and passwords unless you're sure you're dealing with an official (and not just an official-looking) site!

Shielding Your Children from Inappropriate Content

The Internet contains an almost limitless supply of information on its tens of billions of web pages. Although most of these pages contain useful information, it's a sad fact that the content of some pages can be quite offensive to some people—and that there are some Internet users who prey on unsuspecting youths.

As a responsible parent, you want to protect your children from any of the bad stuff (and bad people) online, while still allowing access to all the good stuff. How do you do this?

Using Content-Filtering Software

If you can't trust your children to always click away from inappropriate web content, you can choose to install software on your computer that performs filtering functions for all your online sessions. These safe-surfing programs guard against either a preselected list of inappropriate sites or a preselected list of topics—and then block access to sites that meet the selected criteria. After you have the software installed, your kids won't be able to access the really bad sites on the Web.

The most popular filtering programs include the following:

- Circle Home Plus (www.meetcircle.com)

- CYBERsitter (cybersitter.27labs.com)

- Net Nanny (www.netnanny.com)

- Qustodio (www.qustodio.com)

In addition, many of the big Internet security suites offer built-in content-filtering modules.

Encouraging Safe Computing

Although using content-filtering software is a good first step, the most important thing you can do, as a parent, is to create an environment that encourages appropriate use of the Internet. Nothing replaces traditional parental supervision, and at the end of the day, you have to take responsibility for your children's online activities. Provide the guidance they need to make the Internet a fun and educational place to visit—and your entire family will be better for it.

Here are some guidelines you can follow to ensure a safer surfing experience for your family:

- Make sure that your children know never to give out identifying information (home address, school name, telephone number, and so on) or to send their photos to other users online. This includes not putting overly personal information (and photos!) on their Facebook, Snapchat, or other social media pages.

- Provide each of your children with an online pseudonym so they don't have to use their real names online.

- Don't let your children arrange face-to-face meetings with other computer users without parental permission and supervision. If a meeting is arranged, make the first one in a public place, and be sure to accompany your child.

- Teach your children that people online might not always be who they seem; just because someone says that they're a 10-year-old girl doesn't necessarily mean that person really is 10 years old or a girl.

- Consider making Internet surfing an activity you do together with your younger children—or turn it into a family activity by putting your kids' PC in a public room (such as a living room or den) rather than in a private bedroom.

- Set reasonable rules and guidelines for your kids' computer use. Consider limiting the number of minutes/hours they can spend online each day.

- Monitor your children's Internet activities. Ask them to keep a log of all websites they visit or check their browser history; oversee any chat sessions they participate in; check out any files they download; even consider sharing an email account (especially with younger children) so that you can oversee their messages.

- Don't let your children respond to messages that are suggestive, obscene, belligerent, or threatening—or that make them feel uncomfortable in any way. Encourage your children to tell you if they receive any such messages, and then report the senders to your ISP.

- Install content-filtering software on your PC and set up one of the kid-safe search sites (discussed earlier in this section) as your browser's start page.

Teach your children that Internet access is not a right; it should be a privilege earned by your children and kept only when their use of it matches your expectations.

THE ABSOLUTE MINIMUM

Here are the key points to remember from this chapter:

- Avoid computer viruses by not opening unsolicited email attachments and by using an antivirus software program.

- Windows 11 includes the Windows Security antimalware utility that guards against computer viruses and spyware.

- Fight email spam by keeping your email address as private as possible and utilizing your email program's spam filter.

- Avoid falling for phishing scams characterized by fake—but official-looking—email messages.

- To protect against inappropriate content on the Internet, install content-filtering software—and make sure you monitor your children's online activities.

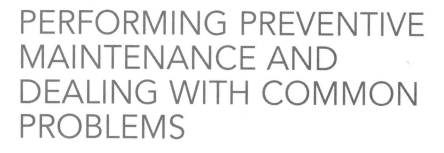

PERFORMING PREVENTIVE MAINTENANCE AND DEALING WITH COMMON PROBLEMS

"An ounce of prevention is worth a pound of cure."

That old adage might seem trite and clichéd, but it's also true—especially when it comes to your computer system. Spending a few minutes a week on preventive maintenance can save you from costly computer problems in the future.

To make this chore a little easier, Windows includes several utilities to help you keep your system running smoothly. You should use these tools as part of your regular maintenance routine—or if you experience specific problems with your computer system.

And if you experience more serious problems—well, try not to panic. There are ways to fix most issues you encounter, without necessarily calling in the tech support guys.

Maintaining Your Computer

Most computers these days, especially those running Windows 11, don't require a lot of handholding to keep them up and running. That said, there's a little bit of routine maintenance you might want to undertake—just to make sure your system remains in its optimal operating condition.

Cleaning Up Unused Files

Most desktop and laptop computers have pretty big hard disks; ultrabooks and tablets do not. But even if your computer has a tremendous amount of storage, it's still easy to end up with too many useless files and programs taking up too much disk space.

Fortunately, Windows includes a utility that identifies and deletes unused files. The Disk Cleanup tool is what you want to use when you need to free up extra hard disk space for more frequently used files.

To use Disk Cleanup, follow these steps:

1. Open File Explorer.

2. Select the drive you want to clean up.

3. Click or tap the See More (three dots) button on the toolbar.

4. Click or tap Cleanup.

5. As you can see in Figure 22.1, Disk Cleanup give you the option of permanently deleting various types of files: downloaded program files, temporary Internet files, deleted files in the Recycle Bin, and so forth. Select which files you want to delete.

6. Click OK to begin deleting.

 NOTE You can safely choose to delete all the files found by Disk Cleanup except the setup log files, which the Windows operating system sometimes needs.

FIGURE 22.1

Use Disk Cleanup to delete unused files from your hard disk.

Removing Unused Programs

Another way to free up valuable hard disk space is to delete those programs you never use. This is accomplished using the Uninstall or Change a Program utilities in Windows. Use the following steps:

 TIP Most brand-new PCs come with unwanted programs and trial versions installed at the factory. Many users choose to delete these "bloatware" programs when they first run their PCs.

1. Open the Start menu and click or tap the Settings icon to open the Settings app.

2. Click or tap Apps on the left side to open the Apps page.

3. Click or tap Apps & Features.

4. Windows now displays all the installed apps on your system, as shown in Figure 22.2. Click or tap the More (three-dot) button for app you want to remove and then click or tap Uninstall.

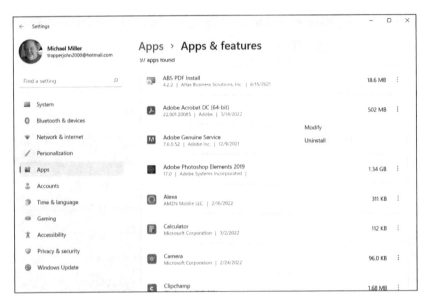

FIGURE 22.2

Uninstall any program you're no longer using.

Optimizing Your Disk Storage

Any time you run an application, move or delete a file, or accidentally turn the power off while the system is running, you run the risk of introducing errors to your hard disk or SSD. These errors can make it harder to open files, slow down your drive, or cause your system to freeze when you open or save a file or an application.

Fortunately, you can find and fix most of these errors directly from within Windows by optimizing your drive. Follow these steps:

1. Open File Explorer.

2. Select the drive you want to optimize.

3. Click or tap See More (three dots) on the toolbar; then select Optimize.

4. Make sure the drive you want to optimize is selected; then click or tap the Optimize button.

Windows scans your hard disk and attempts to fix any errors it encounters. Note that you might be prompted to reboot your PC if you're checking your computer's C: drive.

Updating Windows

Microsoft considers Windows to be a service, which means the operating system is being constantly updated and improved, often in the background. These updates are delivered over the Internet, which means your computer needs to be online and powered on to receive them.

Regular updates are pushed to your computer the second Tuesday of every month. (This is called Update Tuesday.) These updates are typically minor and mainly include bug fixes. Installing one of these updates takes only a few minutes.

There's also one big update in the fall that typically introduces a few new features and interface changes. Installing this more major update may take an hour or so.

All Windows updates, minor and major, are handled by Microsoft's Windows Update feature. You'll receive an onscreen message when a new update is available, and the update will be automatically installed the next time you reboot your computer—or if it reboots automatically.

If you want to control when these updates are installed, open the Settings app and select Windows Update. From here, you can do the following:

- Manually check for updates by clicking the Check for Updates button
- Pause any pending updates for up to seven days
- Change the "active hours" when you use your computer, so Windows will *not* force an update during that time period
- View a history of recently installed updates

Know that installing one of the yearly major updates is a major operation, at least in the amount of time involved. The minor monthly upgrades, even though sometimes require rebooting your machine, don't take that much time to download and install.

Keeping Your Hardware in Tip-Top Condition

There's also a fair amount of preventive maintenance you can physically perform on your computer hardware. It's simple stuff, but it can really extend the life of your PC.

System Unit

The system unit on a traditional desktop PC—or the entire unit of an all-in-one, 2-in-1, laptop, or tablet computer—has a lot of sensitive electronics inside, from memory chips to disk drives to power supplies. Check out these maintenance tips to keep your system unit from flaking out on you:

- Locate your computer in a clean, dust-free environment. Keep it away from direct sunlight and strong magnetic fields. In addition, make sure that your system unit and your monitor have plenty of air flow around them to keep them from overheating.

- Hook up your system unit to a surge suppressor to avoid damaging power spikes.

- Avoid turning on and off your system unit too often; it's better to leave it on all the time than incur frequent "power on" stress to all those delicate components.

- However, turn off your system unit if you're going to be away for an extended period—anything longer than a few days.

- Check all your cable connections periodically. Make sure that all the connectors are firmly connected, and all the screws properly screwed. Also make sure that your cables aren't stretched too tight or bent in ways that could damage the wires inside.

Keyboard

Even something as simple as your computer keyboard requires a little preventive maintenance from time to time. Check out these tips:

- Keep your keyboard away from pets and very young children—they can get dirt and hair and Play-Doh all over the place, and they tend to put way too much pressure on the keys.

- Keep your desktop keyboard or laptop/2-in-1 computer away from dust, dirt, smoke, direct sunlight, and other harmful environmental stuff. You might even consider putting a dust cover on your keyboard when it's not in use.

- Use a small vacuum cleaner to periodically sweep the dirt from your keyboard. (Alternatively, you can use compressed air to *blow* the dirt away.) Use a cotton swab or soft cloth to clean between the keys. If necessary, remove the keycaps to clean the switches underneath.

- If you spill something on your keyboard, disconnect it immediately and wipe up the spill. Use a soft cloth to get between the keys; if necessary, use a screwdriver to pop off the keycaps and wipe up any seepage underneath. Let the keyboard dry thoroughly before trying to use it again.

Display

If you think of your computer display as a little television set, you're on the right track. Just treat your screen as you do your TV, and you'll be okay. That said, look at these preventive maintenance tips:

- As with all other important system components, keep your monitor away from direct sunlight, dust, and smoke.

- With your monitor turned off, periodically clean the monitor screen. Use water to dampen a lint-free cloth, and then wipe the screen; do not spray liquid directly on the screen. Do not use any cleaner that contains alcohol or ammonia; these chemicals may damage an LCD screen. (You can, however, use commercial cleaning wipes specially formulated for LCD screens.)

- Don't forget to adjust the brightness and contrast controls on your monitor every now and then. Any controls can get out of whack—plus, your monitor's performance will change as it ages, and simple adjustments can often keep it looking as good as new.

Printer

Your printer is a complex device with a lot of moving parts. Follow these tips to keep your printouts in good shape:

- Use a soft cloth, mini-vacuum cleaner, or compressed air to clean the inside and outside of your printer on a periodic basis. In particular, make sure that you clean the paper path of all paper shavings and dust.

- If you have an inkjet printer, periodically clean the inkjets. Run your printer's cartridge cleaning utility or use a small pin to make sure they don't get clogged.

- If you have a laser printer, replace the toner cartridge as needed. When you replace the cartridge, remember to clean the printer cleaning bar and other related parts, per the manufacturer's instructions.

- Don't use alcohol or other solvents to clean rubber or plastic parts—you'll do more harm than good!

Maintaining a Laptop PC

All the previous tips hold for both desktop and laptop PCs. If you have a laptop PC, however, there are additional steps you need to take to keep everything working in prime condition.

Using the Windows Mobility Center

Let's start with all the various settings that are unique to a laptop PC—power plan, display brightness, presentation settings, and so forth. Windows puts all these settings into a single control panel called the Windows Mobility Center. As you can see in Figure 22.3, you can use the Mobility Center to configure and manage just about everything that makes your laptop run better.

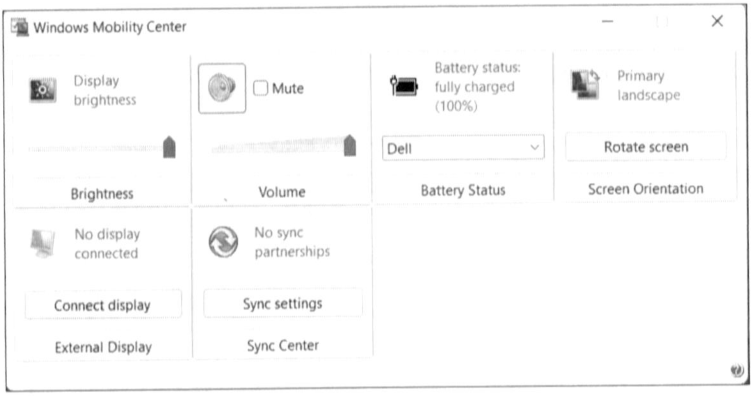

FIGURE 22.3

Manage key laptop PC settings with the Windows Mobility Center.

To access the Windows Mobility Center, right-click the Start button and then click Mobility Center. Click or tap the button or adjust the slider for whichever option you need to change.

NOTE Some laptop manufacturers add their own mobile configuration settings to the Windows Mobility Center.

Conserving Battery Life

One of the key issues with a laptop or 2-in-1 PC is battery life. It's especially important if you use your laptop a lot on the road.

Any laptop, even a desktop replacement model, gives you at least an hour of operation before the battery powers down. If you need more battery life than that, here are some things you can try:

- **Change your power scheme**—Windows includes several built-in power schemes that manage key functions to provide either longer battery life or better performance. (It's always a trade-off between the two.) You can switch power schemes from the Windows Mobility Center, in the Battery Status section.

- **Dim your screen**—The brighter your screen, the more power your PC uses. Conserve on power usage by dialing down the brightness level of your laptop's screen when you're on battery power.

- **Turn it off when you're not using it**—A PC sitting idle is still using power. If you're going to be away from the keyboard for more than a few minutes, turn off the laptop to conserve power—or put the PC into sleep mode, which also cuts power use.

- **Buy a second battery**—If your laptop has a removable battery that gets drained, remove it and plug in a fresh one.

- **Buy a smaller laptop**—Ultrabook models use less power and have longer battery life than do traditional laptops, which in turn are less power-hungry than desktop replacement models. The smaller the screen and the less powerful the CPU, the longer the laptop's battery life.

If worse comes to worst, keep an eye out for an available power outlet. Most coffee shops and airport lounges have at least one seat next to a power outlet; just carry your laptop's AC adapter with you and be ready to plug in when you can.

Securing Your Laptop

One of the great things about a laptop PC is that it's small and easily portable. One of the bad things about a laptop PC is that's it's small and easily portable—which makes it attractive to thieves. Take care to protect your laptop when you use it in public, which may mean investing in a laptop lock or some similar sort of antitheft device. Of course, just being vigilant helps; never leave your laptop unattended in a coffee shop or airport terminal.

In addition, be careful about transmitting private data over a public Wi-Fi network. Avoid the temptation to do your online shopping (and transmit your credit card number) from your local coffee shop; wait until you're safely connected to your home network before you send your private data over the Wi-Fi airwaves.

Troubleshooting Computer Problems

Computers don't always run perfectly. It's possible—although unlikely—that at some point in time, something will go wrong with your PC. It might refuse to start, it might freeze up, and it might crash and go dead. Yikes!

When something goes wrong with your computer, there's no need to panic (even though that's what you'll probably feel like doing). Most PC problems have easy-to-find causes and simple solutions. The key thing is to keep your wits about you and attack the situation calmly and logically—following the advice you'll find in this chapter.

No matter what kind of computer-related problem you're experiencing, there are six basic steps you should take to track down the cause of the problem. Work through these steps calmly and deliberately, and you're likely to find what's causing the current problem—and then be in a good position to fix it yourself:

1. **Don't panic!**—Just because there's something wrong with your PC is no reason to fly off the handle. Chances are there's nothing seriously wrong. Besides, getting all panicky won't solve anything. Keep your wits about you and proceed logically, and you can probably find what's causing your problem and get it fixed.

2. **Check for operator error**—In other words, *you* might have done something wrong. Maybe you clicked the wrong button, pressed the wrong key, or plugged something into the wrong jack or port. Retrace your steps and try to duplicate your problem. Chances are the problem won't recur if you don't make the same mistake twice.

3. **Check that everything is plugged into the proper place and that the system unit itself is getting power**—Take special care to ensure that all your cables are *securely* connected—loose connections can cause all sorts of strange results. In addition, flick the wall switch to make sure the outlet you're plugged into is turned on.

4. **Make sure you have the latest versions of all the software installed on your system**—While you're at it, make sure you have the latest versions of device drivers installed for all the peripherals on your system. (Conversely, if you've just installed a new program or update, you might try removing it. Chances are it may have caused a problem.)

5. **Try to isolate the problem by when and how it occurs**—Walk through each step of the process to see if you can identify a particular program or driver that might be causing the problem. If you've just installed a new app (or updated an old one), consider that this might be the cause of your problem.

6. **When all else fails, call in professional help**—If you think it's a Windows-related problem, contact Microsoft's technical support department. If you think it's a problem with a particular program, contact the tech support department of the program's manufacturer. If you think it's a hardware-related problem, contact the manufacturer of your PC or the dealer you bought it from. The pros are there for a reason—when you need technical support, go and get it.

CAUTION   Not all tech support is free. Unless you have a brand-new PC or brand-new software, expect to pay a fee for technical support.

Troubleshooting in Safe Mode

If you're having trouble getting Windows to start, it's probably because some setting is wrong, or some driver is malfunctioning. The problem is, how do you get into Windows to fix what's wrong when you can't even start Windows?

The solution is to hijack your computer before Windows gets hold of it and force it to start *without* whatever is causing the problem. You do this by watching the screen as your computer boots up and pressing the F8 key just before Windows starts to load. This displays the Windows startup menu, where you select Safe mode.

Safe mode is a special mode of operation that loads Windows in a simple configuration. When in Safe mode, you can look for device conflicts, restore incorrect or corrupted device drivers, or delete apps that might be causing the problem.

 NOTE   Depending on the severity of your system problem, Windows might start in Safe mode automatically.

Reacting When Windows Freezes or Crashes

Probably the most common computer trouble is the freeze-up. That's what happens when your PC just stops dead in its tracks. The screen looks normal, but nothing works—you can't type onscreen, you can't click any buttons, nothing's happening. Even worse is when Windows crashes on you—just shuts down with no warning.

If your system freezes or crashes, the good news is that there's probably nothing wrong with your computer hardware. The bad news is that there's probably something funky happening with your operating system.

This doesn't mean your system is broken. It's just a glitch. And you can recover from glitches. Just remember not to panic and to approach the situation calmly and rationally.

What Causes Windows to Freeze?

If Windows up and freezes, what's the likely cause? There can be many different causes of a Windows freeze, including the following:

- You might be running an older software program or game that isn't compatible with your version of Windows. If so, upgrade the program.

- You might be running an app or game that needs more powerful hardware than you have. This is often the case with newer PC games that need a lot of oomph in terms of CPU and video processor power; your PC might try to run the game but keep slowing down or freezing.

- A memory conflict might exist between applications or between an application and Windows. Try running fewer programs at once or running problematic programs one at a time to avoid potential memory conflicts.

- You might not have enough memory installed on your system. (Advice: 4 GB is never enough.) Upgrade the amount of memory in your PC.

- You might not have enough free space on your computer drive. Delete any unnecessary files to free up more space.

- If your computer has a hard disk drive, it might be developing errors or bad sectors. Check your hard disk for errors, as described in the "Optimizing Your Disk Storage" section earlier in this chapter.

Dealing with Frozen Windows

When Windows freezes, you need to get it unfrozen and up and running again. The way to do this is to shut down or reboot your computer.

In older versions of Windows, you could force a shutdown by holding down the Ctrl+Alt+Del keys. That doesn't work in Windows 11; instead, you need to press the Windows key and your PC's power button simultaneously. If that doesn't work, just press and hold the power button until the PC shuts down.

If your system crashes or freezes frequently, however, you should call in a pro. These kinds of problems can be tough to track down by yourself when you're dealing with Windows.

Dealing with a Frozen Program

Sometimes Windows works fine but an individual software program freezes. Fortunately, recent versions of Windows present an exceptionally safe environment; when an individual application crashes or freezes, it seldom messes up your entire system. You can use a utility called the Windows Task Manager to close the problem application without affecting other Windows programs.

When a Windows application freezes or crashes, press Ctrl+Alt+Del, and when the next screen appears, click or tap Task Manager; this opens the Windows Task Manager. To display everything there is to display, click More Details; you now see a series of tabs, as shown in Figure 22.4. Select the Processes tab, go to the Apps section, and click the task that's frozen. Click the End Task button and wait for the app to close.

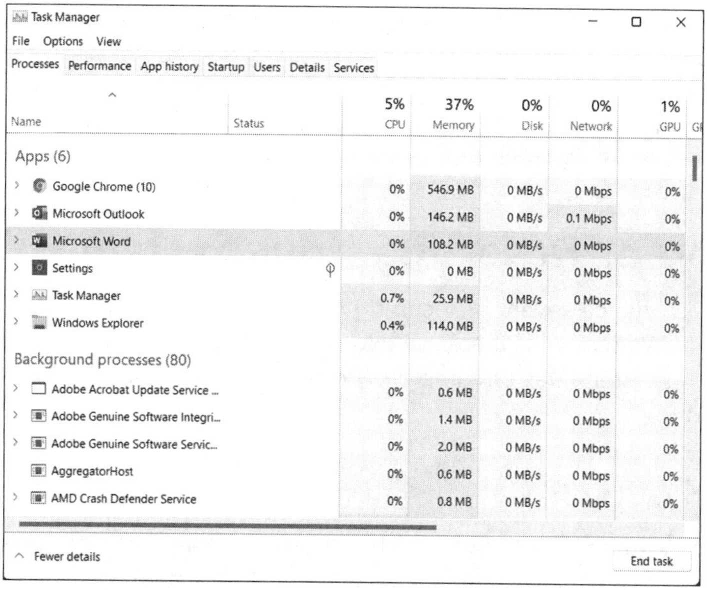

FIGURE 22.4

Use the Windows Task Manager to end nonresponding programs.

If you have multiple applications that crash on a regular basis, the situation can often be attributed to insufficient memory. See your computer dealer about adding more RAM to your system.

Dealing with a Major Crash

Perhaps the worst thing that can happen to your computer system is that it crashes—completely shuts down—without warning. If this happens to you, start by not panicking. Stay calm, take a few deep breaths, and then get ready to get going again.

You should always wait about 60 seconds after a computer crashes before you try to turn on your system again. This gives all the components time to settle down and—in some cases—reset themselves. Just sit back and count to 60 (slowly); then press your system unit's "on" button.

Nine times out of ten, your system will boot up normally, as if nothing unusual has happened. If this is what happens for you, great! If, however, your system doesn't come back up normally, you need to start troubleshooting the underlying problem, as discussed previously.

Even if your system comes back up as usual, the sudden crash might have done some damage. A system crash can sometimes damage any software program that was running at the time, as well as any documents that were open when the crash occurred. You might have to reinstall a damaged program or recover a damaged document from a backup file.

Refreshing or Resetting Your System

If you experience severe or recurring system crashes, it's time to take serious action. In Windows 11, there are two options for dealing with serious problems— refreshing system files or completely resetting your system to its original factory condition.

Refreshing System Files

When a system file gets corrupted or deleted, it can cause all sorts of Windows-related issues—including a complete freeze. Fortunately, Windows 11 provides the ability to "refresh" your system with the current versions of important system files. The Refresh PC utility works by checking whether key system files are working properly. If it finds any issues, it attempts to repair those files—and only those files.

 NOTE The Refresh PC utility doesn't remove any of your personal files or documents, even though it does delete all your installed apps. It refreshes only Windows system files.

To refresh your system, follow these steps:

1. Click or tap the Start button to display the Start menu; then select Settings to open the Settings app.

2. Click or tap System in the left panel.

3. Click or tap Recovery.

4. Go to the Reset This PC section and click or tap the Reset PC button.

5. When prompted to choose an option, click Keep My Files.

Windows prepares your system for the refresh, which might take a few minutes. Your computer eventually restarts. When you see the Start screen, your system is refreshed.

Resetting Your System to Its Original Condition

Resetting your system is more drastic than simply refreshing it. The Reset PC utility wipes your hard disk clean and reinstalls Windows from scratch. That leaves you with a completely reset system—but without any of the apps you've installed or the files you created.

 CAUTION   The Reset PC utility completely deletes any files, documents, and programs you have on your system. Back up your files before taking this extreme step, and then restore your files from the backup and reinstall all the apps you use.

To reset your system, follow these steps:

1. Click or tap the Start button to display the Start menu; then select Settings to open the Settings app.

2. Click or tap System in the left panel.

3. Click or tap Recovery.

4. Go to the Reset This PC section and click or tap the Reset PC button.

5. When prompted to choose an option, click Remove Everything; then follow the onscreen instructions.

Windows begins resetting your system by deleting everything on your hard drive and reinstalling the Windows operating system. This might take some time. When the process is complete, you need to re-enter your Windows product key and other personal information—but you'll have a like-new system, ready to start using again.

THE ABSOLUTE MINIMUM

Here are the key points to remember from this chapter:

- Dedicating a few minutes a week to PC maintenance can prevent serious problems from occurring in the future.

- Windows includes a number of utilities you can use to keep your hard drive in tip-top shape.

- Microsoft updates Windows on a regular basis with a mix of bug fixes and new features. You can control these updates, to some degree, with the Windows Update utility in the Settings app.

- Make sure that you keep all your computer hardware away from direct sunlight, dust, and smoke, and make sure that your system unit has plenty of ventilation.

- If you have a laptop PC, take appropriate steps to conserve battery life—and keep your PC safe from thieves!

- You can shut down frozen programs from the Windows Task Manager, which you display by pressing Ctrl+Alt+Del.

- Some problems can be fixed from Windows Safe mode; to enter Safe mode, restart your computer and press F8 before the Windows Start screen appears.

- If your system has serious problems, you can opt to refresh or completely reset Windows to its original factory condition.

Index

C

Answers to Your Technology Questions

The **My...For Seniors Series** is a collection of how-to guide books from AARP and Que that respect your smarts without assuming you are a techie. Each book in the series features:

- Large, full-color photos
- Step-by-step instructions
- Helpful tips and tricks
- Troubleshooting help

For more information about these titles, and for more specialized titles, visit **informit.com/que**

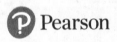